Luce Irigaray

Luce Irigaray

Philosophy in the Feminine

Margaret Whitford

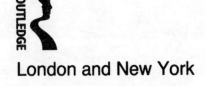

London and New York

First published 1991
by Routledge
11 New Fetter Lane, London EC4P 4EE
29 West 35th Street, New York, NY 10001

© 1991 Margaret Whitford

Typeset in 10/12pt Baskerville by Selectmove Ltd, London
Printed in Great Britain by Clays Ltd, St Ives plc

British Library Cataloguing in Publication Data
Whitford, Margaret
    Luce Irigaray: philosophy in the feminine.
    1. French philosophy. Irigaray, Luce
    I. Title
    194

Library of Congress Cataloging in Publication Data
Whitford, Margaret.
    Luce Irigaray: philosophy in the feminine/Margaret
        Whitford. p. cm.
    Includes bibliographical references and index.
    1. Feminist theory.   2. Irigaray, Luce.   3. Psychoanalysis
    and feminism. I. Title.
    HQ1190.W48 1991
    305.42'01—dc20   90–40947
                                                 CIP

    ISBN 0–415–05968–2
         0–415–05969–0

Contents

Acknowledgements

The first impetus for this book came several years ago when Luce Irigaray, on her first visit to England, suggested that I might like to attend the series of seminars she had been invited to give at the University of Bologna in May–June 1985. At that time, I had only the sketchiest acquaintance with her writing, though I had seen some of the articles and references to her work that were appearing here and there. The seminars in Bologna were most illuminating for me. It became clear that whatever Irigaray was setting out to do, it did not correspond with the majority of accounts of her work that I had seen up to then. I started trying to make sense, to myself and to others, of what had suddenly begun to seem an immensely complex *oeuvre*, whose problems were the problems at the heart of feminist and postmodernist debates. It has been a slow process and I am indebted in many ways to many people.

The second impetus came from co-editing the collection *Feminist Perspectives in Philosophy*. The experience of writing from within feminism has given me a sense for the first time of belonging to a real intellectual community. For many years, it felt as though I was working in a desert; now I find myself part of a much wider network whose existence makes all the difference. It will be clear from the bibliography and from the names of the people it is my pleasure to thank (in the following pages) that this study is indebted in significant ways to women's research and scholarship. Above all, the existence of the Women in Philosophy group was a quite irreplaceable source of support and stimulation.

Luce Irigaray herself has encouraged the project throughout and has generously supplied me with unpublished papers, transcripts of interviews, and even books. I was perhaps excessively scrupulous in wishing to develop an interpretation of her work on the basis of the texts alone; this has meant, however, that I have not at any point consulted Irigaray about the *contents* of this book, and it won't necessarily receive her imprimatur – in fact, she may well want to disagree with some of my interpretations.

A lot of other people assisted directly or indirectly in the writing of this book – by inviting me to give papers or write articles, reading or commenting on drafts, allowing me to read their unpublished work, procuring or indicating books and articles, and innumerable other, less academic, kindnesses. I should like to thank in particular: Kirsteen Anderson, Alison Assiter, Margaret Atack, Caroline Bailey, Christine Battersby, Jay Bernstein, Malcolm Bowie, Rosi Braidotti, Teresa Brennan, Carolyn Burke, Tina Chanter, Dianne Chisholm, Linda Fitzsimmons, Morwenna Griffiths, Jean Grimshaw, Elizabeth Grosz, Valerie Hannagan, Joanna Hodge, Diana Knight, Sabina Lovibond, Toril Moi, Michael Molnar, Perrine Moran, Marie-Christine Press, Anita Roy, Naomi Schor, Anne Seller, Susan Sellers, Paul Julian Smith, Elizabeth Wright. I have a particular debt to Morwenna Griffiths, Elizabeth Grosz, and Toril Moi who made comments on the final draft at very short notice. My colleague Jim Andon provided invaluable assistance with the classical Greek quotations in *Speculum*. Special thanks to Mrs J.M. Boswell, without whom I would not have been able to write about psychoanalysis or perhaps even write at all.

Earlier versions of some of the chapters were given at the University of Wales, the University of Essex, the University of Kent, the Women in Philosophy group, the University of Cambridge Social and Political Sciences seminar, the University of Nottingham, the University of Warwick, the French Studies conference at Swansea, the University of Oxford, the University of York and the Hull Centre for Gender Studies. The comments of the different audiences have helped me to clarify certain points, not least in giving me a clearer picture of the readers the book is primarily aimed at.

I should also like to thank: the library staff at Queen Mary College (now Queen Mary and Westfield College), especially at the inter-library loan desk, who were particularly patient in tracking down difficult-to-obtain non-European material; the staff at the Bibliothèque Marguerite Durand in Paris who were equally helpful; and my editor at Routledge, Janice Price, for taking me on trust and leaving me to get on with it. Lastly, I should like to take this opportunity of thanking the women of Bologna who welcomed me in May 1985 during the period of Irigaray's seminar at the University of Bologna – Anna and Enrica from *Librellula* and Antonia, Marina and Cristina in the via delle Belle Arti.

London
March 1990

*

I should like to thank Oxford University Press for permission to reprint material from my review article 'Luce Irigaray: The Problem of Feminist Theory' (*Paragraph* 8, 1986). An earlier version of Chapter 2 appeared in *Radical Philosophy* 43 (1986) under the title 'Speaking as a woman: Luce Irigaray and the female imaginary'. An earlier version of Chapter 3 appeared in Morwenna Griffiths and Margaret Whitford (eds) *Feminist Perspectives in Philosophy*, Macmillan, and Indiana University Press 1988. An earlier version of Chapter 4 appeared in Teresa Brennan (ed.) *Between Feminism and Psychoanalysis*, Routledge 1989. Translations of quotations from Luce Irigaray, *Sexes et parentés*, and Luce Irigaray, *Amante marine* are copyright forthcoming Columbia University Press and are used by permission. Translations of quotations from Luce Irigaray, *Speculum*, Luce Irigaray, *This Sex Which Is Not One* and Luce Irigaray, *Ethique de la différence sexuelle* are copyright Cornell University Press.

Abbreviations

Freud

SE followed by volume number: *Standard Edition of the Complete Psychological Works of Sigmund Freud*, trans. and ed. James Strachey, London: The Hogarth Press 1951–73.

Irigaray

English texts

B	'Language, Persephone and Sacrifice', interview in *Borderlines* (1985–6)
GP	'The Gesture in Psychoanalysis' (1989)
QEL	'Questions to Emmanuel Levinas' (1991)
SE	*Speculum* (1985)
TS	*This Sex Which Is Not One* (1985)
WE	'Women's Exile' (1977)
WSM	'Women, the Sacred and Money' (1986)
WWT	interview in *Women Writers Talking*, ed. Janet Todd, 1983.

French texts

AM	*Amante marine* (1980)
CAC	*Le Corps-à-corps avec la mère* (1981)
CE	'Créer un Entre-Femmes' (1986)
CS	*Ce Sexe qui n'en est pas un* (1977)
E	*Ethique de la différence sexuelle* (1984)
EQ	'Egales à qui?' (1987)
FPE	Interviews 1 & 11 in *Les Femmes, la pornographie et l'érotisme*, ed. Marie-Françoise Hans and Gilles Lapouge (1978)
LD	*Le Langage des déments* (1973)
OA	*L'Oubli de l'air* (1983)
PE	*Passions élémentaires* (1982)
PN	*Parler n'est jamais neutre* (1985)

SF   *Speculum* (1974)
SP   *Sexes et parentés* (1987)
TD   *Le Temps de la différence* (1989)

Full bibliographical references can be found in the bibliography at the end. Dates of English texts given here refer to the date of first publication in English. I have used (and occasionally modified) English translations where readily available. All other translations are my own.

Introductory remarks

How many people recognize Irigaray as a philosopher? Because, of course, philosophy has often seen itself as the 'highest' of the disciplines, the one which aspires to the realm of the transcendental, above mere empirical concerns and political passions, and most of all, neutral, universal, sexually indifferent. While doing some background research for this book, I looked up Irigaray's name in the extremely exhaustive *Répertoire bibliographique de la philosophie* published as a supplement to the *Revue philosophique de Louvain*. It is the most extensive bibliography of publications in philosophy that I know of, covering books, articles, and review articles in nine languages. It claims to be completely exhaustive in its coverage of books, if not quite exhaustive in its coverage of articles, which are more difficult to track down in the enormous and wide-ranging journal output. What I found was quite significant. Irigaray was first noticed with the publication of her articles on linguistics; in 1969 the *Répertoire* recorded 'Communications linguistiques et spéculaires' (first published in 1966 and reprinted in *Parler n'est jamais neutre*) and 'Négation et transformation négative dans le langage des schizophrènes' (published in *Langages* in 1967 and also reprinted in *Parler n'est jamais neutre*). The French publication of *Speculum* is not recorded, although in 1977 there is a reference to an article which Irigaray published in the Parisian journal *Digraphe* (no.1, 1972: 31–60) on 'L'*ustera* de Platon' (which subsequently became the final section of *Speculum*). Then nothing for several years. *Ce Sexe qui n'en est pas un* [*This Sex Which Is Not One*] is predictably not referred to (it is not obviously philosophical). But, no doubt corresponding to Irigaray's increased fame and reputation, *L'Oubli de l'air*, *Amante marine*, *La Croyance même*, *Ethique de la différence sexuelle* and *Parler n'est jamais neutre* are all duly noted (although these are not all obviously philosophy either).

The European countries which seem to take her work most seriously as philosophy are Holland and Italy. According to the *Répertoire*, *Krisis* (Amsterdam) published a special issue in 1981–2 on contemporary French philosophy ('Franse Filosofie') which included an article on Irigaray among the following line-up of French philosophers: Barthes, Deleuze, Guattari, Irigaray, Derrida, Foucault, Bertrand-Henri Lévy and Glucksmann (a list which is as significant in whom it leaves out as in whom it includes).[1] Another article appeared in the Dutch journal *Kritick* in 1982. In Italy, Irigaray was invited to speak at the Congress of Milan on 'Sexuality and Politics' in 1975, a year after the publication of *Speculum*. Her Italian translator, Luisa Muraro, published a translation of 'Misère de la psychanalyse'[2] in the philosophy journal *Aut Aut* (Milan) in 1977. *Aut Aut* also published an article in 1978 and an interview: 'Desiderio femminile et pratica analitica' in 1980. In Britain and the States, although there has been a wide reaction to Irigaray in writing about feminism, literature and feminist psychoanalysis, philosophy seems to be a watertight category. I did not find any references to articles on Irigaray in philosophical journals. The same is true of France. Although some of Irigaray's own articles are occasionally recorded – because they have appeared somewhere 'respectable'[3] – many of them (published in quite various places from the explicitly feminist *Cahiers du Grif* to the more literary journal *Critique*) are simply not noted. And from the evidence of the *Répertoire* alone, it would seem that in philosophy, in these countries, no one has written about her. Strictly speaking this is not true – there has been some response from women in philosophy (as we shall see later) but the *Répertoire* has not been recording it. As a result, the scholar or student seeking to find out more about the debates kindled by Irigaray's work has their work cut out simply trying to locate the most important articles.

For Irigaray, the boundaries between philosophy and other domains are not clearly demarcated. Perhaps for this reason, the status of her work as philosophy is suspect. However, I would want to claim that she is engaged in that most philosophical of enterprises: philosophy examining its own foundations and its own presuppositions. In addition, she is trying to work out the conditions of ethics and to rethink the social contract, both recognizable philosophical endeavours. But her emphasis on the historical determinants of philosophical discourse, her political stress on the realities of women's lives, her attempt to bring the transcendental back to earth, her insistence on bringing in psychoanalysis and the question of the *sex* of the philosopher – all of this appears to be deeply unsettling. It might be thought that, at a moment when philosophy as a discipline is being questioned from all sides and in all sorts of ways, it may not be a good idea to claim for Irigaray membership of a category to which in any case she might not want to belong. If, as Michèle Le Doeuff argues, philosophy is constructed by exclusion and in particular the exclusion of women, how can women enter it without contradiction?[4] But Irigaray herself, although she is profoundly critical of a certain kind of philosophy, explicitly situates herself as a philosopher with a clear sense of philosophy as 'the work of the universal' (SP: 162) with stringent ethical requirements.

This book is not intended to be a comprehensive introduction to Irigaray's work. It offers a reading of her that on the whole (with some notable exceptions)[5] has been missing from the public debate. I want to present her as a *feminist philosopher* with the emphasis on *both* terms, and to address her work directly, rather than seeing her as one of an allegedly more or less homogeneous group of proponents of *écriture féminine* who can then be critiqued generically without regard to their differences. I should thus stress from the outset the parameters of this study. This is not primarily a study of genesis, debts, sources, and roots. It offers an interpretation of Irigaray's texts, based on close readings, and supplemented with a general acquaintance with western philosophy, contemporary theory in France, psychoanalytic theory and feminist theory. Her method, as I will show later, implies a certain parasitism; it is quite clear, for example, that a large number of Irigaray's central terms derive from either Lacan or Derrida – often she is explicitly reworking or redefining them. Some time, someone will want to do the detailed work of showing these derivations and the transformations each has undergone. This detailed work will enrich our understanding of Irigaray. But I have not undertaken it. In addition, it is obvious that German philosophy – Kant, Hegel, Heidegger, Nietzsche – has been extremely important for Irigaray. Here too, I have not done more than register a textual presence. Although Irigaray's relation to Hegelian and post-Hegelian philosophy is undoubtedly one of the perspectives which would shed considerable light on her formulations of questions of desire, subjectivity, identity, and death, it is not my theme in this book. For in order to examine her from this perspective, it would be necessary to see her first as a philosopher, and this is the position that I want to establish here.

Crucially, Irigaray differs from her philosophical predecessors in her feminist commitment, and that difference is what I want to focus on. I think I have been able to put forward a reading of Irigaray which will make her work more available for debate and discussion, and indicate directions for future research and study. What I intended to do in this book was to put Irigaray as a thinker into wider circulation so that her importance, and in particular her value to feminist thinking, can begin to be assessed and measured. I found it disappointing, when I began work on Irigaray, that she had been so often dismissed without much understanding. A woman *speaking as a woman* deserves a fair hearing, and it may be that she is not so easily heard, for all the kinds of reasons that we are now familiar with.

This reading is neither comprehensive nor conclusive; it is interpretation in process. I wanted to display the internal logic of her thought, a network of preoccupations and connections, in the belief that we cannot seriously start subjecting Irigaray's ideas to analysis and critique until we have some detailed understanding of what those ideas are. I hope this study goes some way in this direction, though I know it to be incomplete. If it stimulates others to the kind of scholarship that any other major thinker or cultural theorist can expect as a matter of course, then it will have achieved at least one of its aims. My intention was to make Irigaray's work available as a resource for feminists. I am interested in the creative relationship between reader and text, rather than in idealizing the text itself (which tends to lead to unprofitable discussions of *less* and *more*: is Irigaray more important than Derrida, or vice versa, and so on). At the moment what interests me is what Irigaray makes it possible for us to think.

My own position is provisionally this. Far from feeling in tune with Irigaray, on the contrary it has taken me a long time to understand her. My own immediate sympathies go rather towards the position taken up by a philosopher like Michèle Le Doeuff, particularly her argument that 'the vocation of feminism is towards universality; it should reveal realities which do not necessarily concern *women only*' (Le Doeuff 1989: 275, my trans.) and her ethical stance: 'an ethics of solidarity and the obligation to assist whoever is in danger' (ibid.: 343). Michèle Le Doeuff's work is lucid and accessible, her commitments to ethics and rationality both forcefully expressed and eminently appealing. Irigaray fascinates me despite myself and in a completely different way. She is more than a little inaccessible; she is associative rather than systematic in her reasoning; it has been a struggle to read and elucidate her, and to come to some understanding of her critique of rationality which appeared to go against my whole intellectual training. She represented an otherness about which I could not say in advance: this is important and valuable, or else: this is not going to be of any use. In addition, one is constantly assailed by the doubts engendered when other writers, whose views one respects, explain why we need not study her further. However, I have come to the conclusion that, albeit from a completely different perspective, Irigaray is *also* committed to 'the work of the universal' and to the centrality of ethics, preoccupations which have been somewhat obscured by the reception of her work, and indeed by the difficulty of the language in which she presents them.

Despite the dismissals, the challenge represented by her work refuses to go away. In more or less all of the critiques I have come across, there is a simultaneous attraction and rejection. These critiques represent a range of political positions. They include views such as the following: Irigaray's inaccessibility makes her elitist; she does not recognize the contribution of other women; she is not really a feminist; she reduces the diversity of women to a falsifying unity by ignoring forms of otherness – racial and class differences for example – which are not sexual otherness; she is essentialist, hypostatizing 'woman'; her theory is not materialist. These objections can be found directed both against Irigaray in particular and against *écriture féminine* in general.[6] They seem to me often to be critiques directed at feminist theory in the name of the women's movement. In summary form, they indicate the fear not only that feminist practice and feminist theory are antithetical, but also that certain kinds of theory may act as a positive brake on action. The tension between feminist theory and political action is a real one, and most feminists find themselves at one time or another attempting to negotiate it at at a personal or collective level. As I shall argue later, I think Irigaray has begun to theorize *dissent* and *dissension* within the women's movement in a way which might enable feminists to understand further the tension between theory and action, particularly in relation to unthought and unsymbolized drives. She has a theory which addresses directly the problem of conflict – whether located as internal to the self, or the group, or expelled and situated in some other (men, other feminists, other women). So for the moment, I shall just make the following general comments. There is no membership requirement for feminism: its diversity is its strength. Feminism is like Merleau-Ponty's heap of sand; each grain individually is minute, but the total sandbank may block a river. We cannot afford to ignore interventions at any level. We do not know clearly in advance which interventions will have been decisive. And, in the process, the goals themselves may change. Because diversity is essential to the women's movement, Irigaray alone is not enough; she cannot fulfil all our needs. But at the same time Irigaray is too important to ignore; she is trying to *think* sexual difference in the strong sense of the term – to bring into existence the unthought and the unsymbolized, an endeavour she shares with more grassroots activists.

However, there is a contradiction inherent in being a 'star'.[7] Critics are simultaneously suspicious of Irigaray's stardom, and yet expect her to be, or see her as, more than the average grain of sand. So it is necessary to stress that the women's movement is what gives Irigaray's work its major contemporary significance, and that we cannot judge her with the eyes of posterity. We simply do not know how important she will turn out to have been, in retrospect. There is no sense in which we can definitively arbitrate on priorities – there is too much to be done, everywhere, both in theory and in action. Trying to think the unthought is an enterprise of colossal difficulty and unpredictability. I want to argue that Irigaray *needs* her readers and interpreters, and that this need is inherent in her theory, as I shall explain later. She cannot, on her own, bring about change in the symbolic order. So far from being an impediment, the effort of understanding needed to read her may be part of the cost of change. I want to insist on *the time of understanding*, and to reject the idea that immediate intelligibility is always and under every circumstance a desirable goal, since it does not allow for the possibility either of the reader changing over a period of time (and understanding at one moment what was obscure at another), or of being changed as a result of reading, not in an immediate flash but in a slow process of making connections. I suggest that the diversity of interpretations to which Irigaray's work has given rise is itself an indication of a fertility and complexity which should encourage us not to discard too quickly this feminism of difference, with all its problems.

*

The critiques which I shall be discussing in most detail in this book are the philosophical ones. These take a number of forms – for example, the argument that Irigaray has not grasped the implications of the work of Lacan or Derrida; or that she is an essentialist (this includes attributing to her the view that women are closer to the imaginary, or should 'return' to the imaginary). Another version of the philosophical critique is that made by Michèle Le Doeuff, who attributes to Irigaray the view that the 'main enemy' is the philosophical *logos* because of its legislative status with respect to other discourses (Le Doeuff 1989: 70).[8] Le Doeuff argues that philosophy itself is not immune from influence. Meaghan Morris explains:

> Le Doeuff [insists] that the circulation of elements does not necessarily go *from* philosophy to other discourses and practices – and that to 'imagine' it does would be to repeat the 'philosophicocentric proposition' that so-called popular culture is the by-product of a process of degradation.
>
> One immediate implication of Le Doeuff's argument here is that the dismantling of 'philosophical discourse' *in general* need not be of first priority for feminist theoretical work. (Morris 1988: 89)

I am not sure to what extent Irigaray does in fact hold the strong thesis that Le Doeuff credits her with. This reading is presumably based on the statement in *This Sex Which Is Not One* that philosophical discourse 'lays down the law to all the others' (TS: 159; CS: 154–5). But Irigaray also writes in *Ethique de la différence sexuelle* that popular movements such as feminism are evolving faster than philosophical thought and discourse (E: 114). However, in a sense it does not matter if Le Doeuff is correct in her reading of Irigaray. The specific and textually detailed interpretations of philosophical texts that Irigaray offers do not depend rigorously on the premise that the dismantling of the philosophical *logos* ought to be a feminist priority. I will suggest in Chapter 1 that Irigaray can be read in different ways, and that interpretations can either immobilize or energize. I link these readings to the two broad types of utopian writing, the static and the dynamic. I will argue that it is more valuable to choose the dynamic interpretation, rather than imprisoning Irigaray in the limitations of her own perspective. The important thing is to engage with Irigaray *in order to go beyond her*. I also put forward an argument about feminism and utopia in general and, under this heading, discuss briefly the materialist critique of Irigaray.

In Chapter 2 I outline Irigaray's method of 'psychoanalysing the philosophers' and her use of psychoanalysis as a dynamic model. I look at the question of how we might understand speaking (as) woman. This chapter does assume that the reader has already come across Irigaray's work and is familiar with the terminology. However, if this is still fairly new, it might be helpful to read Chapters 3 and 4 before Chapter 2, to understand the use and complexities of terms such as 'imaginary' and 'symbolic'. In Chapter 3 I discuss the antecedents, connotations, and deployment of the concept of the imaginary. The principal aims of this chapter are to explicate what is meant by the claim that rationality is imaginary, and to indicate the implications of Irigaray's notion of the female imaginary in relation to rationality. In Chapter 4 I discuss some of the problems thrown up by the discussion in the previous chapter, in particular the articulation of the symbolic and the imaginary. Although not strictly related to philosophical issues, this chapter discusses Irigaray's claim that woman (the maternal-feminine) provides the unsymbolized basis of masculine theoretical constructions. The first four chapters provide the groundwork; they set out the terms in which I think Irigaray needs to be discussed.

The next four chapters discuss in different ways the marginalization of women in the symbolic and social order, the complicity of philosophy in their marginalization, and the conditions for their inclusion. Chapter 5 argues that for Irigaray it is a single gesture which constitutes women's double exclusion from philosophy and from the polis. It traces Irigaray's interpretation of the philosophical phantasies which perpetuate this conceptual and social gesture. Chapter 6 discusses Irigaray's account of identity, and attempts to provide a framework for understanding why Irigaray insists on identity despite powerful opposition to the notion coming from the direction of modern theory. Chapter 7 discusses Irigaray's view that philosophical conceptualization does not provide women with an imaginary and symbolic world which would 'house' them, and looks at some of her tentative suggestions for the conceptualization of a female imaginary. The final chapter makes the links in Irigaray's thought between the body, the imaginary and the social contract. It concludes by linking the difficulties of her writing with her aim to effect a shift in the position of the subject of enunciation. The second half of the book designates Irigaray's project as 'philosophy in the feminine', that is to say, philosophy which does not regard the social situation and struggles of women as something external or irrelevant to its discourse. I argue that Irigaray is a philosopher who is redefining the terrain of philosophy by investigating and exploring what philosophy until now has been unable to allow in. It is an act of land reclamation on her part, which is intended to be of immediate relevance to the lives of women and to the symbolic organization of society as a whole.

I have used notes liberally, to make connections with other feminist thinking, debate with other views on Irigaray and, in general, to acknowledge my sources. However, my interpretation of Irigaray should be quite clear without the notes, and readers wishing for a more uninterrupted reading should find that this is possible.

On the question of terminology – male/female, masculine/feminine, 'men'/ 'women', man/woman etc. – I throw up my hands in despair. There has been a proliferation of strategies, in which inverted commas and terminological precautions, informed by a range of political sympathies and ideological commitments (and the explanation that it's different in the French), are meant to shield or disarm, and occasionally lunge at a real or imaginary opponent. I just hope that my arguments in general will be clear enough for the reader to forgive the occasional inconsistency or ambiguity.

Chapter 1

Feminism and utopia

Un discours peut empoisonner, entourer, cerner, emprisonner ou libérer, guérir, nourrir, féconder. (*Parler n'est jamais neutre*)
A discourse may poison, surround, encircle, imprison or liberate, heal, nourish, fertilize.

There is no mistaking the urgency of the issues which Irigaray is raising. Feminists turn to her work eagerly and as often turn away again in frustration and disappointment. Interpretations of Irigaray which try to pin down and/or *fix* her meaning have often been quite dismissive: Janet Sayers calls her a biological essentialist (1982: 131; see also 1986: 42–8); Lynne Segal calls her a 'psychic essentialist' (1987: 132); Toril Moi thinks that she is making the mistake of trying to give a definition of 'the feminine' (1985: 148); for Monique Plaza, Irigaray is an anti-feminist who echoes patriarchy's recuperation of feminist subversion (1978).

Irigaray faces a dilemma which could be defined as follows: on the one hand, as Moi forcefully points out, 'it still remains *politically* essential for feminists to defend women *as* women in order to counteract the patriarchal oppression that precisely defines women *as* women' (1985: 13), so to that extent it is necessary to define a female identity or specificity; on the other hand, how does one define female specificity without getting locked once again inside the patriarchal metaphysical framework one was trying to escape from? It seems to me that readers of Irigaray are looking for some kind of solution to this dilemma, hoping that she can provide a way out, and so are searching for some statement, some 'theory of woman' that somehow evades the snares and pitfalls of other such theories. But Irigaray herself writes: 'For the elaboration of a theory of woman, men, I think, suffice' (TS: 123; CS: 122); 'Speaking (as) woman is not speaking of woman. It is not a matter of producing a discourse of which woman would be the object or the subject' (TS: 135; CS: 133); 'But there is simply no way I can give you an account of "speaking (as) woman": it is spoken, but not in meta-language' (TS: 144; CS: 141). Irigaray does not intend to tell us what 'woman' is: this is something which women still have to create and invent collectively. What she sets out to do in her work is to expose the foundations of patriarchy and in particular to show it at work in what has traditionally been taken to be the high discourse of universality and reason: philosophy. In the process, the conception of what philosophy consists of (or should consist of) is profoundly shaken. For Irigaray is investigating the *passional foundations of reason*.

More or less simultaneously, her work is presented as both accessible and inaccessible (and either way, it comes under fire). On the one hand, she has been assimilated, along with Kristeva and Cixous, under the heading of *écriture féminine* (women's writing or sometimes 'writing the body'). This strand of Anglo-American criticism tends to make her work sound like little more than a heroic and inspiring but ultimately rather utopian manifesto. Against this view, one needs to point out that in fact her work is steeped in the history of philosophy from the pre-Socratics to the post-structuralists. To read *Speculum*, for example, we really need to know not only Freud but also, among others, Plato, Aristotle, Kant, Hegel, Derrida. To read *Ethique de la différence sexuelle*, one needs to know the Greeks, Descartes, Spinoza, Kant, Hegel. She has written a whole book as a dialogue with Nietzsche, another one as a dialogue with Heidegger, and has also engaged with contemporaries: Lacan, of course, but also Derrida, Merleau-Ponty, and Levinas. She is working primarily in philosophy, but she is also a psychoanalyst; to understand what she means by speaking 'as a woman', one needs to take the psychoanalytic dimension of her work seriously. The fact that she is, or has been, a practising psychoanalyst seems to me not merely an incidental feature of her *curriculum vitae*, but as essential to understanding her work as it has been recognized to be in the case of Lacan. And she has also done research in linguistics: her first book was a study of the disintegration of communicative ability in men and women hospitalized with a diagnosis of senile dementia, and her work at the Centre National de Recherches Scientifiques in Paris has been linguistic research, initially on the language of the mentally ill, latterly on sexual difference in language. After *Ethique de la différence sexuelle*, she has become more and more involved in empirical research projects, designed to show the ways in which language is gendered beyond our conscious volition (see for example the special issue of *Langages*, 'Le Sexe Linguistique' (1987), edited by Irigaray).

Ironically, however, some of those who do recognize this erudite background reproach her for it, as Eléanor Kuykendall points out:

> The first question for a political analysis of Irigaray's psychologic and mythic proposals for matriarchy is whether it is elitist, hence in its very form an undercutting of a feminist politics, separating women from one another by class ... Simone de Beauvoir, for example, ... has suggested that *écriture féminine* is an inappropriate way to do feminist political work, which would be more effectively accomplished by using

everyone's language, ordinary language . . . I found no one, up until a year after its publication, who had been able to read *Amante marine*, with its complex literary allusions. . . . What, then, is the political force of a writing style inaccessible to all but those highly trained academically? (1984: 269–70)[1]

This critique raises the question of Irigaray's relation to feminism and feminist politics.

The complexity of her work is nicely illustrated by the fact that whereas for some women, her work provides a celebration of femininity (Kuykendall 1984; Suleiman 1986), however problematic, for others she falls into the trap of victimology,[2] and fatally ends up presenting woman as innocent and untainted by any trace of phallocentric culture (Berg 1982: 18); for others again, she may not even deserve the name of feminist (Plaza 1978). It's possible that some of the range of views ascribed to her are largely preoccupations of the ascribers; the opacity of her texts elicits a considerable degree of projection and imaginary identification, or aggressive rejection. My own view is that it is a mistake to attribute to Irigaray a static notion of 'woman' or 'femininity' – whether it is woman as essence, woman as morally pure victim, woman as outside history, woman as closer to the imaginary, and so on. Where, then, does Irigaray stand in relation to feminism?

French women theoreticians are reluctant to adopt a label with so many metaphysical implications (see also Chapter 6). 'Woman' is a concept implicated in the male/female oppositions of patriarchal metaphysics. The relation of women to 'woman' is precisely what needs to be rearticulated, and there is a danger of co-option or collusion with what one is trying to undermine, if one accepts a designation that is linked to an assumption of essence that was challenged as early as 1949 by Simone de Beauvoir in *The Second Sex* when she wrote: 'One is not born a woman, one becomes one.' Irigaray has a further reason for having reservations about the term 'feminism': 'It is the word by which the social system designates the struggle of women. I am completely willing to abandon this word, namely because it is formed on the same model as the other great words of the culture that oppress us' (WWT: 233). But she goes on to say that to criticize 'feminism' is likewise an equivocal gesture; what needs to be done is to reclaim the term and redefine what one means by feminism: 'the struggles of women' and their 'plural and polymorphous character' (ibid. and cf. TS: 164, CS: 158–9). So I am going to use the term to describe her work, because I believe that she is committed to women's struggles, and that this is the adjective which best expresses that commitment, whatever its misuse and misapplications.

Her relations with the women's movement have not always been easy, as so often happens when a woman attains a certain visibility, and is then taken by academia or the media to be a kind of spokeswoman. Since women have so often been silenced by those who purported to speak in their name and define them, it has been a principle of 'second-wave' feminism that one does not speak for others, and in particular not for 'women' as a group. So there has been some uneasiness about the political positionality of Irigaray's discourse: where is she speaking from? Who is she speaking for? (see Felman 1975; Plaza 1978). The marginal position which she has assumed – maintaining her independence from any specific women's group or political orthodoxy, while remaining committed to the ideals and aims of the women's movement – has not always made her popular, and although she has received a lot of support and recognition internationally, she has also been bitterly attacked in her own country. She has suggested a theoretical account of these attacks (see Chapter 4), locating their source not purely in individual or group hostilities and rivalries, but in the patriarchal symbolic order and, at the same time, trying to theorize the conditions for an *entre-femmes*, or a sociality among and between women. The danger for women, she suggests, is that of falling back into 'a language and a social organisation which exile and exclude us' (CE: 39). It is clear that she does not have much time for the attempt to 'reverse the order of things' (TS: 33; CS: 32), to simply reverse the balance of power between men and women. What she is concerned with is to promote and encourage the development of a social form specific to women. Separatism, while not a long-term goal – since ultimately she desires a world in which women and men can live together without oppression – can be an effective short-term strategy, imperative even, for some women (see EQ: 435). And certainly an *entre-femmes* is a necessary, though not sufficient, condition for the creation of female identity and subjectivity. Women need to learn to love themselves and each other as an indispensable step towards autonomy (TS: 164; CS: 159).

She does not recommend that women enter the political arena as it at present exists (see TS: 165; CS: 159–60), although again she accepts that there can be a strategic necessity (see WWT: 235). The danger is always that in accepting the terms of the system currently in force, women will become 'men'. Fighting for equal wages and equal rights, against discrimination, the fight for equality, is in the end subordinate for her to the much bigger struggle which is to 'challenge *the foundation of our social and cultural order*' (TS: 165; CS: 160). Whatever equality means, it doesn't mean becoming like men.[3] Here she rejoins the feminist mainstream, for few feminists would now regard equal rights as an adequate goal.[4] It would be very easy to misread this position; the problem of a feminism of difference is that women's difference has always in practice been used against them. In fact, Irigaray suggests that we need to distinguish between struggle and critique on the one hand, and the long-term vision on the other. The local struggles are important, even essential, but to lose sight of that larger objective would mean that women become assimilated to the world of men and then have nothing to contribute *as women* (as is made clear by the problems inherent in applying classical liberal theory to women). At the local level it is often necessary to fight on the terrain of *human* rights rather than *women's* rights.[5] Irigaray is not dictating or even suggesting what strategies any particular women or group of women should adopt (TS: 166–7; CS: 161). Her scepticism about equal rights is not a matter of contesting equal rights per se; as she points out in *Speculum*, equal rights or their approximation may be a necessary condition for the larger question of sexual difference to be raised at all.[6]

To intervene *as a woman*, then, in the discourse of philosophy, is Irigaray's initial aim, and the one which I am going to discuss in this study. It seems to me that this aim is an explicitly feminist stance. In particular, Irigaray diverges sharply from a certain kind of postmodernist feminism in her insistence on struggle.[7]

Feminist philosophy is political and committed; it explicitly desires change (see Griffiths and Whitford 1988), but to provide a blueprint in advance, explaining exactly what the nature of those changes will be, is to fall back into completely traditional methods of philosophy, as Moira Gatens (1986) shows. Gatens points out that ethical and political philosophy in the past depended essentially on a notion of what a human being was: 'In other words, the kind of social and political organisation and the ethical and legal principles that are to govern that organisation are deduced from what a human being is thought to be, what its needs, desires, capabilities and limitations are' (1986: 27). First you start with the definition of the human being, then you move towards the definition of the kind of society in which this human being would ideally live. This is what Rousseau did, for example; in the *Discourse on the Origins of Inequality* he began by defining the essential needs of the human being as freedom, self-sufficiency and independence, its essential emotions a kind of basic self-love or survival instinct (*amour de soi*) and compassion and pity for others. He then tried to show how society as we know it is the product of an inevitable degeneration in the course of which the fundamental human being had become unrecognizable and distorted. In his subsequent works (*The Social Contract, Emile, The New Héloïse*) he made various (incompatible and contradictory) attempts to create in imagination a society in which the human being, as originally defined, might be happy.[8] However, modern theory is pushing feminism towards the notion that the subject, the human being, is socially constructed. Not that biology, for example, is not one of the parameters or constraints on this process of construction, but that human beings have no essential self; they are created in the process of socialization, and that there is therefore no ideal society. So a certain feminist utopianism, the attempt to define the future ideal society, comes into conflict with the theory that we are the sort of persons we are because society has largely (or at least significantly) made us that way. If a human being is at least partly a social product, then to project our current version of ourselves into the future would be to arrest change, to see the future as an alternative version of the past. Such a future would be closed to the possibility of new social or ethical forms still to be invented. Irigaray warns against projecting too far ahead, writing definitive programmes for the future (E: 16; TS: 124; CS: 123). In response to an interviewer, she replied:

> In this question, I hear a desire to anticipate and codify the future, rather than to work here and now to construct it. To concern oneself in the present about the future certainly does not consist in programming it in advance but in trying to bring it into existence. . . . Your remarks seem to assume . . . that the future will be no more than the past.[9]

Each moment of change brings about a new situation, which requires a new response, and in the process the meanings attached to 'man' and 'woman' can begin to alter significantly. What this means in terms of feminist philosophy is that it is not static; it is not an attempt to arrive at a final once-for-all truth, beyond patriarchy, but is a continuous process of critical engagement. It is necessary to stress this dynamic aspect, because Irigaray has so often been seen as having a deterministic theory of woman.

There are two main readings of Irigaray that have been current in Britain. The first is that she is a biological essentialist, that she is proclaiming a biologically given femininity, in which biology in some unclear fashion simply constitutes 'femininity'. Very briefly, the charge of biological essentialism assumes that Irigaray posits an unmediated causal relation between biological sex and sexual identity, leaving out completely the imaginary dimension, in which sexual identity may be related in an unstable and shifting way to the anatomical body, or the symbolic, linguistic dimension, in which sexual identity may be constructed. Further, biological essentialism, in the form in which it is usually attributed to Irigaray, is a deterministic and often simplistic thesis which makes change impossible to explain. The second reading is the Lacanian account of Irigaray as a 'psychic essentialist', a term coined by Lynne Segal (1987: 132). The Lacanian reading argues that Irigaray has misunderstood or misrepresented the implications of Lacan's theories (see for example Ragland-Sullivan 1986: 273), that she takes the feminine to be a pre-given libido, prior to language, in which specific female drives are grounded, thus positing two distinct libidos – a masculine and a feminine. The two-libido theory would imply that psychosexuality, again in some unclear fashion, flows from, or is determined by, some pre-given essence of masculinity and femininity. Against this pseudo-Irigaray, it is then argued that Lacan has shown that 'there is no feminine outside language' (Rose 1986: 80) and that Irigaray has not grasped the Lacanian symbolic dimension and what it means for the construction of sexual difference.

What I will argue, against these readings, is that Irigaray's project is an attempt to effect change in the symbolic order, and that what she has been interpreted as advocating or positing in fact resembles more closely her diagnosis of what is wrong with the symbolic order. She is not pre-Lacanian, but post-Lacanian. The Lacanian reading confuses description with prescription. So whether she is celebrated for her new vision of the feminine, or attacked for it, the readings miss the most important point, which is that Irigaray is a theorist of change.[10]

I shall argue in this book that Irigaray is a philosopher of change, and that she is attempting to begin to state the conditions under which the status of the 'female' in the symbolic realm might be altered. She has a strong thesis, and for that reason, her analysis and strategy are not of the kind that impose themselves without discussion; this makes her controversial, not least in that her chosen terrain – philosophy – could be seen as marginal to the daily struggles of the majority of women. Perhaps particularly controversial is the utopian aspect of her work, for utopia in the twentieth century has come to have pejorative connotations (linked either to totalitarian fantasies on the one hand, or to totally implausible and unrealizable visions of harmony and perfection on the other). In Irigaray's case, the critique tends to assume that she is advocating a kind of regressive retreat to a conflict-free pre-Oedipal state of imaginary closeness between women. One of the reasons for this interpretation is perhaps the thematic affinities between Irigaray and radical or lesbian feminism, the strands of feminism which have on the whole been the most sympathetic to Irigaray up to now.[11] Her uncompromising stress, not on the obliteration and overcoming of sexual differences, but on sexual difference itself, seems to align her with radical feminism and separate her from socialist and materialist versions of feminism. It then becomes difficult to focus on the philosophical presuppositions which make her position distinct from both radical and socialist versions of feminism. In particular, it is clear that both strategically and theoretically, Irigaray finds herself in opposition to the socialist feminist current.

One of the standard positions taken by socialist or materialist feminism is that gender differences are a product of patriarchy and that we should fight for their elimination as part of the fight against the patriarchal order. For example, in a recent collection of essays entitled *Feminism as Critique*, Drucilla Cornell and Adam Thurschwell write that: 'Gender differentiation is in and of itself an evil, because it circumscribes difference and denies access to the "other" in each one of us' (1987: 157). For Monique Plaza, a French socialist feminist, it is patriarchy which sexualizes all relations and makes sexual difference carry all the weight of significance that it bears at present. In her critique of Irigaray she writes:

> the 'patriarchal ordering' . . . places the dimension of sex to the fore, but simultaneously sets it up as being a forbidden dimension. This ordering sets up men and women as different (i.e. man as 'positive', woman as 'negative of the positive') and extends the dimension of sex to the entire universe: sex is everywhere but sexual relation impossible. (Plaza 1978: 22)

Thus she sees Irigaray as a voice propping up patriarchal relations. For Lynne Segal, likewise, the differences between the sexes are seen as a construct of patriarchy and repressive of both men and women. In her recent state-of-feminism book, *Is the Future Female?*, she quotes the following remarks from Cynthia Cockburn:

> All the true diversity that people are capable of experiencing and expressing, of needing in their sexual, domestic and working lives and of contributing to society, is repressed by gender. . . . Gender difference is not true difference at all. . . . The good qualities deemed masculine – courage, strength and skill, for instance – and the good qualities seen as feminine – tenderness, the ability to feel and express feelings – should be the qualities available to all and recognised and acclaimed wherever they occur, regardless of the sex of the person. . . . Any society we set out to organise anew would surely be a celebration of multiplicity and individual difference. (Quoted in Segal 1987: xiv–xv)

Thus Lynne Segal, in the same book, goes on to criticize Irigaray specifically on the grounds that: 'The writings of Irigaray are most readily interpreted as strengthening and celebrating traditional gender ideologies of fundamental biological difference between women and men' (1987: 133).

Now this critique, as I understand it, is a critique based on the fear that Irigaray is offering an ahistorical and therefore essentialist definition of female specificity and thereby positing a femininity which is not constructed by society, and which would therefore fall outside the realm in which one may work for change – in particular changes in the status or position of women in society. Feminists who adopt this critique are usually asking us to work towards a society in which sexual and sexist stereotypes will disappear. The emphasis is placed on the social practices which create masculinity and femininity. Not only is this critique suspicious of Irigaray's stress upon sexual difference, but also it reads her utopianism as stasis. However, despite the very real differences between the different feminisms, I would argue that, from the point of view of their utopian visions, they have more in common than is at first apparent.

Western feminism in all its forms is an inheritor of the Enlightenment and its contradictions.[12] This is true both of socialist feminism and of Irigaray's feminism. Irigaray criticizes the heritage of the Enlightenment in the name of Enlightenment values. In the first place, it is clear that Enlightenment values have not been applied to women. Feminism's appeal to emancipation and autonomy, justice and equality, is an appeal for the extension of revolutionary ideals to women too.[13] Second, and to a certain extent in contradiction with the first goal, there is a critique of those same values, focusing on the notion of the unified humanist subject. Among his other defects, the humanist subject is the atomistic individual of liberal political thought, the participant in the social contract; he is always male (see Pateman 1988). Equally central is the critique of the desire for rational understanding and control; the faith in reason underestimated the non-rational elements in the human mind and its will to power, to control, manipulate, and destroy in the name of the rational. Irigaray is perhaps more thoroughgoing than others in her identification of this reason as peculiarly male, but here again, she is not alone. Another contradiction is that both the aspiration to universality and the politics of identity emerge from the Enlightenment, the latter in its demands that the rights to equality and so on be extended to groups other than the white bourgeois male. Modern forms of racism and political sectarianism are as much products of the Enlightenment as feminism. In addition, scientific and secular progress has also brought efficient and extensive persecution and exploitation, rather than putting an end to it. Humanism has not proved an adequate brake on the exploitation of nature, the earth or different categories of humanity. Reason has not lived up to its emancipatory promises. As a result, the desire for social change has to come to terms with the pessimism engendered by these contradictions.

To point out that the world as it is at present is not designed with the interests of women in mind is to do no more than state the obvious, and does not in itself imply any particular form of a different world. Sometimes Irigaray accepts this, when she writes for example that we cannot programme the future, we can only begin here and now to construct and create it (E: 16). At other times she does speak as if she had a more positive conception – a conception with a more concrete and specifed content – of the kind of world that might correspond to women's needs, and therefore of what might be better for them. As soon as she does this, the question becomes open to discussion – it is a modern form of that ancient philosophical question concerning what constitutes the good life. And in fact it is difficult to imagine that a critique which was not completely nihilistic could do otherwise. The critical moment is in many ways easier to pursue; it does not commit one to any affirmative statements about women's nature. Yet in order to move to the constructive moment, it might be felt that a commitment to some affirmative position is necessary; and it is perhaps here that feminists will find agreement more difficult. It is probably easier to follow Irigaray in her remorseless analysis and exposure of the western psyche as it is materialized and given perceptible form in philosophical texts. When she attempts to hazard some more positive indication about where to go next, or what women might need or want, then she enters the domain of the controversial – and this is how it should be. But at the same time, because of the power of her critique, she runs the risk of being taken for a guru, someone with special powers of insight, who can be expected to pronounce with authority on every social issue from nuclear power to test-tube babies. So Nancy Fraser, for example, distinguishes between the specific and the global in Irigaray's critique:

We might enthusiastically embrace Irigaray's brilliant critical readings of specific androcentric texts while demurring from her global hypothesis about their collective import. For example, feminists could applaud her stunning deconstruction of Freud's essay on 'Femininity' without accepting her view that the logic deconstructed there underpins all symbolic expression in Western culture. Then it would be possible to replace the view that phallocentrism is coextensive with *all* extant Western culture with a more complicated story about how the *cultural hegemony* of phallocentric thinking has been, so to speak, erected. (Fraser 1989: 3)

The wariness about global visions is something which has emerged from the disillusionment of the twentieth century and the loss of belief in totalizing strategies.

Utopia is the space where the contradictory inheritance of the Enlightenment appears in one of its clearest forms. Utopias, while not invented in the Enlightenment, certainly flourished in the eighteenth century and persisted into the nineteenth century, when a number of socialist and socialist-feminist utopias proliferated, both literary utopias and also attempts at utopian communities.[14] But by the twentieth century, the problems of implementing the ideal state or community have become so obvious that the more characteristic and certainly the most well-known form of the genre would seem to be dystopia: Zamyatin's *We*, Aldous Huxley's *Brave New World*, George Orwell's *1984*. Women's utopias, until recently, were not well known. However, feminists seeking to reconstruct women's history have unearthed a utopian tradition which is quite distinctive,[15] and have also pointed out that the rise of 'second-wave' feminism coincides with a fresh wave of utopian fiction (including both visions of different worlds and also allegorical satire) (Albinski 1988).

In all forms of feminism there is a tension between the critique of an unsatisfactory present and the requirement, experienced as psychological or political, for some blueprint, however sketchy, of the future.[16] The utopian visions to which this tension gives rise produce in turn a further tension – between two views of utopia, either a kind of political romanticism (harmony with nature, Elysian future) or else a view of the future 'in process', the struggles taking different forms, but never finally eliminated. The first kind has rightly been criticized from within feminism. Thus from a political point of view, Nora Räthzel writes:

It is not only romanticized versions of the past that take the contradiction out of life, but also rosy visions of the future. . . . To me, a vision of this kind appears both abstract and sickly-sweet . . . sickly sweet, in that it presents a Utopia in which there are no struggles, no arguments, no contradictions. Yet struggles are not directed solely against exploitation and oppression. We struggle against our own mistakes as well. And to make no mistakes is to do nothing whatsoever – to opt out of living. (In Haug et al. 1987: 263)

Another warning against utopias is sounded by Kristeva:

> If the archetype of the belief in a good and pure substance, that of
> utopias, is the belief in the omnipotence of an archaic, full, total,
> englobing mother with no frustration, no separation, with no break-
> producing symbolism (with no castration, in other words), then it
> becomes evident that we will never be able to defuse the violences
> mobilized through the counter-investment necessary to carrying out
> this phantasm, unless one challenges precisely this myth of the archaic
> mother. (Kristeva 1986: 205)

The implication is that this phantasy has to be recognized and abandoned
in favour of a more realistic assessment of possibilities in the real world
(an acceptance of separation and symbolic castration). Otherwise, one of
two consequences will occur. Either women will identify with the social
order, and be incorporated by it rather than challenging it; or feminism
will mobilize in its turn a counter-violence that in no way overcomes
the violence of the social contract, but may simply escalate it.[17] On this
view, feminist utopianism is phantasy, part of that Enlightenment baggage
which any self-respecting citizen of postmodernity, unsentimental and hard-
headed, should have abandoned along with the belief in universality or in
the transcendence of truth and reason.

But there is another strand in feminist utopian reflection which argues
powerfully that we *need* utopian visions, that imagining how things could be
different is part of the process of transforming the present in the direction
of a different future. Critique in itself is not enough, and leaves one in
permanent opposition, where one does not have to take responsibility for
one's mistakes. Feminist utopian visions, whether fictional or non-fictional,
try to 'imagine the unimaginable – namely, where we're going before we're
there' (Kessler 1984: 7); but 'the idea of utopia changes in the search for
it' (Baruch in Rohrlich and Baruch 1984: xi). The strongest element to
emerge from contemporary feminist utopias is the stress on uncertainty
and unpredictability; it is certainly not uniquely the vision of static future
harmony. 'Utopia is process. It is found in neither past arcadias nor future
Elysiums' (ibid.: 207). One of the most valuable formulations to the credit of
feminism is the argument that one can usefully distinguish between two sorts
of utopian vision; between the kind that sees utopia as a moment of static
perfection, in which any change can only be for the worse, and the other
kind which is a utopia of process: 'Whereas the old dystopia or utopia was
complete, fixed and final in its gloomy inexorability or its boring perfection,
the new accepts that struggle is continuous and interesting' (Rose 1988: 121);
'[utopia] is not, finally, any one place or time, but the capacity to see afresh –
an enlarged, even transformed vision . . . a vital utopia requires change and
interaction with alien forces; otherwise it becomes a barren and useless idea'
(Khanna 1984: 273, 275).

I would thus agree with Marcelle Marini's comment on Irigaray that: 'The value of a utopia is not to programme the future but to help to change the present' (1978: 621). Irigaray, as I pointed out earlier, argues quite strongly that one cannot map out the future without projecting into it one's present. Any linear development, any teleology would re-enact in the future (whether real or imaginary) the scenarios of the present. A genuinely different future cannot be entirely foreseen, certainly not predicted in any detail; it can only be the product of freeing our genuine creative abilities. However, at the same time, this view is itself subject to uncertainty, in its belief in the possibility of a radically different future. From this point of view, it seems to me that between Irigaray and Cynthia Cockburn (who stands here momentarily as a representative of socialist feminism), between the view that: 'the good qualities deemed masculine . . . and the good qualities seen as feminine . . . should be the qualities available to all and recognised and acclaimed wherever they occur, regardless of the sex of the person etc.' and Irigaray's commitment to the vision of a future where there would be harmonious coexistence of men and women in the fertile conjunction of two sexual economies, we are standing between two phantasies, two versions of the conditions for the future good life between which we cannot and do not need to arbitrate definitively.[18] (I shall discuss the Irigarayan phantasy in more detail in subsequent chapters.) In psychoanalytic terms, they are operative phantasies which, as Silverman (1988) suggests, may be essential to feminism, providing the libidinal basis and motive force for feminist action. Feminist utopian visions, then, are mostly of the dynamic, rather than the programmatic kind; they do not seek to offer blueprints of the ideal future, still less of the steps towards attaining it. They are intended more to bring about shifts in consciousness (paradigm shifts). For this reason they may be particularly vulnerable to materialist critique.

Irigaray and socialist feminism are in agreement that the regime of difference as it at present exists is an evil. Where they disagree is on the question of strategy.[19] Irigaray has been criticized, for example, for her lack of political analysis (Kuykendall 1984), for omitting any materialist analysis of power (Moi 1985). Her critics reproach her for refusing 'to consider power as anything but a male obsession. For her power is something women are *against*' (Moi 1985: 147–8). Moi goes on to argue:

> Women's relationship to power is not exclusively one of victimization. Feminism is not simply about rejecting power, but about transforming the existing power structures – and in the process, transforming the very *concept* of power itself. To be 'against' power is not to abolish it in a fine post-1968 libertarian gesture, but to hand it over to somebody else. (1985: 148)

It is of course true that Irigaray quite explicitly locates her work within the domain of the symbolic and claims that 'contrary to the implications of Marxism . . . in order to change the economic structure, it is necessary to change the structure of language' (B: 30). The possible articulation of material and symbolic is not worked out by Irigaray *except at the junction of the two in language and in the bodies of women*.[20]

However, Marxism too has its roots in the utopian tradition, and recent theory has been attempting to confront the implications of the failure of traditional utopian strategy, that is, the implementation of a global programme in the name of an as yet unrealized golden future ('after the Revolution'). As Sheila Rowbotham pointed out in *Beyond the Fragments* (1979), this strategy has enabled Marxists consistently to set aside feminist demands on the grounds that 'after the revolution' there will be sexual equality. Feminism has responded by arguing that the revolution is not a distant and cataclysmic 'event' but can begin in everyday life here and now. Irigaray is not the only person to point out that Marxist politics makes feminism secondary to class struggle; it has traditionally paid scant attention to women's exploitation (TS: 165; CS: 160). The polarity of 'bad' utopian thought and 'good' materialist analysis is a misleading alternative.

What Irigaray is countering is the more or less exclusive interest of modern political culture in production and economic relations (see Benhabib and Cornell 1987) which obscures the domain of symbolic relations and relations of exchange.[21] Women need to 'interpret their present situation and status not only in economic terms but also in symbolic terms' (TD: 56). If feminism had not taken this domain seriously in the first place, feminism itself would hardly have come into existence (see Rowbotham et al.(1979) on 'Consciousness' and 'Prefigurative Political Forms'). Its emphasis from the beginning has been on the symbolic and the ideological as well as on concrete material conditions.[22] Irigaray is suggesting that there is a problem with Marxist paradigms, that these paradigms are implicated in the dominant monosexual symbolic order, and therefore that women's difference cannot be thought within them. Since she is putting forward a critique of Marxist categories, one cannot simply use those categories in one's objections; first the critique has to be taken into account, and as far as I know, this has not yet been done.[23]

Unlike classical utopianism (and some forms of Marxism), Irigaray's thought makes no claims to totalization and explicitly rejects 'phenomena of hierarchization, claims of orthodoxy' (TS: 164; CS: 159). It recognizes a multiplicity of strategies. (In the French context, at least one of its targets is the effect of Lacan's pessimistic account of the determining force of the symbolic order.) This is a strategy that seems to me to owe more to Foucault than to traditional Left forms of organization,[24] as does the view that language may have material effects.

I will argue then that Irigaray is addressing the issue of *change*: how to alter women's status in western society. The problem with which she is dealing is that of creating the conditions in which change can take place. For, as she writes in *This Sex Which Is Not One*, 'There is no simple manageable way to leap to the outside of phallogocentrism, *nor any possible way to situate oneself there, that would result from the simple fact of being a woman*' (TS: 162; CS: 157). Her aim, I believe, is not to formulate a programme, but to set a process in motion. However, there might seem to be a contradiction here between the strategy (setting a process in motion) and the assertion of sexual difference, between the recommendation of specific and local struggles and the global overview of the state of play between the sexes and the direction in which women should proceed. For, rather than minimizing sexual difference, Irigaray thinks that the only way forward is to assert it. As Lucienne Serrano and Elaine Hoffman Baruch put it in 1983: 'While many feminists are minimalists, denying sexual differences beyond the purely reproductive, Irigaray might be called a maximalist' (in WWT: 232). For Irigaray, the culture of the west is monosexual; the status of women is that of 'lesser men', inferior or defective men. There is no neutral or universal in this culture, she says repeatedly; what is taken to be neutral – the discourse of science or of philosophy – is in fact gendered: it is the discourse of the male subject. This is difficult to see in the absence of a different, female, discourse, as she points out in *This Sex*. One of the audience at a seminar asks her: 'I'm saying that beyond a certain point I simply fail to understand the masculine–feminine opposition. I don't understand what "masculine discourse" means' (TS: 140; CS: 138). Irigaray replies: 'Of course not, since there is no other. The problem is that of a possible alterity in masculine discourse – or in relation to masculine discourse'. In the light of the preceding discussion on utopias, we might now see that Irigaray is trying to 'imagine the unimaginable' and it is in this light that we should understand her view that to aim for a state 'beyond sexual difference' without rearticulating our present organization of male and female would only maintain the deceptive universality of the male, while the status of women in our society would continue to be secondary. Rather than minimizing sexual difference, then, Irigaray thinks that the only way in which the status of women could be altered fundamentally is by the creation of a powerful female symbolic to represent the *other* term of sexual difference.[25] What is at stake is the ethical, ontological, and social status of women.

Irigaray is often asked about her relation to the women's movement (see for example TS: 163–7; CS: 158–61; WWT). It is clear that she believes that its multiplicity and diversity are essential:

> I think the most important thing to do is to expose the exploitation common to all women and to find the struggles that are appropriate for each woman, right where she is, depending upon her nationality, her job, her social class, her sexual experience, that is, upon the form of oppression that is for her the most immediately unbearable. (TS: 166–7; CS: 161)

Although I shall later go on to argue that 'multiplicity', so often associated with Irigaray's 'feminine', must not be confused with the 'multiplicity' of the postmodern male philosophers, it does seem to be the key to understanding Irigaray. Jan Montefiore, I think accurately, suggests that it gives us a clue to reading and interpreting Irigaray's work:

> Irigaray's insistence on women's fluidity and plurality of speech is, then as much a prescription for the reader's response as a description of female identity; it describes an approach as well as the thing approached. Correspondingly, her discursive method very often consists in offering and at the same time withdrawing a list of definitions of the feminine, none of which quite fit. (Montefiore 1987: 152)

Mary Jacobus adds to this when she insists that what Irigaray is doing must be seen as a *political* strategy (Jacobus 1986: 62 ff.). So I want here to link the two types of utopia, the closed and immobile future state and the open-ended uncertain continuous struggle, with two types of reading. These two types of reading have come to be described as 'male' and 'female', though I now think that this is misleading, since it blurs the distinction between reading *like* a woman, and reading *as* a woman (see Chapter 2).

In an article on psychoanalytic literary criticism, Shoshana Felman makes a useful distinction between two aspects of psychoanalysis: interpretation and transference (Felman 1977, and see also Gallop 1985: 22–30). In interpretation, the critic or reader 'interprets' or 'masters' the text (tells us what Irigaray is 'really' saying, what her theory is). This would be a 'male' reading. However, one is also, in relation to the text, in transference, and this position is one of non-mastery. Thus Gallop, for example, both in her reading of Lacan and in her reading of Irigaray, tries to 'do psychoanalytic reading that includes recognition of transference as it is enacted in the process of reading: that is, readings of the symptomatic effects produced by the presumption that the text is the very place "where meaning and *knowledge* of meaning reside"' (Gallop 1985: 30, quoting Felman). Such an alternative reading, which does not attempt to assume a position of mastery and recognizes that the presumption of coherence is an illusion produced by the transference, would be 'female'. It needs to be added here that Irigaray would have us analyse not only the transference of the reader, but also the transference of the writer, 'restaging *both* transferences' (TS: 148; CS: 144).[26] Of course, from a certain point of view, Irigaray is asking for a 'male' reading. But when she insists that we should read 'as a woman', question 'male' writing, look for 'the *blanks* in discourse' (SE: 142; SF: 176), we could apply this process to her own writing, for in so far as she desires to speak 'as a woman', it can only be from a position of non-mastery, and we have to read her transferentially as well as interpreting. In which case, her meaning cannot simply be 'discovered' in the text, because it is at least partly a product of a creative dialogue between reader and text. And who, in this dialogue, could be the 'third party . . . guarantor of an independent truth' (PN: 12)? She has asked us to be on guard against privileging predicative meaning (TS: 147;

CS: 144), and to 'listen with another ear' (TS: 29; CS: 28).

However, this is not a strategy without risks. For change to occur, you have to put yourself into play, you cannot stand back at a safe distance. And this includes the theorist/analyst, not just the reader/analysand:

> Either the unconscious is nothing but what has already been heard by you . . . or the unconscious is desire which attempts to speak itself and as analysts, you have to listen without excluding. However much this listening to everything might bring about callings into question of *your* desire. . . . Whatever the risk of *your* death that might ensue. (PN: 225, trans. Gallop 1982: 102)[27]

There is a dual purpose in Irigaray's work, in that she wishes to occupy the positions of both analyst and analysand. She wishes that is, to speak 'as a woman' (analysand) but also as the analyst to 'read' and 'psychoanalyse' the philosophers. She wants to *persuade* her readers, but she also wants to allow for the possibility of something new emerging from the dialogue between her and her readers. Within her texts, there is a tension between an invitation to create collectively an unknown future and a strong affirmative will, between openness to the other (woman) and the self-affirmation of her own vision. For this reason it is possible to read her as utopian in both senses (which helps to explain Nancy Fraser's comment quoted earlier). Yet this is also, it seems to me, the dilemma of feminism: we have to act as though the ideal future is both imaginable and possible, while yet knowing that the ideal is both incoherent and unreachable, and in any case subject to metamorphosis en route. Diana Fuss suggests the strategy of the 'both at once' (1989: 65),[28] which derives from the image of the two lips (which I shall discuss in Chapter 8). The 'double gesture' is typical of Irigaray, she comments:

> Irigaray proposes a feminist politics that will work on two fronts at once – on one side, a 'global' politics that seeks to address the problem of women's universal oppression, and on the other side, a 'local' politics that will address the specificity and complexity of each woman's particular situation. In order to accomplish 'both at once', Irigaray believes that 'it is essential for women among themselves to invent new modes of organisation, new forms of struggle, challenges'. (Fuss 1989: 74–5)

What these remarks help to understand is the relation between the global and the specific in Irigaray. It is a real and working contradiction, and embodies the risks inherent in her mode of theorizing, since the specific can destabilize the global (leading to fragmentation and dispersal), or the global can immobilize the specific (leading to rigidity and dogmatism).

In the same way, I am proposing a double reading, hovering between the two reading possibilities. Although, in general, I adopt the mode of the 'male' reading, arguing that we should interpret Irigaray in the way I am suggesting, I accept the principle of the 'female' reading, i.e. I accept that my interpretation is provisional and more important for what it enables other readers to see or think than for its definitiveness. Thus I would argue for *engagement* with Irigaray rather than the alternatives of dismissal or apotheosis. It is in the nature of the engagement that Irigaray's own theoretical position (and the reader's too) is thereby put at risk, and that *qua* analyst/theorist, she herself risks 'death'. But ideally, the 'male' and 'female' readings should be linked ('both at once') in a kind of creative and fertile partnership, which would correspond to the amorous exchange that appears so often as an image in Irigaray's work. In the double gesture, neither would be elevated over the other, and interpretation would embody the symbolic possibilities of sexual difference.

Section I

Psychoanalysis

Chapter 2

Subjectivity and language

Mais quelle prison? Où suis-je recluse? Je ne vois rien qui m'enferme.
C'est dedans que je suis maintenue, en moi que je suis prisonnière.
Comment aller dehors? (*Et l'une ne bouge pas sans l'autre*)
But what prison? Where am I cloistered? I see nothing confining me.
The prison is within myself and it is I who am its captive. How to go
outside?

'Psychoanalysing the philosophers'

The immediate context of Irigaray's intervention in philosophy is the so-called
'crisis' in modern thought. One might identify three factors in particular
which characterize an epistemological crisis in contemporary French thought.
One is the assault on the primacy of the conscious, rational self or subject,
and the recognition that the self is not master in its own house; not only
psychoanalysis and Marxism, but also, more recently, structural linguistics
and structural anthropology indicate that we are determined by structures
which precede and exceed the individual, and into which the individual is
obliged to insert him or herself in order to be a social individual at all. This
'decentring of the subject' has obvious implications for philosophy; it puts
the credentials of the knower into question. Second, there is the theorization
of the position that the determinants or conditions of knowledge always lie
outside that knowledge, so that no ultimate foundation is possible. As a
result of these two factors, a further problem has arisen: the problem of
legitimation. To what authority, or source, or guarantee can one refer
if these in turn stand in need of a further guarantee, and so on? One
of the ways in which French thinkers have appeared to react to this
crisis is by the mobilization of 'the feminine' a reaction which has been
documented at length by Alice Jardine (1985) and Rosi Braidotti (1981
and forthcoming). There does seem to have been a kind of incorporation
or cannibalism at work, a sort of colonization of 'the feminine' by philosophy
which Irigaray has resisted perhaps more strongly than any other woman
theorist.

In an article on women and/in philosophy called 'Ethics Revisited', Rosi Braidotti points out that (male) philosophers trying to think the feminine, and (female) feminists do not have the same place of enunciation (1986b: 60; see also Spivak 1983). Male philosophers situate themselves within the tradition of philosophy as speaking subjects. They diagnose the crisis of philosophy, the decentring of the subject, the problems of legitimation. Their interlocutor is the history of philosophy itself, and they attempt to deal with the crisis, 'their' crisis, by a kind of feminization of philosophy, in which the text becomes the unconscious or the feminine (often seen as synonymous). It is the male subject who is in crisis, Braidotti emphasizes, and he is dealing with it by turning towards a hitherto neglected aspect of his *self* – the previously repressed feminine – but not to women, although at the same historical moment, women are making themselves heard with unprecedented forcefulness, demanding their right to co-subjectivity. Women, on the other hand, have never had this relation to philosophy. In order to be the subject of philosophy, women have had to alienate themselves, to take on a male part; the subject of philosophy is male. Since they have never been by right the 'subjects' of philosophy, they are not, like male philosophers, trying to salvage a tradition, to stay in the driving seat. Their position is much more contestatory. From a feminist point of view, what male philosophers are at present engaged in can be seen as an attempt to continue by other means 'the age-long metaphorisation of women by the masculine subject of enunciation' (Braidotti 1986b: 59). The philosophers do not call into question their 'hegemonic model' (ibid.). In the feminization of philosophy, the feminine, as sign of unrepresentability, 'is not structurally different from all the other signs to which the feminine was confined in the classical mode (the irrational, the emotional, etc.)' (ibid.). Suzanne Moore, in a recent article, puts it even more strongly: such philosophers are the pimps of postmodernism. It's 'the new kind of gender tourism, whereby male theorists are able to take package trips into the world of femininity' (Moore 1988: 167).

One might see, therefore, the attempts of male philosophers to incorporate the feminine as a response to the increasing strength and pertinence of feminist discourse and criticism, an attempt to maintain their traditional position of discursive mastery. There is not much evidence of their political commitment to feminism. For feminists, on the other hand, the preoccupations are rather different. They are primarily social and political rather than philosophical, and a feminist philosopher can find herself torn between her attachment to philosophy and her feminist commitment to analysing the ways in which philosophy has been complicit with other patriarchal methods for maintaining power over women (see Le Doeuff 1989). Philosophy is not 'innocent' (see Gatens 1986); theory too is engaged in power struggles. The primary concern of feminists is to change the status of women in society, and in order to do this it will be necessary to fight for fundamental social change. Irigaray's attitude to the 'crisis' will emerge in the course of this study; in brief, she criticizes the philosophers who attempt to annex the feminine: 'don't we run the risk once more of taking back from woman those as yet unterritorialized spaces where her desire might come into being?' (TS: 141; CS: 138), but also suggests that the crisis may create the conditions for the emergence of the feminine. I will argue in this book that it is psychoanalysis which provides Irigaray with her model for approaching philosophy and for theorizing change in the symbolic order.

Irigaray's relation to psychoanalysis is quite complex, characterized both by indebtedness and by critical distance. In particular, one must distinguish between psychoanalysis as an institution; psychoanalysis as a body of theoretical writing, dominated by the work of Freud and, in France, influenced by Lacan's version of Freud;[1] and third, psychoanalytic practice. Irigaray herself has considerable clinical experience. She came to France to train as an analyst, worked for many years with patients at the Hôpital Sainte Anne, and has a private practice. She attended Lacan's seminars at the Ecole Normale Supérieure in the rue d'Ulm (Marini 1986: 136) and until the publication of *Speculum* taught a course in the department of psychoanalysis at Vincennes. When *Speculum* was published, her relations with the psychoanalytic institution changed overnight. She lost her position at Vincennes [2] and found that relations with colleagues had suddenly become complicated (see CAC: 52 ff.). In particular, she was censured for being politically committed (CAC: 58) by psychoanalysts who thought that being a psychoanalyst precluded political commitment. As Irigaray points out, such a position is itself politically determined. She is critical of the institution, because of the way psychoanalysis is transmitted, from father to son as it were, which makes it difficult to raise any radical questions about theory or practice.[3]

Her critique is developed in a powerful article entitled 'The Poverty of Psychoanalysis'.[4] The nature of her critique can be summarized as follows:

1. Psychoanalysis, like any other discipline or practice, is historically determined, and its attitude towards women is historically determined. As it does not recognize this, its phallocentric bias is elevated into a universal value.[5]
2. The social order which determines psychoanalysis rests on the unacknowledged and incorporated mother.
3. Psychoanalytic theory is governed by unacknowledged and uninterpreted phantasies; it purports to analyse the phantasies of others, but meanwhile its own discourse perpetuates the dominant cultural phantasies. Resistance and defences can be found in the theory too.[6]

She is probably best known for her theoretical challenge to Freud and Lacan. The strength of her analysis is that she uses the theories of both Freud and Lacan against them to put forward a coherent psychoanalytic explanation for theoretical bias. She claims that the cultural unconscious only recognizes the male sex, and details the effects of this unconscious belief upon accounts of the psychology of women. However, although it is often recognized that Irigaray has drawn up a formidable indictment of patriarchal psychoanalysis,[7] what is less often realized is the extent to which she is indebted to psychoanalysis herself, and her positive contribution as a theorist to psychoanalytic theory and practice. She speaks of Freud in most positive terms. An interviewer asks her: 'What elements of Freud's theory can be retained in a new psychology of women?' (WWT: 243). Irigaray replies:

> I would say everything, on the condition that one goes beyond. All of Freud's work is to be understood as the work of an honest scientist. He said of women that which he was able to say in describing what he heard, with the ears he had, which probably couldn't hear anything else. What Freud says about feminine desire is heard on the couch. But there are other things that are heard, and the problem is that he stopped at a certain point, that is to say, that he normalized woman in her role, the condition that she had at a certain moment. (WWT: 243)[8]

So she does not for example argue that women should never go into analysis, but that they should treat it with caution. In *Le Corps-à-corps avec la mère*, she suggests a kind of analysands' consciousness-raising group, comparable to the early consciousness-raising groups of the women's movement. Because of the transference phenomenon, it can sometimes be very hard to assess what is really taking place, to differentiate between the objective situation and one's perception of it through powerful unconscious phantasy. Analysis, for example, can mobilize paranoia, which needs to be directed at the person of the analyst in order to be resolved, and under these conditions it is hard for the analysand to disentangle phantasy and reality. Comparing notes on analysts, like consciousness raising, might help women in analysis to assess the benefits of analysis, while subjecting it to political critique. Irigaray has also started rethinking the psychoanalytic 'scene' (the couch, the analyst seated behind the analysand, the code of practice, and so on) in terms of her theory about sexual difference. If the instrument of psychoanalysis is language, and if language is not sexually neutral, then it is not a matter of indifference whether one's analyst is male or female; the dynamic may be quite different and may need to be theorized.[9]

But most importantly, psychoanalysis is a situation in which unconscious change can take place. 'A discourse may poison, surround, encircle, imprison or liberate, heal, nourish, fertilise' (PN: 11). 'The task of the other's word [*parole*] is to unbind/loosen what has petrified [se sclérose]' (PN: 15). Psychoanalysts are like the poet or the lover (ibid.); their instrument is language.[10] Psychoanalysis, she explains in *Parler n'est jamais neutre*, offers a privileged experimental situation, since it works directly on enunciation, the place of the speaking subject, rather than, like the linguist or the psychologist, working on the *énoncé*, the cold data. In this laboratory, with language as the instrument, real and profound changes can take place with significant effects on the life of the analysand. Irigaray is convinced, then, of the powerful potential of psychoanalysis. But it is necessary, she says, to rethink psychoanalysis from women's point of view (CAC: 55). I will contend that one cannot understand her philosophical contribution without taking into account the insights that psychoanalysis has enabled her to formulate.[11] The unconscious, she writes, is 'the storehouse of what may come to be' [la réserve d'un à venir] (PN: 256), a creative source which psychoanalytic theory and practice to date has attempted to stifle. Her project is to use the methods of the psychoanalyst as a heuristic and epistemological instrument in an attempt to dismantle the defences of the western cultural unconscious, to undo the work of repression, splitting, and disavowal, to restore links and connections and to put the 'subject of philosophy' in touch with the unacknowledged mother. The 'subject of philosophy' is narcissistic, closed to the encounter with the Other, while the Other (woman) has not yet acceded to subjectivity.

Irigaray is a kind of cultural prophet, whose account of western society runs something like this. Our society is dominated by a destructive imaginary (whose apotheosis is scientific ideology elevated to the status of a privileged truth)[12] and which is constructed over a buried act of matricide (a matricide more ancient than the parricide of Freud's *Totem and Taboo*). For there to be any hope of renewal, the male imaginary needs to recognize its own unconscious, and cut the umbilical cord which still attaches it to the mother, while the female imaginary needs to find a voice. For this reason, 'sexual difference represents one of the questions if not *the* question of our age' (E: 13). We are entering the west's third era; the first was the Old Testament, the reign of the Father, the second the New Testament, the reign of the Son, the third, still only on the horizon, will be the age of the couple (or copula): the Spirit and the Bride (E: 140).[13] Subtending the rational subject (with his aspirations to universality, neutrality, and objectivity) but unrecognized, there is a subject governed by unconscious desires, powerfully motivated and, above all, *sexuate* (so that the criteria of scientific epistemology should in fact be seen as shaped by the male imaginary). Irigaray's work, then, can be seen as a sort of 'psychoanalysis' of western culture and metaphysics, seeking what underpins its fragile rationality, looking for the 'repressed' or unconscious of culture. In *Parler n'est jamais neutre*, she attempts to demonstrate her thesis by analysis of the enunciation of speaking subjects in order to uncover the 'true identity of the subject who assumes the *énoncé*' (PN: 55), and to theorize the conditions for a *female* subject which could not be simply incorporated back into the male imaginary as its 'other' (the 'feminine' of the male philosophers). Psychoanalysis offers a model for a situation which is precisely designed to break down the narcissism of the subject and open it/him to that Other which 'cannot be subsumed in a system and cannot be reached by a method, however dedicated one is to it' (Heaton 1989: 5).

Thus Irigaray's method of approach to philosophy is to 'psychoanalyse the philosophers', to look for the phantasies that haunt philosophical discourse. Her method is indebted to Lacan's account of the mirror stage, in which the child is offered an image of itself (for example the image in the mirror), its identification with this image allowing the formation of the ego to take place. The mirror stage precedes the assumption of the 'I' in language. The ego is an imaginary unity; it is not coextensive with the subject, and to the extent that the subject takes this ego to be itself, it is necessarily alienated. Irigaray argues, first, that all of western discourse and culture displays the structure of specularization, in which the male projects his own ego on to the world, which then becomes a mirror which enables him to see his own reflection wherever he looks. Women as body/matter are the material of which the mirror is made, that part of the mirror which cannot be reflected, the tain of the mirror for example, and so never see reflections of themselves. The second step is to look for the infrastructure, the mother (who in Lacan's account supports the child who is looking into the mirror). The mother supports the processes of the male imaginary, but is not herself represented, a neglect equivalent to matricide. Whatever philosopher Irigaray approaches (and this is perhaps the reason why she has written only about men), the strategy is always the same – to look for the resistances and defences which conceal the original crime of matricide. The victim comes back to haunt the slayer in the form of persecutory anxiety (so that men are said to fear the power of women, despite the fact that women have minimal social, economic, or political power). These two principles: to look for the specular relationship, to uncover the buried mother, underlie all her analyses of the philosophers. She is seeking the varied phantasies which persist in discourse as symptoms of the patriarchal unconscious.

The parallels between the psychoanalytic method and Irigaray's method, without coinciding point for point, are striking and in my view intentional. In this method, theory has to take second place. For psychoanalytic theory is retrospective; it may inform the analyst's practice, but it is in the analytic situation that the raw material – discourse – is produced. Psychoanalysis as a *practice* does not fit the scientific paradigm. First, there is no outside observer; the situation is quite unlike the conditions of experiments in empirical science, since no 'test' or 'repeat' situation can be set up. Each situation is unique. And it is not clear what 'verification' or 'falsification' would mean in an analytic context. Second, it is a participatory model, not a distanced objective stance, but one in which *both* participants are involved and take risks, unlike the safe detachment of the academic or scientist. Irigaray insists, in the remarks already quoted in Chapter 1, that:

Either the unconscious is nothing but what has already been heard by you . . . or the unconscious is desire which attempts to speak itself and as analysts, you have to listen without excluding. However much this listening to everything might bring about callings into question of *your* desire . . . Whatever the risk of *your* death that might ensue. (PN: 255)

Third, its essential instrument is the *parole*, that powerful *parole* which can imprison or set free, the word addressed to someone by someone, the spoken word of the analyst and the analysand, *as it is spoken*, at the moment at which it articulates (or fails to articulate) the emotion of the response.

When one reads her work in the light of the psychoanalytic model, further implications spring to mind.

1. The female imaginary offers the features of the unconscious. If we look at the descriptions of the female imaginary we can see that in many respects its distinguishing features resemble those said to characterize unconscious processes: its fluidity and mobility; its indifference to the laws of logic (identity and non-contradition); its inability to speak *about* itself. What Irigaray as analyst is listening for is the equivalent of the unconscious.

2. One can see a parallel between the analytic situation and the cultural situation. In *Parler n'est jamais neutre*, Irigaray uses a linguistic model to analyse taped material from psychoanalytic sessions (PN: 55–68). According to her analysis, the obsessional lives in the universe of the 'I'; there is no interlocutor. The hysteric, on the other hand, cannot assume his/her own discourse; everything is referred for validation to the 'you'. The aim of the psychoanalyst is to enable an exchange to take place between the 'I' and the 'you', the two poles of dialogue. Similarly, Irigaray describes western culture as a monologic, monosexual culture in which men speak to men (the universe of the 'I' or the same) and women remain merely the mediators of this exchange, as goods or objects, never partners in a dialogue. For sexual difference to be realized, women would have to assume the 'I' in their own right, and men would need to venture out of the closed world of the 'I'.

3. It therefore seems to me that what Irigaray is trying to do in her writing is to effect an *intervention*, so that her writing would function like the *parole* of the psychoanalyst and set some change in motion. A word needs to be said here about the status of the analyst's interventions. Within the framework of the psychoanalytic session, interpretations are dynamic; that is to say, they are not global descriptions of a person's character or psychic make-up, but an interpretation of what is happening, at the moment (*here and now*) between the analyst and the analysand. They refer only to the moment at which they are being made; they may apply to only part of a session; they may be confirmed or disconfirmed by the response of the analysand; they are essentially aimed not primarily at 'truth' but

at bringing about a change in the psychic situation. An interpretation is not so much an end-product, the fruits of the analyst's understanding, encapsulated and summarized, but the first step towards changing the situation, designed to effect shifts in the unconscious and open up other possibilities for the analysand who cannot effect the shift unaided. Although one can obviously elicit a 'global' picture from Irigaray's work, I suggest that it makes sense to see her writing primarily as discursive interventions or interpretations in much the same way. The point is to recode the imaginary and symbolic structures of the 'patient' – in this case western thought, rather than producing a universalizing and new 'truth' (see on this point Grosz 1989: 117).

4. Since the desire of the analysand is blocked, help is needed to release it. Analysands are in analysis because they could not, unaided, release themselves. The analysand *needs the other*. Similarly, for Irigaray, there is the suggestion that it will not help men (postmodernist philosophers for example) to attempt to investigate their own unconscious; this will not create the kind of dynamic dialogue with the other that is necessary to open up the solipsistic constructions of the male imaginary. Irigaray thus has in mind a major dynamic role for women, as the following remark from a 1986 paper indicates: 'the community of men needs people, who are people in every way [des personnes à part entière] to enable them to understand themselves and find their limits. Only women can play this role' (SP: 201). This is one of the meanings of Irigaray's strategy of mimesis. In their role as analyst of the male imaginary, women have temporarily to occupy – but as a technique this time – the unconscious positions of the male psyche. Just as the analyst first receives and then interprets the unconscious projections of the analysand, women have to be for men what they cannot be for themselves (receive the projections) and then *interpret* the phantasies. (This point will become clear in Chapters 5 and 6 particularly.)

5. Theory is not what is needed here, at least not primarily. The 'power' of a psychoanalytic theory may not be commensurate with its 'correctness'. In therapeutic terms, explanations and therapies based on irreconcilable assumptions seem to produce effects. So perhaps the importance of Irigaray's work does not lie primarily in its theoretical 'correctness'. The 'interpretations' which she offers may be enabling, may create the conditions of possibility for dynamic cultural shifts – although the 'analysand' here may of course refuse to listen; hence the importance of the role of women in making it difficult nòt to hear.

6. One of Irigaray's most disconcerting characteristics is her conceptual imprecision, the absence of definitions, the appropriation and conflation of concepts from a range of quite different conceptual systems. The critique of this imprecision will tend to assume a theoretical inadequacy on Irigaray's part. Again here, I suggest that it is a procedure derived

from psychoanalytic technique, where words are not, and cannot be, used primarily for their scientific and conceptual rigour. They are rather an attempt to grasp phenomena which are mobile, fluid, protean, and unstable, linked by association, condensation, and displacement, for example. (One has only to think of the way in which a dream resolutely slides away from attempts to pin it down linguistically with precision.) It is a technique which enables all kinds of associations to be made, across a range of thinkers. The deliberate omission of references and footnotes, and blurring of the distinction between her own own text and the text she is supposedly 'citing' allows for these associative connections. The concept immobilizes, produces a definition of the 'feminine', for example:

> To claim that the feminine can be expressed in the form of a concept is to allow oneself to be caught up again in a system of 'masculine' representations, in which women are trapped in a system of meaning which serves the auto-affection of the (masculine) subject. If it is really a matter of calling 'femininity'into question, there is still no need to elaborate another 'concept' – unless a woman is renouncing her sex and wants to speak like men. For the elaboration of a theory of woman, men, I think, suffice. In a woman('s) language, the concept as such would have no place. (TS:122–3; CS:122)

She is pointing to the way in which concepts can themselves be used as part of a defence system, in which case countering them with other concepts merely colludes, it does not dismantle the defence. (Anyone reading her work could with profit follow up their own set of conceptual associations; it would almost certainly work as a method for unravelling Irigaray, and the meeting point between her set of associations and the reader's could be an illuminating one.)

7. Her use of the notion of a female imaginary has structural and perhaps strategic parallels with that of the way in which psychoanalysis uses the notion of resistance to deal with certain critiques. To the critical reader who wishes to raise theoretical objections to Irigaray, it could be replied that the criteria in the name of which one is objecting are *male* criteria, and not *universal* or *neutral* criteria, and that she is attempting to allow for the articulation of an alternative structuring to which these criteria would not be applicable. This argument would then function to forestall any immediate 'recapture within the economy of purely masculine desire' (TS: 158; CS: 154).

8. Finally it is important to stress the symbolic, that vital Lacanian concept. The symbolic is the junction of body, psyche, and language, where the descriptive fields of psychoanalysis and linguistics (or semiotics) meet, and it is what enables Irigaray to use the psychoanalytic model. If it is in language that one becomes a subject, then to say that the subject is male is not polemical rhetoric, it is a precise theoretical statement concerning

the Oedipal structure of the symbolic and the structure of subjectivity. From this point of view, one is not talking any more about individual men and women, male philosophers and female hysterics/feminists, but rather about a monosexual structuration of subjectivity that, because it is an overarching symbolic structure, determines individual subjectivity.[14] In this structure, to be a subject is to take up the male position in the Oedipus complex, to identify with the Father (the Law), and thus, for women, to find themselves in conflict, potentially at odds with their mother, other women, and their self, for lack of an identificatory support in the symbolic order that would confirm them as female subjects. Hence the 'I' in the epigraph to this chapter is the voice of the would-be female subject ('I see nothing confining me') and yet women are 'captives' of the symbolic order. This is why, when Irigaray speaks of the future advent of the female speaking subject, of a different subject position, critics are quick to speak of regression, of failure to understand Lacan, of a threat to the symbolic order with a risk of psychosis. But what Irigaray is positing is that this Oedipal structure is not immutable, that perhaps the unconscious has a history, certainly that discursive representations have a history, and that in any case one can intervene, make 'interpretations' of the symbolic's unconscious. That is why subjectivity and language are inextricably linked in Irigaray's writing, and why one cannot therefore say that the 'feminine' is there already just waiting to find expression. On the contrary, it has to be created, to be given symbolic form. I will go on then to look briefly at the question of speaking (as) woman, before discussing the imbrication of language and subjectivity in Irigaray's work.

Speaking (as) woman

It is interesting that, although Irigaray has often been associated with *écriture féminine*, women's writing, in fact the terms which she privileges are not about writing at all: *parler-femme* and *la sexuation du discours* (translated by Catherine Porter and Cardyn Burke in *This Sex Which Is Not One* as 'speaking (as) woman' and the 'sexualization of discourse'). As far as I know, she does not use the term *écriture féminine* at all; it is a label which has been attached to her by others. What is to be understood by *parler-femme*? To begin with, it was not at all clear what *parler-femme* might mean (witness the rather puzzled reactions to the idea in 'Questions' in *This Sex*). Associated with writing the body, it was taken to refer to a kind of natural and unmediated expression, involving (probably) a regression to the pre-Oedipal relation to the body of the mother. The famous, or infamous, description in *This Sex* (TS: 29; CS: 28), which made it sound as though women, when speaking as women, were destined to be hysterical, incoherent, and irrational, did not help; it did not sound a particularly attractive option for women.

Initially, in 1986, when I first started writing about Irigaray, I hypothesized that one could make an analogy between *parler-femme* and what emerged during a psychoanalytic session, in which something of the unconscious can make itself heard and more importantly lead to change in the structures of the unconscious itself. I wrote as follows:

> It is of course difficult to understand what a woman's language could be, except by analogy with what we already know as language and therefore, as Jacqueline Rose points out, it sounds as though the desire for a different language is self-defeating, because it would break the conditions for any signifying or symbolising at all. But if we keep in mind the model of the psychoanalytic session, we might understand the idea of a woman's language as the articulation of the unconscious which cannot speak *about* itself, but which can nonetheless make itself heard if the listener is attentive enough. Irigaray defines discursive, theoretical or meta-language as 'male', and says there is no 'female' meta-language: 'there is simply no way I can give you an account of 'speaking (as) woman'; it is spoken, but not in meta-language.' (TS: 144; CS: 141; Whitford 1986)[15]

I now think it is possible to enlarge on that definition. Irigaray's thesis of women's language arose initially out of her work on the language (and language disturbances) of senile dementia. She says that she discovered quite unexpectedly – it was not one of the variables that she was controlling for (E: 128) – that there were significant differences between the impairments of women's speech and those in men's speech. Although in both cases one could register various linguistic breakdowns, they were not always the same for both sexes; women lost the linguistic function in different ways. The aim of *Le Langage des déments* (1973) was to classify the speech of senile dementia, to provide a grammar of dementia that would enable a clinical definition based on the nature of the linguistic disturbance in addition to the physiological factors registered by medical investigation. In this context, language for Irigaray means primarily enunciation,[16] i.e. the ability to generate new responses (LD: 348), the ability to respond to the speech of the other speaker. Her analysis of the language of senile dementia shows that, allowing for loss of memory and physical deterioration, the most serious misfunction in senile dementia is the loss of the ability to speak as a subject of enunciation in response to another 'pole' of enunciation – the other speaker – and to generate new responses in relation to the other and to the world. Dead language has taken over. Her patients have little or no metalinguistic ability and cannot use the corpus of language as an object to be manipulated. She concludes: 'The pole of enunciation in the case of senile dementia appears to be language [langage] and not the 'speaking subject', if, that is, one can still speak of enunciation here' (LD: 351).

In *Parler n'est jamais neutre* (not published until 1985), some of her earlier work on linguistic classification of the mentally ill was reprinted, showing that in addition to analysis of categories of mental illness that fall under primarily medical descriptions, she had also done work on the language of the schizophrenic (both a medical and psychoanalytic category) and the language of hysteria and obsession (both clearly psychoanalytic categories, although hysteria could be medical in another context). It became clear that Irigaray was attempting to establish, and formalize, a correlation between psychic phenomena or syndromes, and linguistic phenomena (manifested in the syntax and discursive flexibility of the enunciatory situation).[17] This leads me to suppose that one way of approaching *parler-femme* is to see it – initially and in a first moment – as a psychoanalytic definition, that is to say, like a diagnosis of a particular pathology (in the case of hysteria or obsession) or of psychic organization (such as identification as male or female).

Diagnosis on the basis of linguistic performance (syntax as well as content) is not an unfamiliar idea. Charles Rycroft, for example, points to

> the ways in which information about the patient's infantile anxiety situations and psychopathology can be deduced from his linguistic habits – a possibility which was first envisaged by Ella Sharpe in her paper 'Psycho-Physical Problems Revealed in Language: An Examination of Metaphor' (1940) and which has since been confirmed statistically in a series of papers by Lorenz and Cobb (1953). Lorenz (1953) suggests that many of our so-called intuitive judgments of others are in fact based on our unconscious perception and evaluation of their linguistic and syntactical habits, and cites examples of the way in which disturbances in object-relations, self-awareness, affectivity, etc., are reflected in habits of speech. (Rycroft 1986: 251)

And in fact much of Irigaray's recent work has been dedicated to demonstrating that differences can be shown to exist. The fact that the definition is psychoanalytic means that what one is looking for is evidence of a particular psychic configuration (which may in any case not be completely stable; shifts in object-relations, affectivity and so on, as Rycroft noted, may be registered in syntax); this rescues the definition from the more deterministic one that is sometimes attributed to her – the idea of a direct relation to the body. Deborah Cameron (1985) takes the latter line and quotes the following objection from *Questions féministes*:

> To advocate a 'woman's language' . . . seems to us . . . illusory . . .
> It is at times said that women's language is closer to the body, to sexual pleasure, to direct sensations and so on, which means that the body could express itself directly without special mediation and that, moreover, this closeness to the body and to nature would be subversive. In our opinion there is no such thing as a direct relation to the body. (Marks and de Courtivron 1981: 219, quoted in Cameron 1985: 130)

But Irigaray was already writing in 1966:

> *The reciprocal integration of language and the body*, in which the imaginary originates, decentres man in relation to himself and marks the beginning of his wandering [*errance*]. The impossible return to the body as the secure locus of his self-identity is its ineluctable corollary. From now on, he is mediated by language and one will only find trace of him in the word of the other. (PN: 15)

This Lacanian statement rejects quite clearly the possibility of a direct, unmediated relation to the body.[18] (The use of the word 'man' here predates the emphasis on sexual difference and I think the context of the article makes clear that it is human beings who are being talked about.) In my view, it doesn't make much sense to interpret Irigaray as falling back on pre-Lacanian positions, as I will argue in Chapters 3 and 4.

A second point about the definition is that if it is in fact a psychoanalytic one, then one could expect (a) variations in language in different interlocutory or communicational situations, and (b) the possibility of unconscious psychic change (such as takes place in psychoanalysis for example) to be registered linguistically. Irigaray's article on the grammar of hysteria and obsession (PN: 55–68) is particularly illuminating in this respect. If you accept that the subject of enunciation speaks through language, that the unconscious makes itself heard through speech (which is the basic presupposition of psychoanalysis); if neurosis can speak; if phantasy can speak without the conscious awareness of the speaker; then it is not surprising if gender can speak too. Assuming the Lacanian presupposition that to take up one's place in language one has to position oneself on one side or another of the male/female divide, that speaking subjects are either male or female, and that there is a difference between the male speaking subject and the female speaking subject (whatever the internal splits and identifications), then it would be odd to find that this one aspect of the unconscious, unlike all the others, left no distinctive marks on the discourse of the speaker. One would expect to find that men, for example, registered less conflict than women, since their subjectivity and their identity are congruent, whereas for women there would be a tension between subjectivity and female identity, which they could only resolve by abandoning one or the other. The marks of this tension, and rather stark choice, would inevitably be visible at certain moments (in analysis perhaps). So I think that *parler-femme* must refer to enunciation. This would also explain why *parler-femme* has no meta-language, since in the moment of enunciation the enunciation is directed towards an interlocutor (even if this direction is in the mode of avoidance), and cannot speak about itself. Enunciation and meta-language are mutually exclusive (E: 166); one cannot comment on one's own enunciatory position while simultaneously occupying it. Meta-language belongs to the *énoncé*. But since the position one takes up in enunciation is always in relation to an interlocutor, and as in analysis subject to an interpretation which has no outside guarantee, there would always be a problem of identifying *parler-femme*, particularly in the absence of a female symbolic.

At a second moment, one would need to distinguish between speaking (as) woman in patriarchal culture, in which that voice is not heard or listened to, and speaking (as) woman in a different symbolic order. (Even if that situation does not yet exist, it is the pole towards which change must orient itself.) The controversial description from *This Sex* would seem to correspond to the first case. The second one raises the question of change in the symbolic order and how it is to be achieved. What Irigaray is above all concerned to work out is the conditions of women's subjectivity – how women can assume the 'I' of discourse in their own right and not as a derivative male 'I'. This presupposes of course that what it is to be 'male' and 'female' is available to change, since they are possibilities provided by the symbolic order. Speaking (as) a woman is not only a psycholinguistic description, it is also the name for something which does not yet exist, the position of the female subject in the symbolic order. As will become apparent, I cannot agree with Kaja Silverman when she writes in her chapter on Irigaray that '[a]lthough Irigaray clings tenaciously to the concept of desire even in the face of its impossibility, she proves herself quite willing to relinquish subjectivity' (Silverman 1988: 160).[19] On the contrary, it seems to me that the question of female subjectivity is *central* to Irigaray's work.

I will have more to say about *parler-femme* and the relation between symbolic and social later in this chapter. For now I want to move on to the question of subjectivity in language. To clarify the discussion, it is helpful to distinguish between a number of different terms which I have been using until now without definition:

language (*langue*)	– the corpus of language available to the speaker
language (*langage*)	– the corpus as used by a particular person or group, e.g. the language of the mentally ill, or the language of lovers
discourse (*discours*)	– systemic instances of language (written or spoken)
enunciation (*énonciation*)	– the position of the speaking subject in the discourse or statement
énoncé (which I will keep in French)	– the content of the statement

It will be helpful to keep these definitions in mind in the following discussion. For when Irigaray talks about a different language, it is *langage* she has in mind, a different utilization of the resources available, both lexical and syntactical, in the way that her mentally ill patients, for example, employed, or failed to employ, a different range of syntactical devices.

There are similar problems with the definition of the subject or subjectivity.[20] One speaks of the subject in philosophy, the subject in psychoanalysis, the subject in language, the subject in culture as a historical agent, the subject of enunciation or of the *énoncé*, the transcendental subject, the empirical subject, and so on. Are they all the same, and what is the relation between them? The subject is a concept which has a history. It has shifted from its theoretical position as constituting ego and unifier of representations through the instability of the phenomenological subject (Sartre's ever-onward-thrusting and non-self-coinciding for-itself or *pour-soi*) to the irrevocably split subject of Lacanian theory. Judith Butler comments as follows:

> The twentieth-century history of Hegelianism in France can be understood in terms of two constitutive moments:(1) the specification of the subject in terms of finitude, corporeal boundaries, and temporality and (2) the 'splitting' (Lacan), 'displacement' (Derrida), and eventual death (Foucault, Deleuze) of the Hegelian subject. (Butler 1987: 175)

Whatever we eventually come to understand by woman-as-subject, it is clear that she has not had the same trajectory as the male subject. The successive adventures and crises of the Hegelian subject were not *her* adventures or crises.

I shall look first at Irigaray's claims that women need a language [langage] of their own, and argue that these are all aspects of the attempt to think woman-as-subject. For Irigaray, woman-as-subject in language and in the symbolic is the condition of the coming-to-be of woman-as-subject in the social, although I think that the relation is more two-way than this formulation suggests, in that the emergence of the women's movement – women's affirmation of themselves as social subjects – has also provided the conditions for the rethinking of subjectivity in language. All the themes I outline in the following pages will be developed in subsequent chapters. Here, by juxtaposing remarks from different parts of Irigaray's work, I attempt to shed light on the link between language and subjectivity.

Now, in imaginary and symbolic terms, language can be seen as a territory, a house or a home: 'men continually seek, construct, create for themselves houses everywhere: grottoes, huts, women, towns, language [langage], concepts, theory, etc.' (E: 133); so women too need a house of language:

> they need language, a language [il leur faut le langage, du langage]. That house of language [langue] which for man even constitutes a substitute for his home in a body . . . woman is used to construct it but (as a result?) it is not available to her (E: 105).

> It is necessary for a symbolism to be created among women in order for there to be love between them. This love is in any case only possible at the moment between women who can speak to each other. Without that

interval of *exchange*, or of words, or of gestures, passions between women manifest themselves in a . . . rather cruel way. (E: 103)

Irigaray's stated aim is to produce change in discourse (SP: 191). I understand her to mean here a shift in the position of the subjects of enunciation (as I discussed earlier in relation to the obsessional and hysterical patients). Now if culture – very schematically – enacts the drama of a hysteric endlessly demanding proofs of affection or validation of her existence from an obsessional male subject, for whom the other has no real existence except as something to be controlled, then no dialogue can get off the ground, and no satisfactory outcome can be foreseen. (This is a combative definition of hysteria, rather than the traditional equation of femininity with hysteria. It does not imply that all women are hysterics (pathology), but that there is no place for woman-as-subject in the symbolic. Pathology is transferred from the individual to the symbolic; it is the symbolic which is sick.) This is Irigaray's well-known picture of the hom(m)osexual culture in which men exchange goods and women. It is also perhaps exemplified in Descartes's classic vision, in the *Discourse on Method*, of the mastery of nature, where nature (woman/other) is posited as something to be mastered and dominated (see E: 78). In each case, one has to attempt to shift the position of the subject of enunciation to allow any kind of dialogue. The ideal dialogue would be one in which neither pole or interlocutor was frozen, immobile, fixed to one position, frozen in a predicate (E: 79), but in which each was able to respond to the other,[21] to provide a symbolic house for the other, to move readily between subject and object positions without being immobilized in either, or in which it was possible to allow the distinction between subject and object to become blurred, as in psychoanalysis, in the transference. However, at the moment, it is women who occupy the object position; in phantasy they are the mother's body; in language, they are the predicate. (It is the structuration of the imaginary which distributes these roles.) This will become clearer if we look at Irigaray's account of predication and language.

Psychoanalysis posits an imaginary equivalence between playing with the body of the mother and manipulating the corpus of language. Men's relationship to the phantasied mother is exemplified by the *fort-da*,[22] the manipulable object which can be thrown away and then retrieved. They can relate to the phantasied mother as to an object, without their own subject-position being put into question. If women learn their identity in the same way, the results are disastrous for that identity: 'The woman cannot reduce her mother to an object without reducing herself to an object at the same time, because they are of the same sex' (SP: 210). If women take the mother's body as a phantasied object, and at the same time a woman *identifies* with her mother, she is forced to take herself as an object too. Then as soon as she starts using language, she is objectifying the mother and herself. Using language then presents a woman with the choice between remaining outside the signifying system altogether (in order to stay with her mother) or entering a patriarchal genealogy in which her position as object is already given. Irigaray envisages that in a different economy: 'A woman would be directly in intersubjective relation with her mother. Her economy is that of the *between-subjects*, and not that of the subject– object relation' (SP: 211). Irigaray wants it to be possible for a woman to enter language as a subject, to make a female identification with her mother that does not objectify her: 'It is necessary for a woman to be able to speak her identity [se dire] in words, in images and in symbols within this intersubjective relation with her mother, then with other women, in order to enter into a relation with men that is not destructive' (SP: 211). A woman's first address to the other, her first 'you' (*tu*) should be to another woman, but for this to be possible the mother and woman *must* be symbolically differentiated. Hence the need for a female homosexual economy, and for a genealogy on the mother's side.

This point is put in another way when Irigaray writes in *Amante marine* that the subject-predicate structure of language presupposes woman as universal predicate (AM: 97). (This, incidentally, is another way of formulating the statement that the subject is male.) This is the context of Irigaray's remarks about bringing the body into language. The body that subtends language is the phantasied body of the mother:

> Language [langage], however formal it may be, is sustained by blood, by flesh, by material elements. Who and what has sustained it? how to pay that debt? (E: 122) ... [How] to bring the maternal-feminine into language [langage]: from the point of view of theme, motif, subject, articulation, syntax, etc. (E: 143)

The relationship is one of maternal sustenance which is related to the formal features of language (syntax) as well as to the content of statements (theme). For the maternal-feminine to enter language, for women to become subjects in language, another 'syntax' would be needed (whatever we understand by this), in which the predication was not simply one-way, in which women were not the 'universal predicate'. There are several comments in *This Sex* to the effect that we need another syntax or grammar of culture; here is one from *Sexes et parentés*:

> We lack, we women with a sex of our own kind [nous sexuées selon notre genre], a God in which to share, a word/language [verbe[23]] to share and to become. Defined as the often obscure, not to say hidden, mother-substance of the word/language [verbe] of men, we lack our *subject*, our *noun*, our *verb* [verbe], our *predicates*: our elementary sentence, our basic rhythm, our morphological identity, our generic incarnation, our genealogy. (SP: 83)

I'll come back to the idea of God a bit later. What I note here is that the absence of the maternal-feminine in language is connected with the position of woman as universal predicate.[24] (Anticipating a future chapter, it needs to be made clear at this stage that, for Irigaray, the symbolic order does not distinguish between the mother and the woman, and that the *mother* is never positioned as a subject, only as a predicate or substratum.)

How should we understand the demand for a different syntax? In *This Sex*, Irigaray comments on 'feminine syntax' as follows:

> what a feminine syntax might be is not simple nor easy to state, because in that 'syntax' there would no longer be either subject or object, 'oneness' would no longer be privileged, there would no longer be proper meanings, proper names, 'proper' attributes. . . . Instead, that 'syntax' would involve nearness, proximity, but in such an extreme form that it would preclude any distinction of identities, any establishment of ownership, thus any form of appropriation. (TS: 134; CS: 132)

(The style here is very definitely Irigaray's 'utopian' mode.) If one interprets the demand for another language as the demand for a language [langue] in which the subject-predicate structure disappears, then it would be rather self-defeating. However, I don't think it is necessary to interpret it in that way, since Irigaray refers elsewhere to the syntax or grammar of *culture* (TS: 143, 155; CS: 141, 151) or *society* (TS: 132; CS: 130), and makes it clear that she is talking about *langage* (TS: 155; CS: 151). This casts a completely different light upon the statement. *Langage* is an articulated communication system, it is not necessarily *langue*, since one can refer, for example, to *le langage des abeilles* (the language of bees). And in *This Sex* it is used to refer to social organization (TS: 132; CS: 130). So if the position of women in culture shifts, if women are no longer predicates in the cultural grammar, then this has an effect on language (*langage* or *discours*). (Culture is a word that Irigaray has recourse to frequently. I speculate that it covers over that difficult to formulate articulation of symbolic (as language) and symbolic (as social formations), implying homologous structure, but without arguing it in specific instances.) It is difficult to see how women might speak a different language if by language one means *langue*, and this seems to block any further understanding. One may admit that the subject-predicate structure obliterates women in language, but the price of bringing women into language then seems to be the end of signifying itself. No doubt this is why one hears the criticism that Irigaray wants to destroy or dissolve the symbolic order.

Shifting the position of the subject of enunciation, however, is more readily intelligible. At the level of enunciation, Irigaray hypothesizes that there could be a two-way predication (*de façon bi-univoque*) (E: 79), or that one might hear the enunciation of a desire which 'is not yet qualified . . . not yet frozen by a predicate' (E: 79). For this, we have to look beyond the third-person statement (the *constat*), although the third-person statement may conceal an enunciation (we shall come to this point shortly). The modalities of enunciation include: 'commands, prayers, appeals, thanks, pleas/benedictions [la grâce], cries, complaints, glorias, anger, questions . . .' (E: 132). These are most often traditionally addressed, not to the other sex, but to God:

> Performatives, the means of access to the presence of the other, to the relation to the other in and through language [langue], across time as well, are most often reserved for the relation between man and his God and not for the exchange between men and women as other. . . .
>
> It is rare for the question 'who art thou?' to be put to someone (male or female) other than God. (E: 132)

If a woman responds to the question, 'she disconcerts the order of discourse' (ibid.). Thus the question of enunciation and the question of the divine are related; they are to do with the other, the non-assimilable to self. Man's other, says Irigaray, has always been conceived of as God, and not the other sex. This brings us back then to the question of the divine, which was raised earlier in relation to *langage*, and to the question of the *sensible transcendental*. This is a central term in *Ethique de la différence sexuelle*, and yet it is not at all easy to see how to understand it. I am going to try and give a provisional definition here, but then come back to it from a different angle in subsequent chapters. The sensible transcendental is glossed in a number of ways. In particular, it is said to be a 'vital intermediary milieu, a perpetual journey [marche], a perpetual transvaluation, a permanent becoming, the immanent efflorescence of the divine' (E: 33, 36; see also E: 28). In its most general sense, I think the sensible transcendental is not a precise concept; it is a condensed way of referring to all the conditions of women's collective access to subjectivity. From one point of view (although this is not an exclusive definition), it can be seen as the symbolic order *in its possibilities of and for transformation*, in other words, language as a field of enunciation, process, response, and becoming, but a field in which there are *two* poles of enunciation, so that the 'I' may be 'male' or 'female', and so may the 'you', so that the speaker may change positions, exchange with the other sex; it follows, too, that the divine other must also be potentially of the female sex. And so we find that the sensible transcendental is also referred to as a *god*.[25]

We saw earlier that God and language could be identified, that *Dieu* and *verbe* could be the same. What links God, language, and woman here is the idea of becoming; God or language is defined in terms of becoming (see SP: 83); woman, or 'being in the feminine' [l'être au féminin] is also defined in terms of becoming (E: 132). And God and language are both defined in terms of a house or habitation (language – E: 105; God – E: 133). What is needed for women, then, is a habitation that does not contain or imprison them; instead of an invisible prison which keeps them captive, a habitation in which they can grow is the condition of becoming, and of becoming 'divine'. The sensible transcendental is a divine whose advent is still ahead of us:

of whose advent *we would be* the mediators and the bridges . . . bringing the god to life through us [à travers nous], between us, as a resurrection and transfiguration of blood and flesh through their language [langage] and their ethic. (E: 124)

To summarize then: the blood and flesh of the phantasied mother/woman, which sustains the language/house of men, must find its own symbolic expression in language, thus becoming the other pole of cultural discourse, and allowing two-way predication, (the 'double syntax'), unfreezing the discourse which has petrified (PN: 15), and at the same time giving to women the cultural and symbolic possibilities previously allowed only to men in patriarchy, including the possibility of divinity.

The sensible transcendental, then, is the flesh made word (in an audacious reversal of the New Testament), but not in a simple predicative sense. Since the definition incorporates consistently the idea of process and becoming, it cannot refer to *langue*, the more or less rigidified corpus, but only to language in its possibilities for exchange and response to the other, to the non-self, the other subject or pole of enunciation. It must then be language (*langage*) as ideally enunciative (though enunciation on its own is not enough; an object of exchange is needed; however, this can now be a language in which the bodies of women are no longer the universal predicate). So the dynamics of enunciation are here given primacy over language which simply conveys information or truth, such as theoretical language (*le constat*). Epistemology is subtended by the subject of enunciation, and it is that subject which concerns Irigaray.

Irigaray conceives of the subject-in-process (to borrow a useful term from Kristeva) as a subject in dialogue, engaged with the other. This explains why knowledge is linked to love, and why love is central to *Ethique de la différence sexuelle*:

contrary to the usual methods of dialectic, love should not have to be abandoned in order to become wise or learned. It is love which leads to knowledge [science]. . . . It is love which leads the way and is the path, both. A mediator par excellence. (E: 27–8)

The change in discourse that Irigaray envisages only takes place when one's deep unconscious feelings are mobilized: in the child's relation with its parents, in the analysand's relation to the analyst, in the relationship between lovers and, perhaps most crucially, in the love between women – as actual or spiritual mothers and daughters or sisters – in subject-to-subject relationships, for which the women's movement has provided new possibilities. Playing with a text, from Irigaray's point of view, is a rather solipsistic activity; it is not a dialogue with the other which includes process and the possibility of change. The conditions of emergence of female subjectivity are simultaneously, then, love between women (a female homosexual economy) which is the matrix which can generate change, and language or discourse as a process of enunciation, a dynamic exchange between interlocutors which can transfigure flesh and blood. This is also the prerequisite for dialogue between the sexes, so that each can offer a house or home to the other.

Irigaray is thus addressing herself both to the philosophers, whom she is trying to 'seduce'[26] into an amorous exchange, and to other women. The first address is not an untraditional one, although as it is *explicitly* mimetic, (she is playing the role of the 'philosopher's wife') it must be read in inverted commas. The second address has no such obvious strategy marked out for it, since the new relations between women are still in the process of creation. I shall go on to suggest one of the possible ways of responding to Irigaray's address.

Woman-as-subject

The problem for feminists is to move from enunciation to epistemology. Men have a 'long-term practice in discursive relations to the world and to the other'(E: 130–1). The male subject of enunciation conceals himself beneath third-person statements. 'The *he/it* is a transformation, a transposition of the *I* ' (E: 130). There is 'a kind of effacing of the enunciation in an edifice of language [langage]' (ibid.). 'The *he/it* also becomes a *there is*, another mask for the *I* ' (ibid.). In the discourse of science and knowledge, apparently no one is responsible. Whereas in analysis, in cases of pathology, Irigaray says, the structure of the apparently neutral third-person discourse becomes clearly visible; one can see the redundance of the 'I' (since all third-person statements are referred back to the self) and the self-confirming process of the enunciation. The women's movement has acted as a kind of social psychoanalysis (E: 130). It has revealed the self-referential quality of epistemology and its hidden subject of enunciation. At the same time, the women's movement, in drawing attention to the male subject of enunciation, has staked a claim for the right of a female subject of enunciation to be an epistemological subject too: 'to become *Is* [des "*je*"] producing truth: cultural, political and religious' (E: 130). So far, Irigaray suggests, women have only reached the threshold of meaning (E: 131), but this is clearly what is at stake. Her analysis of language indicates the immense cultural transformations that will be needed. Hence the distinction between speaking *like* a woman and speaking *as* a woman is vital, since to speak *as* a woman implies not simply psychosexual positioning, but also social positioning. The dual function of the term *parler-femme* can now be noted; not only can it refer to 'feminine' language, it is also a pun on *par les femmes* (by women). The pun is retained in the English translation as 'speaking (as) woman'.

There has been a tendency in recent writing to suggest that the feminine position can be adopted by either sex, and this has led to some politically equivocal gestures. To the extent that we are talking about linguistic representation of a psychic configuration, it is well known that male and female identifications can be made by either sex; this is visible in psychoanalysis, in the transference. But as Irigaray points out, one should not confuse *identification* with *identity* (SP: 210). So when Kristeva or Cixous want to give instances of a different kind of writing, they instance the 'feminine' writing of certain male authors – Mallarmé, Lautréamont, Artaud (for Kristeva) or Kleist (for Cixous, although Cixous has subsequently found an exemplary woman writer, Clarice Lispector). In philosophy too, Derrida claims that he wants to write like a woman: 'I would like to write, too, like a woman. I try to . . .' [J'aimerais bien écrire, aussi, comme (une) femme. J'essaie . . .].[27] (It's rather ambiguous in French because of those brackets; 'comme une femme' means 'like a woman', whereas 'comme femme' is much closer to 'as a woman'.) Commenting on Derrida, Irigaray writes:

> All the philosophers I've mentioned [Nietzsche, Heidegger, Hegel, Levinas and Derrida] – except Heidegger – are interested in feminine identity and in their identity as feminine or women. . . . Turning back towards the moment at which they seized socio-cultural power(s), are men seeking a way to divest themselves of these powers? I hope so. Such a desire would imply that they are inviting women to share in the definition of truth and the exercising of it with them. Up to now, writing differently has not done much to affect the sex of political leaders or their civil and religious discourses.[28]

Not only has writing differently not obviously led to an invitation to women to participate as women in the making of culture, it has also led to the paradoxical conclusion (discussed in more detail in Chapter 6) that feminists are speaking like men. Very roughly, to speak or write like a man is to assert mastery, to be in control of meaning, to claim truth, objectivity, knowledge, whereas to speak like a woman is to refuse mastery, to allow meaning to be elusive or shifting, not to be in control, or in possession of truth or knowledge. So to be assertive, to make claims, to be 'dogmatic', which means to have a thesis, a meaning, a political position, is to take up a 'male' stance, whatever one's sex. So we are left in the rather odd position that men (the philosophers who want to write like women) are better at being women than women are. This is one of the problems that Irigaray's work is addressing.

From Irigaray's point of view, the male philosophers and writers who are attempting to write like women are in practice trying to colonize the space that might become women's. Their 'feminine' is, in Irigaray's terms, 'the other of the same', not the 'other of the other' (these terms will be explained later). They are still within the same hom(m)osexual economy. For this reason, Irigaray now places the emphasis more on woman-as-subject than on *parler-femme*. I think this element has been there all along – it is largely a question of focus. Now what she emphasizes is that occupying the subject-position is not simply a question of the position of enunciation, it must be rooted in social practices too – part of the definition of woman-as-subject is that women must be involved in the construction of the world and the making of culture and sociopolitical reality. One definition of *parler-femme* should therefore be that speaking as a woman should be language (*langage*) or discourse which contributes to making it possible for women to occupy the social and symbolic space as woman-subjects, epistemological subjects, producers of truth and culture. This position is summarized forcefully by Rosi Braidotti as follows:

> Irigaray's strategy consists in refusing to separate the symbolic, discursive dimension from the empirical, material historical one. She refuses to dissociate questions of the feminine from the presence of real-life women and in so doing she may appear to repeat the binary perversion of phallocentrism, by equating the feminine with women and the masculine with men. But the apparent mimesis is tactical. (Braidotti 1989: 99)

Some women have expressed fears that Irigaray's *parler-femme* takes 'the risk of speaking in no voice at all' (Martindale 1987: 18). I think this fear is also implicit in Michèle Le Doeuff's remark that: 'We will not talk pidgin to please the colonialists' (1987: 196). Although the context indicates that she is referring to the 'femininity' of the philosophers, from what she says about Irigaray elsewhere one may infer that this could also be taken as a comment on *parler-femme*. In fact Irigaray makes a clear distinction between the 'femininity' of the philosophers ('the other of the same') and the 'femininity' of *parler-femme* ('the other of the other'). To be a female subject of enunciation is not to speak pidgin. This is to confuse the first moment – the unheard feminine in patriarchy – and the second moment – the demands of women claiming their right to be epistemological subjects too. I think we have to distinguish between these two moments to make sense of Irigaray. However, it is not surprising if the two moments have been confused, for they rely upon a sleight of hand. If *parler-femme* cannot speak *about* itself, for example, then how can a woman be the subject of culture, 'producer of truth'? But, on the other hand, a woman as subject of culture depends for her advent on a collective transformation of the symbolic which in fact is still in the future. Irigaray is speaking *as if*, as Kathleen Martindale points out: 'she writes in the optative mood about a world that is not yet in existence' (1987: 18).[29] These two moments intertwine in the text; but strictly speaking their coexistence is a problem. If Irigaray's diagnosis of patriarchy is correct, what position can she make it from? Logically, since *parler-femme* cannot speak about itself, she can only make it from a position *in the future*. This leads to the paradoxical situation that if she is right, then according to her analysis she should not be able to make that analysis at all. This is not a dilemma unique to Irigaray; it is embodied in feminism itself, in the presupposition that the vision of a hypothetical future can have an effect on the present.

To ask whether Irigaray herself is speaking a masculine or feminine discourse would be to hypostatize a process. To attempt to mine her writing for models of *parler-femme* would be, I think, to miss the point which is that she is initiating a possible dialogue between herself and her readers. I suggest that she is proposing her work as a sort of intermediary between women, as that indispensable third party in any symbolic relationship (which is therefore precisely *not* a dual imaginary relationship), as an object of exchange, especially between women, which we can use in order to avoid one of the common impasses of the attempts at a women's sociality: unmediated (because unsymbolized) affects. In Irigarayan terms, it might create the *espacement* or the 'space between' that is difficult to women who are required to constitute space for men (see Chapter 7). Her work is offered as an object, a discourse, for women to exchange *among themselves*, a sort of commodity, so that women themselves do not have to function as the commodity, or as the *sacrifice* on which sociality is built. Instructions for use of Irigaray would include the message: Do not consume or devour. For symbolic exchange only.

Chapter 3

Rationality and the imaginary

[L'homme] ne se souvient même plus du fait que son corps est le seuil, le portique de la construction de son, ses univers. (*Ethique de la différence sexuelle*)
Man no longer even remembers that his body is the threshold, the porch of the construction of his universe(s).

Irigaray's critique of rationality is not a prescription for female irrationality; to say that rationality is male is to argue that it has a certain structure, that the subject of enunciation which subtends the rational discourse is constructed in a certain way, through repression of the feminine. What I shall suggest in the following two chapters is that Irigaray is proposing, not the abolition of rationality – she is after all adept herself in the manipulation of rational argument – but the *restructuring* of the construction of the rational subject. To understand Irigaray's critique of rationality it is necessary to understand the notion of the imaginary, and in particular to see the ways in which Irigaray has attempted to reclaim the imaginary from its most well-known recent conceptualization in Lacan. For the Lacanian conceptual system offers scant possibility for radical social change; Lacanian discourse implies a deep social conservatism as far as the situation of women is concerned.[1]

One of the points Irigaray makes in her critique of psychoanalysis is that psychoanalysis is 'a possible enclave of philosophic discourse' (TS: 160; CS: 155), and thus that the conceptualization of the unconscious has a history (PN: 254). The unconscious is not *literally* an undiscovered continent and cannot so readily be mapped. To see the function of woman in the theory, one needs first to begin from different presuppositions. This point is clearly exemplified in Irigaray's deployment of the term 'imaginary', a term with multiple conceptual resonances. The briefest working definition of the 'imaginary' is that it is equivalent to unconscious phantasy (see pp.65–6), but to limit its function to this definition would be to deprive it of all its associative richness. I will begin with a brief account of the recent history of the term, before going on to elucidate its function in Irigaray's critique of western rationality. Even a brief survey of its range will serve as a caution against the too rapid reinterpretation of Irigaray's language in terms of the Lacanian framework. For although Irigaray clearly does have some debt to Lacan, she also demarcates herself sharply from his conceptualizations, and redefines the imaginary for her own purposes.

One source of the term 'imaginary' is phenomenology. (One should keep in mind that Irigaray can be situated at least partly in the phenomenological tradition, and indeed sometimes situates herself there.)[2] Sartre, in his book *L'Imaginaire* (1940) [*The Psychology of the Imagination*] made a sharp distinction between the perceiving and imagining functions of the mind, and held (a) that the imagining consciousness was intentional and (b) that it could not be confused with the perceiving consciousness. According to Sartre's definition, the imaginary is the intentional object of the *imagining* consciousness, whether it is an object in the mind (fantasies, daydreams, evocations of absent persons, and so on) or external objects which are products of the imagination (such as novels or paintings). Without retaining Sartre's theory of intentionality, Irigaray does appeal to a phenomenological definition when she looks to myth and poetry for images of the material of which our passions are constructed (see SP: 69 ff.). Unlike Sartre, however, she conflates in a single term the phenomenological definition of the imaginary (the conscious, imagining, and imaging, mind) with the psychoanalytic definition (the unconscious, phantasying mind), and can move fluidly between one and the other. She has never shown any particular interest in Sartre's work; on the other hand, she has written sympathetically on Merleau-Ponty, whose two terms *invisible* and *visible* (Merleau-Ponty 1964) can perhaps be serviceable here. Thus we could say that sometimes the imaginary is an unconscious (invisible) structure and sometimes a structure of the symbolic which can be viewed in its external and visible manifestations in myth, or works of the imagination. Like Merleau-Ponty, Irigaray is interested in pre-discursive experience (E: 143) and how conceptualization of experience brings with it certain ontological commitments: designation of objects in the world, allocation of subjects and objects and so on. However, she criticizes Merleau-Ponty for a kind of solipsism, for failing to take into account the sexual other (E: 148). She goes further than previous phenomenologists in that she conceptualizes the imaginary in terms of sex, either male or female: the imaginary either bears the morphological marks of the male body, whose cultural products are characterized by unity, teleology, linearity, self-identity, and so on or it bears the morphological marks of the female body, characterized by plurality, non-linearity, fluid identity and so on. In this sense, her use of the term imaginary, linking the imaginary with the products of the imagination – art, mythology, poetry, writing – does bring her momentarily close to other so-called proponents of *écriture féminine*. The following remark by Hélène Cixous shows the way in which the phenomenological and psychoanalytic versions of the imaginary may be conflated:

Things are starting to be written, things that will constitute a f&
Imaginary, the site, that is, of identifications of an ego no longer
over to an image defined by the masculine . . ., but rather inver
forms for women on the march, or as I prefer to fantasize, 'in flight',
that instead of lying down, women will go forward by leaps in search of
themselves. (Cixous 1981: 52)

It is important to note that the (unconscious, invisible) identifications require
external sites (such as writing), *visible* products of the imagination. One can
see Irigaray's own 'poetic' writing as attempts to mobilize a possible other
(female) imaginary.

Another source of 'the imaginary' is Bachelard. Although Irigaray never,
as far as I know, mentions Bachelard, within the French intellectual
context the resonances of the term imaginary are clearly Bachelardian.
In addition, Irigaray's use of the four elements seems to echo Bachelard's,
below. The imaginary, for Bachelard, as for Sartre, is a function of
the imagination. It is that faculty of the mind which alters the images
provided by perception and *distorts* them. This distortion may be creative
in the case of the literary imagination, but it contaminates the effort to
acquire scientific knowledge. A sharp distinction is therefore made, as in
Sartre, between two functions of the mind which either cannot (Sartre) or
should not (Bachelard) be confused. Knowledge has to purify itself of the
images supplied so readily by the imagination in order to achieve genuine
objectivity. The image offers apparent and seductive solutions to problems
of knowledge which must be resisted if real knowledge is to be won. In
a number of works, Bachelard classes these images in terms of the four
elements: earth, air, fire, and water, and argues that these are primitive and
basic categories of the imagining mind. Irigaray makes a similar argument:

When I wrote *Amante marine, Passions élémentaires, L'Oubli de l'air*, I
intended to make a study of our relations to the elements: water,
earth, fire, air. I wanted to return to those natural materials which
constitute the origin of our body, our life, our environment, the flesh
of our passions. . . . Our daily life still takes place in a universe which
is composed of and can be described in terms of four natural elements:
air, water, fire, earth. We are built of them and we dwell in them. They
determine, more or less freely, our attractions, our affects, our passions,
our limits, our aspirations. (SP: 69)[3]

Bachelard suggests that creative writers have a preference for one element
over another, and that there in usually one in which they feel most at home. For
example he devotes a whole chapter of *L'Air et les songes* (1943) [*Air and Dreams*]
to Nietzsche's 'dynamics of ascension' (air), whereas Irigaray, in her book
on Nietzsche, looks rather for what is absent (the repressed mother/woman)
and takes Nietzsche's work as a point of departure for a meditation on the
flight from water and from the unacknowledged nurturant element. Here the

Bachelardian analysis of a dominant element is linked to her aim to 'go back through the masculine imaginary, to interpret the way it has reduced us to silence' (TS: 164; CS: 159). For, whereas for Bachelard there is a disjunction between knowledge and imagination, with knowledge having to be separated off sharply from the imagination which would otherwise distort it, Irigaray argues that the disjunction from the imaginary cannot finally be made, that knowledge always bears the marks of the imaginary, and that what we take to be universal and objective is in fact male, so that the four elements in their turn are subtended by a more basic schema than Bachelard's, namely the male/female division. Bachelard's attempted disjunction depends on the male splitting off from the female and then claiming universality (knowledge); the female remains repressed and mute, excluded from knowledge and universality. There can thus be no question of purification by getting rid of the sexual imaginary; knowledge is irrevocably marked by its imaginary (male) morphology. The belief that knowledge can purify itself in this way is itself an imaginary belief.[4]

A third source of the 'imaginary' is the confluence of political and psychoanalytic discourses in the work of Althusser and Castoriadis, particularly the latter. Castoriadis is known both as a critic of classical Marxism and a critic of Lacanian psychoanalysis. He is, or was, a member of a psychoanalytic group, *Le Quatrième Groupe* [The Fourth Group] formed in 1969 after disagreements with Lacan (Marini 1986: 22), and he has since become one of Lacan's most outspoken critics (Castoriadis 1978). In particular, Castoriadis attacks Lacan's definition of the imaginary for its conservatism. In *L'Institution imaginaire de la société* (1975), he proposes a definition of the imaginary which (a) argues that there is an imaginary more primordial than that conceptualized by Lacan, an imaginary of which the mirror stage imaginary would be but a secondary derivation, and (b) deploys the concept of the imaginary in an explicit attempt to understand the persistence of social formations and the possibility of changing them. One of the names he gives to this primordial creative source is 'magma' (1975: 253), a term which is also used by Irigaray. Castoriadis's theorization of the imaginary, which uses the same term to cover both the imaginary as a primordial creative source or magma, and the imaginary as a social formation, is probably the closest to Irigaray's imaginary but does not coincide with it. Castoriadis does not discuss sex as a dimension of the imaginary. From Irigaray's point of view, while she admits that Marxism, for example, was a precondition of her own thought, she does not believe that the current political (and non-feminist) discourses offer any place for thinking sexual difference.[5]

Whenever we find the term 'imaginary' in Irigaray's work, then, we have not only to look for the network of associations *within* her work that give the term its meaning, but also to bear in mind the network of associations circulating in the intellectual context within which she is writing and being read. In summary, the imaginary is a term which has a connotative range in recent French thought that has no equivalent in English. English-speaking readers tend to be familiar with the imaginary primarily via Lacan who gives the Imaginary a major role in his theory. My view is that Anglo-American feminists have tended to assimilate and then dismiss Irigaray's work too quickly, in part because the concept of the imaginary (and its corollary, morphology)[6] has not been closely examined. Either the imaginary has been ignored altogether, in which case Irigaray is mistakenly described as a biological essentialist, or else it has been interpreted as purely and simply a Lacanian concept, in which case the conclusion is that Irigaray has misunderstood or misread Lacan, and has not taken on board the implications of his theory (see Mitchell and Rose 1982: 54–6; Rose 1986: 136, 140; Ragland-Sullivan 1986: 273–80). In either case, the critique of Lacan has not been noticed or taken seriously, and the challenge to the western conception of rationality has largely been ignored.

In the first section, I will begin with a description of the difference between the male and female imaginary as characterized by Irigaray, without at this point trying to say exactly what the imaginary is, or to explain or account for the elements in the description. In the second section I will examine the evolution of the concept of the imaginary in Irigaray's work, and its origins in psychoanalytic theory. This section will clarify the initial description of the imaginary and show what is meant by the claim that rationality is imaginary. In the third section I will return to the categories of male and female as applied to the imaginary, and argue that Irigaray does not see them primarily as empirical descriptions which can be 'read off' the world, but as reconceptualizations which might help us change and transform our society in a direction which is less inimical to women. Although Irigaray eschews the domain of politics as commonly thought of, her reconceptualizations can be seen as a contribution to feminism as a political and social movement in which what is at stake is not simply philosophy but the lives and futures of women (and men).[7]

The symbolism of male and female

There have been a number of discussions recently, which I shall not attempt to summarize here, about whether it makes sense to talk of the 'maleness' of philosophy (see Harding and Hintikka 1983; Lloyd 1984; Grimshaw 1986, ch.2). Very briefly, the argument concerns what it would mean to describe philosophy, or rationality, as male. Lloyd, for example, argues that 'our ideals of Reason have historically incorporated an exclusion of the feminine, and . . . femininity itself has been partly constituted through such processes of exclusion' (1984: x). Grimshaw suggests that conceptions of masculinity are built into certain philosophical theories, arguing, for example, that Kant defines moral worth in such a way that women – as described by him elsewhere – are incapable of it (1986: 42–5). From the point of view that

concerns me here, the problem is that conceptions of rationality seem to have
been based on exclusion models. Male/female symbolism has been used 'to
express subordination relations between elements of a divided human nature'
(Lloyd 1984: 28) and reason, conceptualized as transcendence, in practice
came to mean transcendence of the feminine, because of the symbolism
used, despite the fact that 'it can of course be pointed out that mere bodily
difference surely makes the female no more appropriate than the male to
the symbolic representation of "lesser" intellectual functions' (Lloyd 1984:
32).

Irigaray's work constitutes an attack upon such exclusion models, drawing
for its symbolism on psychoanalysis. There is a view in psychoanalytic
theory, based on clinical evidence, that psychic health may be conceived
of, unconsciously, as a state in which both parents, i.e. both the male
and the female elements, are felt to be in creative intercourse within the
psyche. Along these lines, then, Irigaray argues that for rationality to
be fertile and creative, rather than infertile and sterile, it must not be
conceived of as transcending or *exclusive of* the female element. The model
is that of a creative (sexual) relationship in which the two elements in
intercourse bring forth offspring, rather than a domination/subordination
model in which one part of the self is repressing another part (as reason
may be said to dominate the passions, for example). For Irigaray, the
conceptualization of rationality is inseparable from the conceptualization
of sexual difference; thus the imbalance in the symbolization of sexual
difference is a clue to other forms of imbalance that have far-reaching
consequences: sexual difference is 'a problematic which might enable us
to put in check the manifold forms of destruction of the world. . . . Sexual
difference could constitute the horizon of worlds of a fertility which we
have not yet experienced' (E: 13). The critique of rationality is couched,
at least partly, in the vocabulary of fertility/sterility, creation/destruction,
health/sickness; rationality as we know it is implicated in a whole cultural
pathology.

Although the terms 'male' and 'female' are sometimes used to refer
to biological males and females, it is much more common to find the
pair being used as a kind of basic and fundamental symbolism (of which
Genevieve Lloyd gives many examples in the history of philosophy and
Alice Jardine (1985) in contemporary French thought). Irigaray would argue
that rationality in the western tradition has always been conceptualized or
symbolized as male. She adds a psychoanalytic dimension to this – which
I will explain further in the next section – by making a connection between
the morphology of the body and the morphology of different kinds of
thought processes. It must not be assumed here that the body here is
the empirical body; symbolism (or representation) is selective;[8] and it is
clear from *Speculum* that Irigaray is talking about an 'ideal morphology'
(SE: 320; SF: 400), in which the relationship to anatomy is metaphorical,

somewhat schematic, a 'symbolic interpretation of . . . anatomy' (Gallop 1983: 79). Anticipating, one might say that it is an imaginary anatomy. So she can say that in the phallomorphic sexual metaphoricity (SE: 47; SF: 53–4) of western rationality, there is 'no change in morphology, no detumescence ever' (SE: 303; SF: 378). The imaginary morphology of western rationality is characterized by: the principle of identity (also expressed in terms of quantity or ownership); the principle of non-contradiction (in which ambiguity, ambivalence, or multivalence have been reduced to a minimum); and binarism (e.g. nature/reason, subject/object, matter/energy, inertia/movement) – as though everything had to be either one thing or another (PN: 313). All these principles are based upon the possibility of individuating, or distinguishing one thing from another, upon the belief in the necessity of stable forms.[9] An equation is made between the (symbolic) phallus, stable form, identity, and individuation. Irigaray explains in *This Sex* that the logic of identity is male because it is phallomorphic:

> The *one* of form, of the individual, of the (male) sexual organ, of the proper name, of the proper meaning . . . supplants, while separating and dividing, that contact of *at least two* (lips) which keeps woman in touch with herself. (TS: 26; CS: 26)

For the female imaginary, there is no 'possibility of distinguishing what is touching from what is touched' (TS: 26; CS: 26). The possibility of individuating is absent; woman '*is neither one nor two*' (ibid.):

> Perhaps it is time to return to that repressed entity, the female imaginary. So woman does not have a sex organ? She has at least two of them, but they are not identifiable as ones. Indeed she has many more. Her sexuality, always at least double, goes even further: it is *plural*. (TS: 28; CS: 27)

> But if the female imaginary were to deploy itself, if it could bring itself into play otherwise than as scraps, uncollected debris, would it represent itself, even so, in the form of *one* universe? (TS: 30; CS: 29)

It is not that the female is unidentifiable, but that there is 'an excess of all identification to/of self' (SE: 230; SF: 285). The principle of non-contradiction does not apply. The female imaginary is mobile and fluid: 'a proper(ty) that is never fixed in the possible identity-to-self of some form or other. It is always fluid' (TS: 79; CS: 76). In *Ethique*, the undifferentiated maternal-feminine is described as that which underlies 'all possibility of determining identity' (E: 98). Like the womb, it is the 'formless, "amorphous" origin of all morphology' (SE: 265; SF: 330; trans. adapted).

The reader will note the correspondence between the descriptions of the male and female imaginary, and the Pythagorean table of opposites, described by Aristotle in the *Metaphysics* (986a). About this table, Genevieve Lloyd comments:

In the Pythagorean table of opposites, formulated in the sixth century BC, femaleness was explicitly linked with the unbounded – the vague, the indeterminate – as against the bounded – the precise and clearly determined. The Pythagoreans saw the world as a mixture of principles associated with determinate form, seen as good, and others associated with formlessness – the unlimited, irregular or disorderly – which were seen as bad or inferior. There were ten such contrasts in the table: limit/unlimited, odd/even, one/many, right/left, male/female, rest/motion, straight/curved, light/dark, good/bad, square/oblong. Thus 'male' and 'female', like the other contrasted terms, did not here function as straightforwardly descriptive classifications. 'Male', like the other terms on its side of the table, was construed as superior to its opposite; and the basis for this superiority was its association with the primary Pythagorean contrast between form and formlessness. (Lloyd 1984: 3)

This correspondence between Irigaray's description of the imaginary, and the ontological categories of the pre-Socratics, is not, of course, accidental. I interpret the description of the female imaginary, for example, not as an essentialist description of what women are really like, but as a description of the female as she appears in, and is symbolized by, the western cultural imaginary. The implications of this apparent ahistoricism are not entirely clear. (I say 'apparent' because almost all of Irigaray's analyses are of specific texts; they are not wildly unsubstantiated universalist claims.) It may be that, as Joanna Hodge interestingly suggests, for Irigaray, *women have no history;*[10] or it may be that the philosophical imaginary has no history.[11] My own (provisional) interpretation is that Irigaray is displaying what she regards as *patriarchy's* view of women: that they are 'natural' and therefore outside history. In short, the imaginery is open to some of the same objections as the concept of patriarchy;[12] it is an extremely useful concept, but also a controversial one.

Although the theoretical constructions of the symbolic may be highly sophisticated and abstract, the underlying imaginary is much more simplified; it deals with the primitive material of experience: life and death, kin relationships, and the body (either the body surface or speculations about what might be inside). It is also passional through and through; none of these figures is affectively neutral (dreams are often the nearest we can usually come to the experience of these basic feelings and thoughts). Irigaray seems to be positing that to rethink the cultural imaginary it may be necessary to bypass the sophistication of theoretical constructions, whose imaginary is so well and so deeply concealed, and to return to the elemental, 'those natural materials which constitute the origin of our body, our life, our environment, the flesh of our passions' (SP: 69). The exploration of the elemental, then, belongs to a more constructive aspect of Irigaray's work, and not simply to its critical moment.[13]

I said earlier that the coincidence between the conceptualization of the imaginary and the ontological categories of the pre-Socratics was not accidental; it is part of her attempt to 'go back through the masculine imaginary'. Without implying a return to the pre-Socratic world-view, the elemental offers also a number of strategies for bypassing the sophisticated defensive structures of theory. In the first place, it provides a vocabulary for talking in the most basic terms about the material of passional life, about opposition and conflict, or love and exchange, about fertility and creativity, or sterility and death, a vocabulary which is more immediate and direct in its language than the abstractions of conceptualization, yet without the immobilizing tendencies of the concept. It is a discursive strategy which allows for fluidity. Elizabeth Grosz explains:

> Empedocles' representation of the four elements provides a startling yet apposite metaphor of the meeting of different substances, a perilous meeting which, through Love, can bring productivity and unexpected creation, and through Strife can break down apparent unities and stable forms of co-existence. It is thus a rich metaphor for contemplating the possibilities of autonomy and interaction between the two sexes. (Grosz 1989: 169)

The texts which draw on the elemental vocabulary – *Amante Marine, L'Oubli de l'air, Passions élémentaires*, but also others such as *L'Une ne bouge pas sans l'autre* [And the One Doesn't Stir Without the Other], 'When Our Lips Speak Together' in *This Sex*, 'Fecundity of the Caress' in *Ethique* and 'Femmes Divines' [Divine Women] in *Sexes et parentés* – explore the realization or failure of love, whether the creative love between the sexes that I mentioned earlier, or the love between those of the same sex (which will be discussed further in subsequent chapters). For 'love should not have to be abandoned in order to become wise or learned' (E: 27). The same point is made in both the more theoretical and the more poetic texts. This is how Irigaray describes love in *Passions élémentaires*:

> Love may be the becoming which appropriates the other for itself by consuming it, introjecting it into itself, until the other disappears. Or love may be the motor of becoming which allows each its own growth. For the latter, each one must keep its body autonomous. Neither should be the source of the other. Two lives should embrace and fertilize each other, without the other being a preconceived goal for either. (PE: 32–3)

There is a sense in which this love can be said to be divine;[14] it has the features of the sensible transcendental: it is embodied and it allows for growth and becoming, not immobilizing either lover in his/her own growth. This is the ideal towards which Irigaray's critique of the western cultural imaginary tends; its precondition is the possibility of a specific female imaginary which would not simply be the scraps or debris of the masculine. This creative and loving imaginary relationship is the new (as yet non-existent) base which Irigaray proposes for the renewal of thought and rationality.

In the second place, I suggest, the recourse to the elemental provides a vocabulary for talking about the passions, including the erotic passions, without depending on the erotic vocabulary currently available. Discourse about the bodies of women is inevitably recaptured by the dominant sexual economy. Elizabeth Grosz again (she is talking about religion, but I think her remark applies equally to the erotic): 'it is not possible to position female-oriented images in place of male ones where the underlying structure accords no specificity to the female' (Grosz 1986c: 6).

The elements allow Irigaray to speak of the female body, of its morphology, and of the erotic, while avoiding the dominant sexual metaphoricity which is scopic and organized around the male gaze; she can speak of it instead in terms of space and thresholds and fluids, fire and water, air and earth, without objectifying, hypostatizing, or essentializing it. These terms are not so easily reduced to the body of one sex or the other. They are more pliable, accessible to the imagination of others and available for their private mental landscapes. They have both an individual and a collective dimension. The advantage too of the vocabulary of the elements is that one is less likely to confuse the imaginary with real objects in the world (such as the body).

Third, there may be a political as well as a theoretical rationale. In the traditional repartition of roles, women *represent* the body for men. The resulting split between intelligible and sensible then becomes difficult to shift, because it appears to be the basis of all thought. This is why, I think, Irigaray does not want to oppose yet another theory, but tries instead to reach the imaginary more directly. I hypothesize that the elements, in their simplicity, may have an access to the imaginary of others that more theoretical accounts lack. (In addition, the vocabulary of the elements, as building materials of art, writing, and poetry, is accessible to all, and not just to the theoretically sophisticated.) The role Irigaray attributes to poetry in this respect is significant. Poets, like psychoanalysts (or lovers) may speak the liberating word. The elements, then, can represent an unstructured and fluid psychic space, less constrained by the dominant imaginary, more open to other possibilities. It is the poet who takes the risk of exploring these spaces, and who can then presumably offer glimpses of previously undreamt-of horizons.

However we interpret the strategies involved, I think there is no doubt that the exploration of the imaginary and the vocabulary of the elements are linked, and are related to the project of *thinking sexual difference*.

The imaginary

In this section I shall trace briefly the development of the imaginary in Irigaray's work. It seems to me that between *Speculum* and the work which follows it Irigaray becomes more confident; the initial fairly cautious appropriation of the term in a relatively uncontroversial way is succeeded by a bolder and more extensive deployment with much more far-reaching connotations. The points to which I want to draw particular attention in this section are:

- the importance of the imaginary body in philosophy;
- the introduction of the notion that the imaginary may be male or female;
- the description of rationality as imaginary.

As most readers of French theory know by now, the imaginary is a psychoanalytic concept developed by Lacan in his reading of Freud. The concept, if not the term, is introduced by Lacan in his article entitled 'The Mirror Stage as Formative of the Function of the I as Revealed in Psychoanalytic Experience' (Lacan, 1977: 1–7). The imaginary is a moment in the formation of the Ego or 'I': the baby, whose experience of its body until then had been fragmented and incoherent, is enabled, by means of a mirror (or an image of itself mirrored from a parental figure or figures) to see a reflection of itself as a whole body or unity, with which it can then identify 'in anticipation' (1977: 4). However, it must be stressed that Lacan's imaginary has its origins in Freud's theories of the Ego and of narcissism,[15] and for my purposes here, it is the Freudian corpus which is initially more pertinent.

Freud does not use the term Ego entirely consistently (see the editorial comments in SE XIX: 7–8), but it is possible to pick out three strands which shed light on Irigaray's concept of the imaginary. First, the Ego is something which develops: 'a unity comparable to the ego cannot exist in the individual from the start; the ego has to be developed' (SE XIV: 77). Freud describes it as 'a coherent organization of mental processes' (SE XIX: 17). Thus the unity of personal identity is constructed out of a preceding state of lack of organization of mental processes, which is described variously by psychoanalysts as undifferentiation, fragmentation and so on. (Lacan describes identity as illusory.) What is important is that it is not given from the beginning of life, but is developed in the context of the profound and literally life-giving relationship with the parental figure(s), and is thus completely suffused with affect. Since it is something which develops, it is therefore capable of modification under certain conditions in later life (such as psychoanalysis).

Second, the Ego is not equivalent to consciousness; part of the Ego is unconscious (SE XIV: 192–3); SE XVIII: 19; SE XIX: 17–18). Third, the Ego is a bodily Ego. This third point needs explaining in some detail. Freud's comment that 'the ego is first and foremost a bodily ego' (SE XIX: 26) is expanded by a later footnote as follows:

I.e. the ego is ultimately derived from bodily sensations, chiefly from those springing from the surface of the body. It may thus be regarded as a mental projection of the surface of the body, besides . . . representing the superficies of the mental apparatus. (SE XIX: 26)

Freud describes at several points how in phantasy, the ego represents its activities (mental and physical) to itself as equivalents of bodily activities. Probably the most well-known example of this is the identification whereby gifts or money (gold) or babies are equated with faeces (see SE VII: 186, 196; SE IX: 173–4, 219–20; SE XVII: 128 ff., 130–3). These equations or identifications may be shifting and provisional, or they may stabilize during the course of a person's development into a particular set of characteristics, as Freud describes in his paper 'Character and Anal Erotism' (SE IX: 167–75).[16]

A more pertinent example of phantasy here is Freud's essay on 'Negation' in which the intellectual faculty of judgement (such as the capacity to assign truth or falsity to an assertion) is traced to this very primitive type of thinking in which everything is perceived/conceived on the model of the body:

> The function of judgement is concerned in the main with two sorts of decisions. It affirms or disaffirms the possession by a thing of a particular attribute; and it asserts or disputes that a presentation has an existence in reality. The attribute to be decided about may originally have been good or bad, useful or harmful. Expressed in the language of the oldest – the oral – instinctual impulses, the judgement is: 'I should like to eat this', or 'I should like to spit it out'; and, put more generally: 'I should like to take this into myself and to keep that out.' That is to say: 'It shall be inside me' or 'it shall be outside me'. (SE XIX: 236–7)

To judge that something is true is, in phantasy, to swallow it or to incorporate it; to judge that something is false is to spit it out or to expel it. Freud comments on the way in which a repressed thought may return in the form of a negative assertion: 'That is *not* what I was thinking', which is a kind of phantasy expulsion of the forbidden or repressed thought.

This is not a reductive account; to show the origins of conceptual thought in bodily phantasy does not entail any judgement about the truth or falsity of that thought, but is to do with the unconscious affect or emotion attached to it. Phantasy is neither true nor false, and truth and falsity are judgements which belong to a different order, and are governed by different rules. Further, as Freud shows in his paper on the sexual theories of children (SE IX: 205–26), phantasmatic representations are not necessarily accurate representations of biological or social processes, but *interpretations* of them. These unconscious (mis)representations can coexist in the mind with the knowledge acquired at a later stage, providing an affective substratum which determines a person's feelings (often unconscious) towards that later knowledge. (I will return to this point in the final section.)

The Freudian account of the (bodily) ego and its relation to more intellectual activities in (unconscious) phantasy is explicitly assumed by Lacan under the explanatory concept of the imaginary: 'the symbolic equation [e.g.

money = faeces] . . . arises from an alternating mechanism of expulsion and introjection, or projection and absorption, that is to say, from an imaginary game' (Lacan 1975a: 96, trans. Rose 1986: 174–5).[17] What pre-Lacanian psychoanalysis describes as unconscious phantasy, Lacan describes as imaginary (though he then goes on to build a much more complicated edifice on the imaginary and its relation with the symbolic and the real).

Let us return now to Irigaray. In *Speculum*, she takes the Lacanian term imaginary, and applies it to what psychoanalysis had previously called unconscious phantasy. This can be seen clearly in that she attributes anachronistically the imaginary to Freud himself, referring to Freud's 'imaginary economy' (SE: 101; SF: 125); at another point, she comments: 'elsewhere, Freud insists that in the childish imaginary the production of a child is equated with the production of feces' (SE: 36; SF: 39). In this section on Freud, she does not discuss Lacan head-on. However, when, throughout *Speculum*, she examines the idea of the mirror, she is clearly addressing Lacan's theory of the imaginary and the role of the mirror in the construction of subjectivity. But rather than giving an alternative account of women's psychosexual development (although that element is there by implication), she is offering a critique, or a deconstruction, of a dominant conceptualization or representation of sexual difference. Taking Lacan's mirror as an image of representation, she asks why he used a flat mirror, 'in that the flat mirror reflects the greater part of women's sexual organs only as a hole' (SE: 89 note; SF: 109 note). The body which is reflected in this flat mirror, and thus the imaginary body subtending subjectivity, is either a male body (with male sexual organs) or else a defective male body (a male body without sexual organs, hence 'castrated'). The flat mirror does not reflect the sexual organs and the sexual specificity of the woman. For the exploration of woman's sexual specificity, a different sort of mirror (literal or symbolic) would be needed – a speculum for example. Elsewhere she suggests that women cannot appear reflected in this flat mirror; they are the components of which the mirror is made, the tain of the mirror (TS: 151; CS: 147).

This is a point about conceptualization, rather than directly about women. What Irigaray is doing in the first section of *Speculum* is psychoanalysing the psychoanalysts, analysing *their* imaginary, the unconscious phantasies underlying the Freudian or Lacanian explanatory systems. Her interpretation is that Freud's account of sexuality is anal, and that in the Freudian phantasy, the stage in which children are believed to be born through the anus (see e.g. SE IX: 205–26) continues to underlie his theorization.[18] Freud's model of sexuality is male, according to Irigaray. And since his phantasy is anal, a phantasy in which the role of women in childbirth is not recognized, women inevitably appear in this scenario as defective males.

The point is also that an anatomical difference is perceived in the light of the conceptual frameworks already available. Freud's phantasy is not an idiosyncrasy peculiar to him, it is the imaginary of the ruling symbolic. In an important transition (and incidentally using Lacanian conceptualization against itself) Irigaray goes on to argue that this is not an example of the individual phantasy of any particular philosopher or psychoanalyst, but that speculation itself in the west is dominated by anality (what she refers to elsewhere as a kind of 'ontology of the anal' – E: 100); sexuality and thinking, in an imaginary operation, have become equated both with each other and with one and the same bodily activity. The diagnosis of an anal imaginary, then, moves at this point out of the domain of the technically psychoanalytic into the domain of social explanation, and becomes a social imaginary signification which, as Castoriadis explains, has almost unlimited extension:

> Compared with individual imaginary significations, [social imaginary significations] are infinitely vaster than a phantasy (the underlying schema of what is referred to as the Jewish, Greek, or Western 'world-picture' has no bounds) and they have no precisely located existence (if that is to say one can ascribe to the individual unconscious a precisely located existence). (Castoriadis 1975: 200–1)[19]

By appropriating the term imaginary for his particular version of Freudian theory, Lacan was colonizing a term which was already in current use in aesthetics and literary criticism (though not, as far as I know, in psychoanalysis), and changing or extending its meaning radically. Irigaray, in a similar fashion, wrests Lacan's concept out of its Lacanian context in order to extend its significance; the imaginary emerges from its relatively subordinate[20] position in *Speculum* to become, in *This Sex* and *Ethique*, one of the key notions of an ambitious *social* critique.

To put it as succintly as possible, the problem as defined by Irigaray is that the female has a particular function in symbolic processes: to subtend them, to represent that which is outside discourse. Using the language of bodily phantasy and of the representations of the female body, one could say that: 'She functions as a *hole* . . . in the elaboration of imaginary and symbolic processes' (SE: 71; SF: 85).[21] Any organization of the world, whether it be linguistic, social, or individual, is an organization which carves out of an undifferentiated continuum a set of categories which enable the world to be grasped. But it is impossible to organize the world in this way without residue. The emergence of distinctions, determinate identities, or social organizations always implies something else, that original state of non-differentiation from which they have emerged, such as a pre-social nature[22] or the unconscious[23] or Castoriadis's magma.[24] This outside, which is non-graspable in-itself, since it is by definition outside the categories which allow one to posit its existence, is traditionally conceptualized as female (the unlimited or the formless of the pre-Socratics). Within this sexual symbolism, the determinate, that which has form or identity, belongs to the other half of the pair, and is therefore male.

Within this schema, rationality falls on the determinate and male side.

Referring to this traditional conceptualization, then, Irigaray describes women as a 'residue' (TS: 114; CS: 112; AM: 98), or as a 'sort of magma . . . from which men, humanity, draw nourishment, shelter, the resources to live or survive for free' (E: 102). In *Speculum*, she had already described this 'outside' of discourse as the womb (*le matriciel*) and by extension the maternal body: 'formless, "amorphous" origin of all morphology' (SE: 265; SF: 330); in *Ethique*, she adds that the undifferentiated maternal-feminine underlies 'all possibility of determining identity' (E: 98). Or women are described as resembling/being the unconscious: 'thus we might wonder whether certain properties attributed to the unconscious may not, in part, be ascribed to the female sex, which is censured by the logic of consciousness' (TS: 73; CS: 71).

The unconscious is a realm in which the laws of identity and non-contradiction do not apply. So when Irigaray writes that for the female imaginary too, the laws of identity and non-contradiction (A is A, A is not B) do not apply either, it may sound like a dangerously irrationalist description of women that merely reinforces a traditional denigration. The practical value of these principles, without which rationality would be inconceivable, is so evident that it appears unquestionable. The logic of identity is the prerequisite of any language or society at all. However, the point is that there will always be a residue which exceeds the categories, and this excess is conceptualized as female:

> In other words, the issue is not one of elaborating a new theory of which woman would be the *subject* or the *object*, but of jamming the theoretical machinery itself, of suspending its pretension to the production of a truth and of a meaning that are excessively univocal. Which presupposes that women . . . do not claim to be rivalling men in constructing a logic of the feminine that would still take onto-theo-logic as its model, but that they are rather attempting to wrest this question away from the economy of the logos. They should not put it then, in the form 'What is woman?' but rather, repeating/interpreting the way in which, within discourse, the feminine finds itself defined as lack, deficiency, or as imitation and negative image of the subject, they should signify that with respect to this logic a *disruptive excess* is possible on the feminine side. (TS: 78; CS: 75–6)

From Irigaray's point of view, she is not *prescribing* what the female should be, but *describing* how it functions within western imaginary and symbolic operations, in order to show how what is taken to be the unalterable order of reality (discursive or otherwise) is in fact *imaginary* and therefore susceptible to change. In the following chapter we shall see how the female imaginary can be understood in more than one sense: there is the position of the female in the male imaginary; there are the scraps or debris of what might be an alternative imaginary (a fragmented female imaginary); there is the anticipation of a more fully deployed female imaginary which might exist in creative intercourse with the male.

For the moment, I want to look briefly at her critique of Lacan. There is some disagreement about Lacan's potential value for feminist politics. Some critics argue that Lacan's 'symbolic determinism' offers no possibility of any theory of change, particularly in the situation of women (see Macey 1988 ch. 6; Leland 1989), while others are more optimistic.[25] For Irigaray, what Lacan's work does is to take up once again, and renew, the familiar theme of the female as support or substratum of the male subject. So she comments on Lacan that: 'The topology of the subject as it is defined by certain theoreticians of psychoanalysis (cf. the *Ecrits* of Jacques Lacan . . .) . . . would use the symbolisation of the feminine as a basis or basement for the (masculine) subject' (E: 103).

Any particular organization is taken to be reality in an imaginary operation, since the world cannot be grasped without the framework of a set of categories. However, if one takes the imaginary to be equivalent to reality, and implies for example that reality is coextensive with the categories of discourse, then of course the only possibilities for change will be permutations within the same set of categories; no totally different reorganization would be possible. (This is the objection that Castoriadis makes to Lacan.) Irigaray's objection, then, is the way in which Lacan takes a particular discursive organization to be unchangeable: 'What poses problems in reality turns out to be justified by a logic that has already ordered reality as such. Nothing escapes the circularity of this law' (TS: 88; CS: 87).

This *ahistorical* (TS: 100, 125; CS: 97, 124) conflation of the present categories of western discourse with reality, thus eliding the question of social change, indicates the presence of Lacan's *imaginary* (TS: 99; CS: 96),[26] which is also the imaginary of western metaphysics. For,

> we note that the 'real' may well include, and in large measure, *a physical reality* that continues to resist adequate symbolization and/or that signifies the powerlessness of logic to incorporate in its writing all the characters of nature. (TS: 106–7; CS: 105; trans. adapted)

Her particular argument against Lacan is that he excludes in advance the possibility of any real social change, because he does not ask the question about the relationship between real women and women in the symbolic. For the problem for those people who are designated women by the symbolic is that although they may be symbolized as the outside of discourse, they are not *in fact* outside the society they live in and its symbolic structures.

Lacan argues that 'there is no pre-discursive reality' (1975b: 33) but this is a statement which is more ambiguous than it might appear. If it is interpreted as a statement about the necessity of symbolic castration (as in Silverman 1988: 7–8),[27] then there is probably no real disagreement between Irigaray and Lacan here, for symbolic castration is a condition of sanity (see Brennan

1989: 2–6). When Irigaray is criticized for locating woman in the imaginary, outside the symbolic order, it is because the critic takes her to be rejecting symbolic castration. If symbolic castration is taken, as it standardly is, as a condition of sanity, then any suspicion that Irigaray is rejecting it would feed the charge of irrationalism. (But note that the conceptualization of sanity in terms of symbolic 'castration' may still remain problematic, because the *representation* still takes the male body as norm.)[28] I shall discuss this charge further in the next chapter.

But Lacan's statement can also be interpreted, as Castoriadis interprets it, as a conservative thesis, about the nigh-impossibility of symbolic change, since in order to accede to subjectivity we have to insert ourselves into an already existing and preceding symbolic order, which we cannot then reject except by falling into meaninglessness or insanity. Or it can be interpreted, as Dews interprets it, as a conflation of symbolic with social which evades the issue of the possibility that the symbolic could mask or conceal relations of force (Dews 1987: 105), which are then presumably thrust out into the Lacanian 'real' or left unsymbolized. In these interpretations, it becomes impossible to understand the emergence of a social organization that did not previously exist. Such a new social organization is not a question of an (impossible) return to a pre-discursive reality, but a question of the possibilities for change provided by the symbolic order itself (see Castoriadis 1975, passim).

When Irigaray states her interest in pre-discursive experience (E: 143), she is positing that what has been excluded by the symbolic as its residue or waste (woman) could in fact be symbolized differently, that the categories in terms of which we apprehend the world could be different (see Chapter 4). She is also positing that to understand the symbolic we need to understand its *imaginary*. The coherence of a conceptual system does not imply its *truth*, but may be the coherence of its phantasy. We need to look at the phantasies underlying the propositional statements of psychoanalysts and philosophers.

In summary, then, Irigaray begins with an analysis of the imaginary of western philosophical and psychoanalytic discourse (*Speculum*), aiming to show that the conceptualization of sexual difference in this discourse is governed by an imaginary which is anal, that is to say, which interprets sexual difference as though there were only one sex, and that sex were male (women are defective men). For our culture, identity, logic, and rationality are symbolically male, and the female is either the outside, the hole, or the unsymbolizable residue. At most, she may occupy the maternal function. In *This Sex* and *Ethique*, Irigaray goes on to suggest that the imaginary is not confined to philosophers and psychoanalysts, but is a social imaginary which is taken to be reality, with damaging consequences for women who, unlike men, find themselves 'homeless' in the symbolic order. Unlike Lacan, she does not believe this imaginary to be irreducible; like Castoriadis, she is arguing that radical transformations in the social imaginary *could* take place, and that a new and previously unimaginable configuration could take shape.

In 1966, in an early paper on the imaginary, Irigaray referred to 'the impossible return to the body' (PN: 15). In *Ethique*, she deplores the modern neglect of the body, and emphasizes the fact that 'man's body is the threshold, the porch, of the construction of his universe(s)' (E: 99). Is there a contradiction here? Not if one remembers that the relation to the body is always an imaginary or symbolic one. The importance of the imaginary body is that it underlies western metaphysics; the imaginary body of the subject is male. Thought is still, as it were, in the anal stage; sexual difference does not yet exist in the social imaginary of the west;[29] the female body has not acceded to the symbolic, except in residual, fragmentary form. 'But this fault, this deficiency, this "hole", inevitably affords woman too few figurations, images or representations by which to represent herself' (SE: 71; SF: 85).

There might be another problem here. Since Lacan describes identity as imaginary, and if identity, according to Irigaray, is male (as described in the first section): either the idea of a female imaginary is self-contradictory, or the female imaginary, in so far as it attributes identity to the female, would still fall within the parameters of male thought. I think Irigaray's answer to that would be that first what we need to analyse is the unconscious of western male thought (the female imaginary in the first sense – see p.67). Not until this repressed has been more adequately symbolized, will we be able to articulate the relation between male and female elements in a different way. And at that point we might be able to consider the female imaginary in a different light, because identity might no longer mean exactly the same thing. This leads on to the question of strategy and the final section.

The politics of male–female symbolism

In the previous section I argued that Irigaray's imaginary, although a concept which derives from psychoanalysis, cannot be understood in purely psychoanalytic terms, but also has an irreducible social dimension; its anatomical reference is also a symbolic and cultural one. Irigaray is not referring to a direct and unmediated relation to the body, but to an imaginary and symbolic representation of the body, an 'ideal morphology' which, as she puts it, leaves residues that are unsymbolized (or in which the female body may be symbolized as residue). I now want to conclude by discussing briefly the implications of using male–female symbolism to describe rationality as male and the female as unconscious/magma/residue in what might appear to be a symbolically retrograde move. Is it not politically dangerous to regard women as the irrational, or as the unconscious of culture?

The problem is that one cannot alter symbolic meanings by *fiat*;[30] one cannot simply step outside phallogocentrism, simply reverse the symbolism or just make strident or repetitive claims that women are in fact rational. For this reason, Irigaray adopts the strategy of mimicry or mimesis:

One must assume the feminine role deliberately. Which means already to convert a form of subordination into an affirmation, and thus begin to thwart it. . . . To play with mimesis is thus, for a woman, to try to locate the place of her exploitation by discourse, without allowing herself to be simply reduced to it. It means to resubmit herself – inasmuch as she is on the side of the 'perceptible', of 'matter' – to 'ideas', in particular to ideas about herself that are elaborated in/by a masculine logic, but so as to make 'visible' by an effect of playful repetition, what was supposed to remain invisible: recovering a possible operation of the feminine in language. (TS: 76; CS: 73–4; trans. adapted)

Several things need to be said about this strategy. In the first place, since metaphoricity itself, according to Irigaray, is male, there are problems about using metaphors of the female. Readers do not hesitate to use the term 'metaphor' when they discuss Irigaray's work; some, but not all, realize that there is a problem here.[31] The difficulty Irigaray faces was indicated with great clarity by Elizabeth Berg as far back as 1982:

For Irigaray, if woman is given an image – if she is represented – this representation must necessarily take place within the context of a phallocentric system of representation in which the woman is reduced to mirroring the man. On the other hand, the presence of the woman as blank space – as refusal of representation – only serves to provide a backdrop or support for masculine projections. Thus the feminist theorist is caught in a double bind; whether she presents an image of woman or not, she continues the effacement of woman as Other. Irigaray attempts to steer a third course between these two alternatives by fixing her gaze on the support itself: focusing resolutely on the blank spaces of masculine representation, and revealing their disruptive power. At the same time, however, she is obliged to advance some image of woman if only to hold open this blank space. The images she proposes – of fluids, caves, etc. – are empty ones. . . . (Berg 1982: 17)

It is this deliberate mimetic assumption of male metaphors, male images of the feminine which has led to accusations of essentialism and logocentrism. But as Rosi Braidotti insists, for Irigaray the route *back through* essentialism cannot be avoided: 'The apparent mimesis is tactical and it aims at *producing* difference' (Braidotti 1989: 99).

Another way to approach the same issue is through the link which Irigaray makes between mimesis and hysteria (see for example SE: 71–2; SF: 85–6). In hysteria, the subject of enunciation whose discourse is always directed towards the 'you' for validation is willing to produce symptoms, if that will obtain the desired result (love). The tactic of mimesis can be seen as a kind of deliberate hysteria, designed to illuminate the *interests* which are at stake in metaphors:

Either let Truth carry the day against deceitful appearances, or else, claiming once more to reverse optics, let us give exclusive privilege to the fake, the mask, the fantasy because, at least at times, they mark the nostalgia we feel for something even more true.

We will continue to waver indecisively before this dilemma unless we interpret the *interest, and the interests*, involved here. Who or what *profits* by the credits invested in the effectiveness of such a system of metaphor . . .? (SE: 269–70; SF: 335)

Given that there is no other language in which to talk about representations of women except the essentialist language of metaphysics, Irigaray is proposing that we might be able to turn this to our advantage by assuming it deliberately.[32]

We might note also that of the terms Irigaray uses: *mimésis, mimétisme, masque*, etc., one of them, *mimétisme*, usually translated mimeticism, comes from the domain of animal ethology and means 'camouflage' or 'protective colouring'. I think this may be relevant too. Irigaray may be arguing, I think, that women also need to protect themselves against (re)assimilation and destruction by the masculine economy.

However, the aspect of mimesis that I want to emphasize in this chapter is the psychoanalytic interpretation of it. So I refer back again to the psychoanalytic model. In the individual psyche, unconscious phantasy is determining to the extent that it remains unconscious. When in the psychoanalytic process, it achieves an access to consciousness via language (what Irigaray refers to as symbolization or 'the operations of sublimation'), it becomes possible to effect a shift or change in the phantasy which enables the analysand to change and brings about real transformations in the personality in the direction of greater flexibility and creativity, and less rigidity or repression.[33] I would suggest that one way to read Irigaray is to see her as conceiving of her work as initiating a process of change at the level of the social unconscious (or imaginary), by offering interpretations of the 'material' offered by society in its philosophical or metaphysical discourse:

> This process of interpretive rereading has always been a *psychoanalytic undertaking* as well. That is why we need to pay attention to the way the unconscious works in each philosophy, and perhaps in philosophy in general. We need to listen (psycho)analytically to its procedures of repression, to the structuration of language that shores up its representations, separating the true from the false, the meaningful from the meaningless, and so forth. (TS: 75; CS: 73)

These interpretations would verbalize the unconscious phantasy and begin the process of lifting the repression, a process which, on the model of psychoanalysis, might lead to change. On this reading of Irigaray, what is described as the female imaginary is not the essential feminine, common to all women, but a place in the symbolic structures.

In the first section, discussing the development of the Ego and its phantasies, I pointed out that the individual Ego, in psychoanalytic theory, is said to take shape in the context of a relationship with parental figures. Putting this another way, one might say that the acquisition of one's knowledge of the world is passionately motivated. Later, epistemology loses touch with its sources. This is precisely Irigaray's diagnosis of what has gone wrong with the rationality of the west. In *Ethique*, she suggests:

> contrary to the usual methods of dialectic, love should not have to be abandoned in order to become wise or learned. It is love which leads to knowledge [science]. . . . It is love which leads the way, and is the path, both. (E: 27–8)

As I indicated earlier, for Irigaray the conceptualization of rationality is inseparable from the conceptualization of sexual difference. The scission of epistemology from its sources is linked to a model of rationality (symbolized as male) in which the symbolic female is dominated or repressed, and 'transcended'. Irigaray suggests that this has led to the apotheosis of rationality – modern technology – and to apparently unstoppable processes of destruction.

To describe rationality as male is not to restrict rationality to men. Rather, it is to argue against exclusion models of rationality as Irigaray states more or less explicitly:

> What has been needed, in effect, is a discourse in which sexuality itself is at stake so that what has been serving as a condition of possibility of philosophical discourse, or rationality in general, can make itself heard. (TS: 168; CS: 162)

Exclusion is a process governed by the male imaginary (i.e. identity, or A is A, involves exclusion: A is not B); another way of putting it is to say that it is the way the male imaginary deals with sexual difference. What is important is that rationality is categorized by Irigaray as male, not in order to oppose it, which would be self-defeating, but in order to suggest a more adequate conceptualization, in which, in psychoanalytic terms, the male does not repress or split off the female/unconscious, but acknowledges or integrates it. For the psychoanalytic model, the relation between the different parts of the person, however they are named: reason/passion, body/mind, superego/ego/id, consciousness/unconscious, need not be a clear-cut one; the boundaries may fluctuate, there may be a possibility of intercommunication which is not necessarily experienced as threatening or overwhelming. In Irigaray's terms, the sexual relationship (i.e. the relationship between the imaginary or symbolic male and female) should ideally be like a chiasma, in which each could offer a home (*lieu* or *sol*) to the other (E: 16), in 'exchanges without identifiable terms, without accounts, without end' (TS: 197; CS: 193).

The condition of the advent of woman-as-subject – as subject of philosophy, subject of culture, even subject of science – is creative intercourse within the cultural imaginary. But for that to take place, the monosexual cultural imaginary would have to open up to another sex, to make a space for the female sex; it would have to recognize the Other. It is to that issue that we now turn.

Chapter 4

Maternal genealogy and the symbolic

> toute notre culture occidentale repose sur le meurtre de la mère. (*Le Corps-à-corps avec la mère*)
> the whole of our culture in the west depends upon the murder of the mother.

Several issues were touched on in the previous chapter, which raised a number of theoretical problems, in particular the relation between the imaginary and the symbolic, the meaning of symbolic castration, and the critique that Irigaray is locating woman in the imaginary *outside* the symbolic order. Although apparently tangential to the central theme I am concerned with, it is nevertheless essential to clarify them in relation to Irigaray's thought, if we are to understand her project to effect change in the symbolic order. The sophisticated theoretical constructions of philosophers, according to Irigaray, all depend upon an unacknowledged foundation, the unsymbolized maternal-feminine. Since woman is not recognized by the cultural imaginary, theory, no matter how far-reaching and innovative, goes on perpetuating the founding obliteration. The absence of creative intercourse in the imaginary leads, eventually, to an impasse in thought; thought is condemned to go on repeating over and over again the same gesture of silencing and repression.

Given Irigaray's stress on the imaginary, some of her critics have concluded that the space which she is reclaiming for the feminine is located in the pre-Oedipal and outside the symbolic order. Take the following remarks:

> The tendency in the very important work of Nancy Chodorow, Luce Irigaray and Hélène Cixous, for example, has been to concentrate on the importance of the pre-Oedipal phase of psycho-sexual development – that time before femininity or masculinity when the infant is in a symbiotic relationship with her mother . . . for Irigaray . . . it is the point at which femininity has not yet been repressed by patriarchy and women have not yet become man-made [. . .] There is no space for resistance within the terms of the symbolic order, and women who do not wish to repress their true femaleness can have no access to it. (Weedon 1987: 56, 65)

The term 'psycho-sexual development' indicates the point where misunderstanding arises. I want to emphasize that Irigaray is using a *psychoanalytic* model and not a psychological model.[1] The essential difference here is that whereas a psychological model is developmental and chronological, a psychoanalytic model is structural; though 'stages' may be identified, there is no suggestion that they coincide with, or are necessarily observable in, the stages of development. Whatever pre-Oedipal means, it does not refer to a developmental stage like learning to walk or speak. Psychoanalytic theory employs a number of different sequences; for example oral/anal/ genital; auto-erotism/narcissism/object-choice; paranoid-schizoid position/ depressive position; autism/symbiosis/separation/individuation; imaginary/ symbolic. They are derived, not from observations of child development, but from clinical situations, and are ways of conceptualizing structures of the mind. Irigaray is not offering an alternative version of women's psychosexual *development*.

What I will suggest in this chapter is that symbolic and imaginary form a system, in which we cannot understand one without the other. There *is* no space or time for women to retreat to, without retreating at the same time from language and meaning. If Irigaray appears to be emphasizing the imaginary, this is because she is specifically looking for the unconscious elements of the system; but change in the imaginary *must* bring about change in the symbolic and vice versa. So I shall be discussing here, first, the major and most significant absence in the symbolic: representations of a maternal line or genealogy; and second, the relationship between the systemic elements, of which this absence is a structuring factor. In the first section I want to look at the relationship which the symbolic has bypassed, the mother–daughter relationship, and argue that for Irigaray it is essential to bring that relationship into the symbolic (through interpretations of symbolic – philosophical or cultural – material). Further, I want to suggest that although Irigaray draws on psychoanalytic accounts of the mother–daughter relation, she is not herself offering a psychoanalytic account (i.e. this is not an account primarily of individuals, but of a whole cultural system). In the second section I shall discuss the Lacanian interpretation of Irigaray, and specifically, the questions of representation and symbolic castration. In the final section I shall look further at the articulation of the imaginary and the symbolic.

A note on terminology. I shall be referring on several occasions to the unsymbolized mother–daughter relationship. By describing this relationship as unsymbolized, Irigaray means that there is an absence of linguistic, social, semiotic, structural, cultural, iconic, theoretical, mythical, religious or any other representations of that relationship. There is no maternal genealogy. One can readily think of examples of the mother–son relationship, enshrined in Christian doctrine and iconography. Irigaray argues that we have to go back to Greek mythology to find available, culturally embodied representations of the mother–daughter relationship. This does not mean that there are none – the women's movement has been resuscitating and/or creating literary and artistic representations of relations between women, and one can certainly find denigratory versions (the wicked stepmother) – but they are not adequate; they afford women 'too few figurations, images, or representations by which to represent herself' (SE: 71; SF: 85).

The mother–daughter relationship

Irigaray claims explicitly that the unsymbolized relationship between mother and daughter constitutes a threat to the patriarchal symbolic order as we know it:

> The mother–daughter relationship is the *dark continent* of the *dark continent*. (CAC: 61)

> The relationship between mother/daughter, daughter/mother constitutes an extremely explosive kernel in our societies. To think it, to change it, amounts to undermining [ébranler] the patriarchal order. (CAC: 86)

An unsymbolized mother–daughter relationship makes it difficult if not impossible for women to have an identity in the symbolic order that is distinct from the maternal function, and thus prevents them from constituting any real threat to the order of western metaphysics, described by Irigaray as the metaphysics of the Same. They remain 'residual', 'defective men', 'objects of exchange', and so on. When, as the women's movement has done, one begins to ask questions about women's identity, this is perceived as extremely dangerous to the symbolic order:

> from a feminine locus nothing can be articulated without a questioning of the symbolic itself. (TS: 162; CS: 157)

> For, without the exploitation of the body-matter of women, what would become of the symbolic process that governs society? (TS: 85; CS: 81)

> The culture, the language, the imaginary and the mythology in which we live at present . . . let us look at what foundations this edifice is built on. . . . This underpinning is woman reproducer of the social order, acting as the infrastructure of that order; all of western culture rests upon the murder of the mother. . . . And if we make the foundation of the social order shift, then everything shifts. (CAC: 81)

The alternative to not threatening the patriarchal, symbolic order is for women to remain, in the absence of symbolization, in a state of *déréliction*; this term, which is much stronger in French than in English, connotes for example the state of being abandoned by God or, in mythology, the state of an Ariadne, abandoned on Naxos, left without hope, without help, without refuge.[2] Women are abandoned outside the symbolic order; they lack mediation in the symbolic for the operations of sublimation (E: 70). Irigaray explains clearly in *Speculum*, using Freud's lecture on femininity as an exemplary text, why the difficulty for women of performing the operations of sublimation arises precisely from the unsymbolized relation between mother and daughter. (In other words, being outside the symbolic order is not a condition to which women should aspire; the absence of adequate symbolization is the dereliction in which they already exist.)

Now the practical question for feminism, as Irigaray sees it, is how to construct a female sociality (*les femmes entre elles*), a female symbolic and a female social contract: a horizontal relation *between women*, so that women are no longer left in this state of dereliction. Attempts to do so have revealed the discrepancy between the idealization of women's nature found in some early feminist writing and the actual hostilities and dissensions engendered within the women's movement itself, the 'horizontal violence' between members of an oppressed group, in Mary Daly's (1984) phrase. Irigaray suggests that it may be impossible to negotiate the problems thrown up by the horizontal relationship without attending to the vertical relationship, that prototypical relationship between mother and daughter (E: 106). And it may be impossible to do the latter – collectively at any rate – within the present symbolic order. I will return to this point later.

First of all, here are some of the features, enumerated by Irigaray, of the problems that women face in attempting to create a different social and symbolic order. It will be seen that she does not attribute any special 'natural' virtues to women, and that there is no suggestion that communities of women will automatically be idyllic or irenical spaces from which conflict, aggression, or destruction have been excluded. What she does do is to make a link between certain clichés of psychological or psychoanalytic descriptions (hatred of the mother, rivalry between women, women as women's own worst enemies), and the symbolic order; thus she allows for the possibility that a different symbolization could have effects on women's relationships with each other. So women are prey to:

1. interminable rivalry between women (even if undeclared). This is because there is no room for more than one at a time in the place of the mother:

    Since the place of the mother is unique, to become a mother would mean occupying this place, but without a relation *with her in this place*. (E: 101, my emphasis)

    For women, love for the mother perhaps must only or could only exist in the form of a *substitution*? Of a taking her place? Which is unconsciously suffused with hate? (E: 100)

2. permanent risk of destruction in the absence of a female symbolic (CE: 38);

3. the cruelty which takes place when relations are not mediated by anything, whether by rites, by exchanges, or by an economy (E: 103). So women often become the agents of their own oppression and mutual self-destruction [*anéantissement*] (E: 102);
4. various forms of pathology: flight, explosion, implosion (all forms of immediacy) (E: 111);
5. murder:

> Thus a sort of *international vendetta* is set up, present more or less everywhere, which disorientates the female populace, the groups and micro-societies which are in the process of being formed. Real murders take place as a part of it, but also (insofar as they can be distinguished), cultural murders, murders of minds, emotions and intelligence, which women perpetuate amongst themselves. (WSM: 14; SP: 100)

To summarize all this, one could say that women suffer from 'drives without any possible representatives or representations' (TS: 189; CS: 183) which, for Irigaray, is another way of saying that the relation between mother and daughter is unsymbolized. The problems do not arise from immutable characteristics of women's 'nature', but are an effect of women's position relative to the symbolic order as its 'residue' or its 'waste'. A picture which superficially resembles a stereotypically misogynistic version of women's psychology is in fact attempting to state the conditions under which, say, hate or envy or rivalry might be both operative and inescapable in relations between women – because a way of negotiating them symbolically was not available, and to attribute the acting out of such unmediated feelings directly to the way in which 'woman' figures in the structure of metaphysics and society.

A more familiar way of putting the issue would be to say that women suffer from inability to individuate themselves, from 'confusion of identity between them' (E: 66), from lack of respect for or, more often, lack of perception of, the other woman as different (E: 66). The problem of individuation for women is a theme familiar to us from Nancy Chodorow's work on object-relations theory in relation to women, so it might seem here as though we are on familiar ground. However, the aims and presuppositions of Chodorow and Irigaray are quite different.

Chodorow explains that, at an unconscious level, women often never separate sufficiently from their mother; their identity never becomes distinct from that of their mother, and they remain, unconsciously, in a state of merging or fusion in which it is impossible for them to distinguish between their own feelings and those of their mother:

> Mothers tend to experience their daughters as more like, and continuous with, themselves. Correspondingly, girls tend to remain part of the dyadic primary mother–child relationship itself. This means that a girl continues to experience herself as involved in issues of merging

and separation, and in an attachment characterized by primary identification and the fusion of identification and object choice. By contrast, mothers experience their sons as a male opposite. Boys are more likely to have been pushed out of the preoedipal relationship, and to have had to curtail their primary love and sense of empathic tie with their mother. A boy has engaged, and been required to engage, in a more emphatic individuation and a more defensive firming of experienced ego boundaries. Issues of differentiation have become intertwined with sexual issues. (Chodorow 1978: 166–7)

As long as women mother, we can expect that a girl's preoedipal period will be longer than that of a boy and that women, more than men, will be open to and preoccupied with those very relational issues that go into mothering – feelings of primary identification, lack of separateness or differentiation, ego and body-ego boundary issues . . . (1978: 110)

As a phenomenological description, Chodorow's account is most persuasive.[3] However, from the standpoint which Irigaray adopts, there would be a number of problems with her theory. First, Chodorow does not present the construction of sexual identity as a problem; she does not deal with the unstable nature of sexual identity in the unconscious, and so tends to equate sexual with biological or social identity (and see Rose 1986: 60 note 28). Second, because she is uncritical of the discourse of psychoanalysis, she is unable to confront the way in which psychoanalytic theory itself reproduces the structure of sexual difference as it is deployed in western thought. Third, when envisaging possible ways in which the situation of women could be changed, she makes only a token gesture in the direction of the collectivity; her solution of shared parenting is a familial rather than a social solution, because she is offering a predominantly descriptive account of how individual women acquire the ability to mother. And there is in her picture, implicitly at any rate, a certain inevitability or static quality about the way mothers and daughters relate to each other, as though the *only* way to stave off the suffocating merging of identities were for the father to become involved in parenting too.[4]

Now, Irigaray accepts the clinical view that women have difficulty in separating from their mothers, that they tend to relationships in which identity is merged and in which the boundaries between self and other are not clear. However she presents this psychoanalytic diagnosis as a symptom or result of women's position in the symbolic order, and it is this order which she is primarily concerned to expose. She argues for example that the clinical picture with which we are familiar from the work of feminist and other therapists also applies to metaphysics; in the metaphysical picture too, women are not individuated: there is only *the place of the mother*, or the *maternal function*.

Whereas the fundamental ontological category for men is *habiter* (dwelling), whether in a literal or figurative sense: men live in 'grottoes, huts, women, towns, language, concepts, theories, etc.' (E: 133)[5], women's ontological status in this culture is *déréliction*, the state of abandonment, described significantly in the same terms (*un fusionnel*) as the psychoanalytic term for 'merging' or failure to differentiate and separate. Dereliction is defined as 'a state of fusion [fusionnel] which does not succeed in emerging as a subject' (E: 72). So Irigaray explains:

> If women don't have access to society and to culture:
> – they remain in a state of dereliction in which they neither recognise or love themselves/each other;
> – they lack mediation for the operations of sublimation;
> – love is impossible for them. (E: 70)

> It is necessary for a symbolism to be created among women in order for there to be love between them. This love is in any case only possible at the moment between women who can speak to each other. Without that interval *of exchange*, or of words, or of gestures, passions between women manifest themselves in a . . . rather cruel way. (E: 103)

> . . . they need language, a language. That house of language which for men even constitutes a substitute for his home in a body, . . . woman is used to construct it, but (as a result?) it is not available to her. (E: 105)

It is confusion of identity, then, that leads to pathological phenomena in relations between women. And fusional, non-individuated relationships are a symptom of dereliction. So when one claims that Irigaray is celebrating 'the feminine', one must be wary of how one describes that 'feminine'. When Irigaray describes the female imaginary in *This Sex* as plural, non-identical, multiple, '*neither one nor two*', this is not a recommendation that relationships between women in the real world should be of the kind described by Chodorow as fusional or merged. The imaginary is plural because it is fragmented, in bits and pieces: 'scraps, uncollected debris' (TS: 30; CS: 29). The following remarks from *This Sex* should help to clarify this point:

> In this connection, I would like to raise another . . . question: do women rediscover their pleasure in this 'economy' of the multiple? When I ask what may be happening on the women's side, I am certainly not seeking to wipe out multiplicity, since women's pleasure does not occur without that. But isn't *a multiplicity that does not entail a rearticulation of the difference between the sexes* [my emphasis] bound to block or take away something of women's pleasure? In other words, is the feminine capable, at present, of attaining this desire, which is *neutral* precisely from the viewpoint of sexual difference? Except by miming masculine desire once again? And doesn't the 'desiring machine' still partly take the place of woman and the feminine? Isn't it a sort of metaphor for her/it, that men can use?

> Especially in terms of their relation to the techno-cratic? (TS: 140–1;
> CS: 138)

This warning about the interpretation of multiplicity is echoed in the following
remarks on the mother–daughter relationship, where the 'neither one nor
two' of an earlier essay is shown to be, not a desirable and delightful state
of fluid identity, but a pathological symptom of a cultural discourse in which
the relation between mother and daughter cannot be adequately articulated:

> But there is no possibility whatsoever, within the current logic of
> sociocultural operations, for a daughter to situate herself with respect
> to her mother: because, strictly speaking, they make neither one nor
> two, neither has a name, meaning, sex of her own, neither can be
> 'identified' with respect to the other. . . . How can the relationship
> between these two women be articulated? Here 'for example' is one
> place where the need for another 'syntax', another 'grammar' of culture
> is crucial. (TS: 143; CS: 140–1)

I think therefore it is necessary to insist that statements about the female
imaginary be looked at again and reread in the light of Irigaray's critique of
metaphysics and its discourse.[6] I shall indicate in the final section some of the
reasons why I think that the female imaginary is a concept which is both labile
and refractory, liable to twist and turn in the hands, or theory, of the user.

I think the interpretation of 'multiplicity' is a point worth dwelling on,
because 'multiplicity' in one form or another has become one of the themes
of contemporary French philosophy, and one of the characterizing features
of what has come to be called postmodernism. In particular, I want to
distinguish Irigaray from a number of possible interpretations which could
be attributed to her, in order to show what is specific about her thesis. The
problem is that the 'multiple' can exclude women just as certainly as the
'one' or the 'same'.

For example, when Derrida is asked to state his position on feminism, he
sometimes produces a conception of sexual multiplicity, which I don't think
it would be unreasonable to describe as phantasmatic. Here are a couple of
examples:

> What if we were to reach, what if we were to approach here (for one
> does not arrive at this as one would at a determined location) the
> area of a relationship to the other where the code of sexual marks
> would no longer be discriminating? The relationship would not be
> a-sexual, far from it, but would be sexual otherwise: beyond the binary
> difference that governs the decorum of all codes, beyond the opposition
> feminine/masculine, beyond bisexuality as well, beyond homosexuality
> and heterosexuality which come to the same thing. As I dream of
> saving the chance that this question offers I would like to believe in
> the multiplicity of sexually marked voices. I would like to believe in

the masses, this indeterminable number of blended voices, this mobile of non-identified sexual marks whose choreography can carry, divide, multiply the body of each 'individual', whether he be classified as 'man' or 'woman' according to the criteria of usage ... Then too, I ask you, what kind of advance would there be, or would there be one at all, if the sexes were not exchanged according to rhythms that vary considerably? In a quite rigorous sense, the *exchange* alone could not suffice either, however, because the desire to escape the combinatory itself, to invent incalculable choreographies, would remain. (Derrida and McDonald 1982: 76)

There is a certain neutralization which can reconstruct the phallocentric privilege. But there is another neutralization which can simply neutralize the sexual opposition, and not sexual difference, liberating the field of sexuality for a very *different* sexuality, a more multiple one. At that point, there would be no more sexes ... there would be one sex for each time. (Derrida 1987: 199)

This phantasy is another example of a utopian phantasy, since it abolishes, in thought, the distance between where we are now and where we might be. What has happened here is that the question of sexual difference, as it appears from the side of women, has been elided. In Irigaray's terms, the difference between the sexes has not been *rearticulated*. Leaving aside the question of the *social* forms this phantasy might take, one is still left with the fact that the move from the masculine subject to the disseminated or multiple subject bypasses the possibility of the position of woman-as-subject.

This is not an unfamiliar move, and Christine Battersby, in her recent book *Gender and Genius*, reminds us that something similar has happened before:

As the industrial society was born during the closing years of the eighteenth century, aspects of the mind previously downgraded as 'feminine' were revalued and re-assigned to the psyche of the genius-male. A similar process is occurring now as the industrial fades into the post-industrial age. (1989: 209)

As Battersby tartly points out: 'Postmodernists have proclaimed the death of the author. But for an author to *die*, he must first have lived' (1989: 207). The celebration of a sexually multiple subject is the exploration of aspects of the psyche, which has disturbing similarities to previous aesthetic movements. Women engaged in similar explorations are not in the same situation since (according to modern theory itself) they have never had a subject to lose. The problem for women, then, is that of acceding to subjectivity in the first place. Its dissemination is not an exhilarating or perilously heroic adventure, but an alienating and familiar condition.

Irigaray sees the 'feminine' of the philosophers as an attempt at colonization or territorialization which once more pushes out *women* (as opposed to the feminine) from the cultural space,[7] so that the multiplicity of the philosophers has become a multiplicity which expropriates women yet again. And it is interesting that any attempt on the part of women to resist this expropriation is easily dismissed in terms of essentialism, logocentrism, dogmatism, or whatever it is that the philosophers have renounced. In these terms, then, one can see why Irigaray, while insisting on multiplicity on the one hand, insists on the other hand on the strategic necessity of mimesis and the assertion of (an apparently essentialist) feminine, in order to make a space which resists colonization. If multiplicity is to be celebrated, it has to be *after* sexual difference and not, as at present, by simply bypassing it. From Irigaray's point of view, a precipitate celebration of sexual multiplicity merely confirms the sexual indifference of our culture, in which women's difference is not *represented* in the symbolic.

Women's relation to origin

The Lacanian interpretation of Irigaray depends upon the claim, implicit or explicit, that she rejects symbolic castration.[8] One of the central claims made, for example, is that according to Irigaray women have specific feminine drives which return them to the real of the maternal body (Rose 1986: 79). Now the real of the maternal body, in Lacanian terminology, means psychosis or foreclosure. So Laplanche and Pontalis, glossing Lacan, define foreclosure as follows: 'Foreclosure consists in not symbolizing what should have been symbolized' (1976: 166).[9] What is odd about such an interpretation of Irigaray is that it is raising against her as an objection the very point that she makes herself. Irigaray writes repeatedly and consistently that the problem for women lies in the *non-symbolization* of the relation to the mother and to the mother's body, and that this threatens women with psychosis (cf. SE: 71, 43 note 26; SF: 85, 47 note 28). Another version of this claim is that Irigaray fails to distinguish between symbolic castration and the castration complex (Silverman 1988: 156). Symbolic castration, in its most neutral sense, is a way of referring to what is also called the loss of origin, i.e the entry into language and the symbolic, and thus the definitive loss ('castration') of the original symbiotic relation with the mother. Whatever one thinks of the terminology, the *process* appears to be the only route to growing up and becoming a functioning social human being. If the Lacanians really think that Irigaray is recommending that women turn their back on this process, it is not surprising that they find her theory valueless or incoherent.

What I think the objections miss is that Irigaray is not offering an alternative psychoanalytic theory, but interrogating psychoanalytic conceptualization itself. One of Irigaray's themes in *Speculum* is that *symbolic* castration has been naturalized by projecting lack on to the female body, which enables men to avoid facing their own castration anxiety (SE: 51–2; SF: 59). Castration anxiety is thus palliated (but also confirmed) by the *representation* of the woman as biologically lacking (SE: 51; SF: 59). This makes it difficult even to discuss symbolic castration in the case of women; the very terminology itself seems to make it clear that women are not in the symbolic but in the real (they are really, already, naturally, castrated). The Lacanian theory, whatever its merits in other ways, simply reproduces the same kind of apparently referential language. Whatever its denials and disavowals (the phallus is not the penis, but a *signifier*; woman is not woman but that which exceeds representation), it does not put into question the symbolic representations of women. My main point in this section, then, is that the Lacanians take Irigaray to be talking about feminine specificity at the level of the drives, whereas I take her to be talking about feminine specificity at the level of the symbolic, or representation. Since the symbolic has a structuring effect upon the otherwise unrepresentable drives, this is a rather important distinction. Although some of her formulations could readily be taken to support the Lacanian interpretation, my view is that, in everything she has written, she has been addressing herself to the symbolic and not to the innate. For part of her critique of Lacanian theory is that it illicitly *naturalizes* what is in fact a *representation*. So I want now to look at the analysis of the conceptualization of the mother–daughter relationship in *Speculum* to illustrate this point, and in particular to look at the question of the desire for, and relation to, origin and the loss of origin inherent in becoming a subject.

Jacqueline Rose states that for Irigaray, 'Women are *returned*, therefore, in the account and to each other – against the phallic term but also against the loss of origin which Lacan's account is seen to imply' (Rose 1986: 79). Now look at the way Irigaray discusses the question of the loss of origin. Discussing Freud's essay on 'Femininity' in his *New Introductory Lectures on Psychoanalysis*, Irigaray makes a point about Freud's interpretation of clinical evidence. When the small girl's playing with dolls can be seen as evidence of a desire for a penis, this is interpreted as a manifestation of femininity. When playing with dolls is clearly the child representing to herself her relation to her mother, this is interpreted by Freud as *phallic* (SE XXII: 128) So that for the girl to represent to herself her relation to her mother is not a manifestation of her femininity (SE: 77–8; SF: 92–4). Now it is obviously not a matter of deciding whether Freud's interpretation is correct. How would one decide what constituted a manifestation of femininity, unless one believed one already knew what femininity was? Irigaray comments that it is rather the case that the girl child 'exiles herself from, or is banned from a *primary metaphorization* of her, female, desire in order to inscribe herself in that of the boy child, which is phallic' (SE: 84; SF: 101; trans. adapted). I think one can see how comments of this kind *could* lead to the interpretation of essentialism. The vital point, however, seems to me to be the impossibility of a primary *metaphorization*, i.e. the language in which one represents desire to oneself. Unless one accepts the need for women to be able to represent their relation to the mother, and so to origin, in a specific way, i.e. not according to a masculine model, then women will always find themselves devalued. Neutral/universal/single-sex models always turn out to be implicitly male ones. So I interpret statements about female desire or female specificity as statements about representation.

Irigaray again:

> In fact this desire for re-presentation, for re-presenting oneself in desire is in some ways *taken away from woman at the outset* as a result of the radical devalorization of her 'beginning' that she is inculcated with, subjected to – and to which she subjects herself: is she not born of a castrated mother who could only give birth to a castrated child, even though she prefers (to herself) those who bear the penis? This shameful beginning must therefore be forgotten, 'repressed' – but can one speak at this stage of repression when the processes that make it possible have not yet come into being? Even if woman is sexually repressed, this does not mean that she actively achieved this repression – in order to defer to a valid [valeureuse] representation of origin. . . . (SE: 83–4; SF: 101)

> The girl, indeed, has nothing more to fear since she has *nothing* to lose. Since she has no representation of what she might fear to lose. Since what she might, potentially, lose, has no value. (SE: 84; SF: 102)

Irigaray points out that if one puts side by side Freud's description of the girl's psychic development after her discovery that she is 'castrated' and that her mother is also 'castrated', and his account of the difference between mourning and melancholia, one discovers that many of the characteristics of melancholia can be mapped on to Freud's description of the state of the little girl. The girl child, in certain respects, remains in a state of melancholia; she can never accomplish the work of mourning the loss of the object (separation from the mother), because she has *no representation of what has been lost*. As a result, 'the little girl's separation from her mother, and from her sex [*sexe*], cannot be worked through by mourning' (SE: 67; SF: 80). Irigaray insists that the impossibility of mourning arises from the fact that the girl child cannot grasp consciously what it is that has been lost, so she cannot mourn it: 'In more ways than one, it is really a question for her of a "loss" that radically escapes any representation' (SE: 68; SF: 80). In this process, the little girl may *identify* with the lost object that can never be found (SE: 69; SF: 81–2). (Identification with a lost or abandoned object that cannot even be represented is, then, another way of formulating women's dereliction.)

Freud states that in melancholia, the work of mourning is hindered by the (unconscious) ambivalence, both love and hate, which the person feels for the lost object. Connecting this with the description of the little girl in Freud's account, Irigaray writes:

> Now, the relation of the daughter to her mother is not without ambivalence, and becomes even more complicated when the little

girl realises that her mother is castrated, while the person to whom her love was addressed was – according to Freud – a phallic mother. This devalorization of the mother accompanies or follows, for the little girl, that of her sexual organs. As a result, 'the relation to the (lost) object is no simple one in her case; it is complicated by the conflict due to ambivalence', 'which remains withdrawn from consciousness'. To which it should be added that no language, no system of representations, will be available to replace, or stand in for [suppléer, assister], the 'unconsciousness' in which remain the conflictual relations which the daughter has with her mother and with her sexual organs. As a result we get the 'reminiscences' in the form of somatic complaints that are characteristic of melancholia? Of hysteria as well, of course. . . . (SE: 68; SF: 81; trans. adapted. The quotations within the quotation are taken by Irigaray from Freud's *Mourning and melancholia*.)

It is not simply, as a psychoanalyst might say, that because women lack a penis it is more difficult for them to symbolize lack (loss of origin).[10] The boy child, with his penis but also with a system of representations that is phallic, can more readily symbolize the loss of origin. The girl child has available to her no adequate representations of 'what she might fear to lose', since 'what she might . . . lose, has no value'. So Irigaray sums up:

This effective 'castration' [castration réalisée] that Freud accounts for in terms of 'nature', 'anatomy', could equally well, or rather, be interpreted as the impossibility, the prohibition that prevents woman . . . from ever imagining, conceiving of, representing, or symbolizing . . . her own relationship to beginning. (SE: 83; SF: 100–1; trans. adapted)

This prohibition leads to the non-differentiation (in-difference) of mother and daughter, and thus to the non-symbolization of their relationship. There is no genealogy on the side of women; the generational differences are blurred; the man takes the woman as a *substitute* for his mother (SE: 31; SF: 32–3) while the woman simply takes her mother's place. So that women (in the symbolic) are in a kind of continuous present; they *represent* the death drives (SE: 55; SF: 63), but cannot sublimate their own, because their own relationship to the passing of generations is unsymbolized.

Although Irigaray is criticized for simply substituting a maternal metaphor for the Lacanian paternal metaphor, in fact what she argues is that this non-differentiation between women becomes inevitable because the relation to origin (*désir d'origine*) is not referred to the relation between man and woman. But in order for a relation between the sexes to be cathected, first two sexes must exist and this is the crux of the problem:

Will there be no possible cathexis of the relation *between* the sexes? (SE: 40; SF: 44, trans. adapted)

... the lack of differentiation between the daughter and the mother or the maternal function ... is inevitable when the desire for origin is not referred back to a relation between a man and a *woman* – a relation that implies in turn a positive representation of femininity (not just maternity) in which the little girl can inscribe herself as a woman in the making. (SE: 36; SF: 38)

In the previous chapter I suggested that for Irigaray, Freud failed to conceptualize a maternal genealogy, because for Freud the little girl is, in the imaginary, a little man, as in the sexual theories of children. However, Irigaray also points out that Freud's thought is governed by the terms of classical philosophy (SE: 93; SF: 113), by the metaphysics of presence (SE: 83; SF: 101). Western systems of representation privilege *seeing*: what can be seen (presence) is privileged over what cannot be seen (absence) and guarantees Being, hence the privilege of the penis which is elevated to the status of a Phallus: '*Nothing to be seen is equivalent to having no thing. No being and no truth*' (SE: 48; SF: 54). So the ontological status assigned to women in western metaphysics is equivalent to the status assigned to them by an imaginary that does not recognize sexual difference. Again:

No attempt will be made by the little girl – nor by the mother? nor by the woman? – to symbolize the status of [ce qu'il en serait de] this 'nothing' to be seen, to defend what is at stake, to claim its value/worth. Here again, there seems to be no possible economy whereby her sexual reality could be represented by/for the woman. (SE: 49; SF: 56; trans. adapted)

As a result, 'within discourse, the feminine finds itself defined as lack, deficiency, or as imitation and negative image of the subject' (TS: 78; CS: 76).

Irigaray is not the only person to point to the primacy of *seeing* in Freud's account of the castration complex. The problems with this have been identified by many others: it seems to make the castration complex dependent upon a contingency (whether or not one happens to see); and second, as Lacan points out, there can be nothing 'missing' in the real (quoted by Rose 1986: 66). For Irigaray, it is indicative of a metaphysics, in which the symbolic representations that might enable women to perform certain symbolic operations of sublimation are absent. But there is a problem about 'imagining, conceiving of, representing or symbolizing'. How can one imagine, represent or symbolize when these processes are structured by a male subjectivity which exploits the body-matter of woman for its own symbolic operations? How can one symbolize without objectifying the mother yet again? So Irigaray makes the claim that what is needed is a change in the symbolic. Whatever the problems with this claim, certain things are clear. In the first place, it would imply an interpretation of the maternal genealogy, which would symbolize the relation between the girl-child and her mother in a way which allowed the mother to be both a mother *and* a woman, so that women were not forever competing for the unique place occupied by the mother, so that women could differentiate themselves from the mother, and so that women were not reduced to the maternal function. On a collective level, Irigaray says that women need a religion, a language, and an economy of their own (WSM: 9; SP: 93). I hypothesize that this alternative symbolic is not envisaged simply as a substitute for what we have now, but would be a symbolic which enabled the imaginary creative intercourse between two parents to take a symbolic form. It would be a symbolic which, by making a place for the woman, would enable cathexis of the relation *between the two parents*. It would not *replace* the paternal metaphor with a maternal one, but would allow the woman as lover, and mother as co-parent to enter the symbolic for the first time.

The imaginary and the symbolic

In this final section, I wish to raise some of the problems I have come up against in trying to elucidate what we are to understand by the ideas of a female imaginary, a female symbolic and so on. I outlined in the previous chapter the conceptual mobility of the imaginary. As I suggested earlier, I think that some writers on Irigaray have tried to deal too summarily with the difficulties in conceptualizing the female imaginary, by a precipitate celebration of the female imaginary, which evades the problem of its existence (whether it exists at all, and what kind of existence it might have) within the present symbolic order. Another problem is the relation of imaginary to symbolic, which is often omitted altogether by an exclusive focus on the imaginary.

The imaginary can be described in more than one way. (1) The female imaginary can be seen as the unconscious of western thought – the unsymbolized, repressed underside of western philosophy. In this sense, it falls under the description in *This Sex*: it is plural, because it is 'scraps, uncollected debris' (TS: 30; CS: 29), an imaginary which consists of the remnants or residues left over by the structuration of the imaginary by the dominant symbolic order. It may make its presence felt in the form of 'somatic complaints'. (2) But there is another sense in which the female imaginary should be understood: as something which does not yet exist, which still has to be created.[11] This would be a non-essentialist thesis; the female imaginary would be, not something lurking in the depths of women's unconscious, but a possible restructuring of the imaginary by the symbolic which would make a difference to women. We have the problem here of stating what it is that women need which would not leave them in dereliction – unsymbolized – but which would not be thought of either simply in terms of identity, since an identity that is equivalent to sameness is an integral part of the metaphysics which represses the feminine. In this second sense, I think that one cannot think the female imaginary without thinking the female symbolic. This would also be the sense in which Irigaray's imaginary can be related to

Lacan's future perfect (or future anterior): identifications with oneself in an anticipated future which has not yet been realized:

> What is realized in my history is not the past definite of what was, since it is no more, or even the present perfect of what has been in what I am, but the future anterior of what I shall have been for what I am in the process of becoming. (Lacan 1977: 86)

In other words, the imaginary has a projective dimension, which was discussed in terms of utopia in Chapter 1. (3) Imaginary identity cannot be limited to the unconscious phantasy of an individual. These phantasies are themselves structured by the symbolic, so that identity is also collective and social. One should then conceive of the creation of the female imaginary as a social process, involving intervention in the symbolic. (4) Although the imaginary is related to identity (this issue will be further discussed in Chapters 5 and 6), the female imaginary should not be seen in terms of the 'one' but in terms of the multiple; it is not an attempt to impose a constricting definition on women, but rather the attempt to create a space in which women, in all their multiplicity, can *become*, i.e. accede to subjectivity.

The symbolic can also be interpreted in more than one sense. First, it can be taken in a more or less developmental sense (with qualifications): it is the order of discourse and meaning, the order into which all human beings have to insert themselves and which therefore precedes and exceeds individual subjectivity; it is what enables the subject to break out of the imaginary mother–child unity and become a social being. (It is, then, the 'third term' which makes symbolic castration possible.) But more importantly, it can be interpreted in a structural sense, as that which enables the break from the imaginary to be made at all, at any time. It is clear that the social human being continues to function for most of the time in an imaginary register, locked into various unconscious phantasies, which may or may not find support in the social or interpersonal world. Irigaray makes this point when she writes, for example, that the present symbolic order is completely imaginary: 'The symbolic that you impose as a universal, free of all empirical or historical contingency, is *your* imaginary transformed into an order, a social order' (PN: 269). (The 'you' she is addressing here is 'Messieurs les psychanalystes'.) She makes a similar point when she writes that the 'subject of science', the epistemological subject, has not made the break, but is still governed by a *male* imaginary. Or again, when she explains that western metaphysics is subtended by an anal imaginary. The crucial problem then becomes: how to effect the break from the imaginary. Teresa Brennan points out that it can be effected in two ways; either external reality obstinately refuses to match the phantasy, or, in psychoanalysis, the analyst refuses the imaginary projections of the analysand.[12] It is relatively easy to see how this function might be carried out by the analyst. It is rather more difficult to see how a female symbolic might be created which would serve the function of 'break' to the male imaginary in external reality. I will return to this question in a moment.

It looks, then, as though one needs to think two things simultaneously. The first is that the female symbolic depends upon a female imaginary. If one attempts to bypass the question of the female at the level of the imaginary, by addressing the question at the symbolic level only – stating for example that women are capable of reason too, or pointing out that the fact that the Phallus is the signifier of difference does not imply any inevitable oppression of women within the symbolic and social order[13] – then one is relying on a most precarious position; the break from the imaginary, which is the structural sense of the symbolic, may not have any support in the social; social institutions continue to support the phantasies of the male imaginary. If one abandons the imaginary to the male, women will still be left without *representations*, or *images* or, one might add, institutions, to serve as identificatory supports. But if a female symbolic depends upon a female imaginary, it is also the case that a female imaginary depends upon a female symbolic. The imaginary is an *effect* of the symbolic; it is the symbolic which structures the imaginary, so that there is a sense in which the imaginary does not exist until it is symbolized; one may not even be able to say that it is repressed: 'can one speak at this stage of repression when the processes that make it possible have not yet come into being?' (SE: 84; SF: 101). For this reason, I would not agree with those who equate the imaginary in Irigaray's work with the archaic, maternal, pre-Oedipal space. From a structural point of view, the pre-Oedipal is produced by the symbolic, as well as informing it.

One could put this point more schematically as follows. The question of the relation between symbolic/imaginary and subjectivity/identity can be formulated in this way: (1) subjectivity is a *structure*, or a position of enunciation. It is not identity; (2) but that structure would be empty without the imaginary: representations are what flesh it out. So the symbolic is structure (form) which is given content by the imaginary, and the imaginary pours itself into the available structures to form representations. Subjectivity, then, belongs to the symbolic, but it is empty without the imaginary; identity is imaginary, but it takes a symbolic (representational) form. Although it is possible to make a conceptual distinction, in practice the two overlap, because one never finds one without the other. Language (*langage*) belongs simultaneously to both symbolic and imaginary, so perhaps because Irigaray focuses on language it sometimes seems as though she conflates imaginary and symbolic, at the expense of the symbolic.

Now this idea of a female symbolic is obviously problematic, even if it is put in social and philosophical, rather than psychoanalytic, terms; some people would argue that it is not even coherent. One thing I would suggest is that for Irigaray, that break with the imaginary, in which one is capable of thinking *about* one's own imaginary, instead of being thought *by* it, is unlikely to take a social form as long as there is no real *other*. At the moment, according to

Irigaray, what we have is an economy of the Same, exchange between men – the same, male imaginary with nothing to act as the 'break', except women (i.e. women in external reality refusing the projections of the male imaginary). In other words, for men to make the break with *their* imaginary, another term would be needed – women as symbolic term. So long as women continue to be *objects of exchange* within that imaginary, they cannot be the term that effects the break. They need to 'go to market' in their own right. There is a symbolic castration which men have yet to effect: cutting the umbilical cord which links them to the mother. And they will only be able to do this when it becomes possible to distinguish between the mother and the woman, when the relation between mother and daughter is symbolized.

Another way of understanding this might be through the idea, developed in a paper by Teresa Brennan,[14] that 'social relations can either oppose or reinforce psychical products'. This would be true whether or not one took a certain imaginary to be historical or not, that is, even if the male imaginary, or what Lacan calls the 'psychical fantasy of women', or the child's belief that there is only one sex, were all transhistorical factors. Then one direction for action would have to be the construction of social relations which *opposed* this imaginary, for instance the construction of a women's sociality, or representations of women which directly counter it. There is no reason why the social should automatically be regarded as no more nor less than the psyche writ large, and to do so would be to collapse the social into the psychic. The crucial question of course, and one which can *only* be addressed collectively, is that of how to make changes in the symbolic.

We are brought back here to the question of Chapter 2: the question of change is also the question of women as subjects of epistemology. If knowledge and the production of knowledge are subtended by the unacknowledged mother, what would it mean to acknowledge the mother? One of the ways Irigaray suggests is that a place for maternal genealogy must be made in the symbolic order. This is not the abolition of symbolic castration, but a symbolic recognition that *two* parents are involved in reproduction, and that there is a relation between them. Thus Irigaray argues that she is not putting forward a new 'theory' of woman, but attempting to intervene in and have an effect on the economy of the logos (TS: 78; CS: 75–6, quoted in Chapter 3). For Irigaray, symbolizing the mother–daughter relationship, creating externally located and durable representations of this prototypical relation between women, is an urgent necessity if women are to exist *as women* in the social imaginary. These symbolic representations would constitute an external reality which might block the more damaging effects of the male imaginary and ideally have a creative outcome. For Irigaray, the only way in which the status of women could be fundamentally altered is by the creation of a powerful female symbolic to represent the other term of sexual difference against the omnipresent effects of the male imaginary.

*

Another way of approaching the question of the symbolic female is to look at the relation in Irigaray's work between 'nature' and the symbolic. Irigaray's mobilization of the vocabulary of 'nature' presents her interpreters with certain difficulties. On the one hand, as we shall see, she is arguing that women have had the function 'nature' one-sidedly attributed to them. On the other hand, there is her insistent recourse to the claim that nature itself is sexuate, which seems to lead to the kind of 'origin story' that has been discredited by modern philosophy. The interpretation I will be putting forward in the second half of the book is an attempt to make sense of her strategy. I shall argue that she is thinking through the implications of the 'double syntax' (TS: 132; CS: 130) – the idea that there is a logic or syntax, the logic of the unconscious, which is quite other than the Greek *logos* or rationality. Her main point is about the relation between the double syntax and the symbolic distribution of functions. The double syntax – the divisions between consciousness and unconscious, for example – is, or should be, internal to each sex. But symbolically, the line of cleavage goes *between* the two sexes. Men continue to transcend 'nature' – biology, mortality – by allotting 'nature' to the side of women (leaving aside for the moment the question of what 'nature' means). But because of the operations of the double syntax, the unwanted or transcended functions have been subject to cultural repression and splitting; they are, in a certain sense, unconscious. Sometimes Irigaray calls this simply a symbolic division of labour (*répartition du travail*: E: 114). Sometimes, much more strongly, she refers to it as a 'scission' (E: 121) or a 'schize' (E: 120), a split in which one part remains totally unconscious of the other part and of its existence. The two sides of this split, men and women, thus find themselves in a very different position vis-à-vis the world:

> one part of the world would be asking how to be able to find and speak its meaning [sens], its side of meaning [signification], while the other would be wondering about the meaning [sens] that language, all values and life might still have. (E: 121–2)

Irigaray is arguing for a symbolic redistribution, so that men can accept that part of themselves which is 'nature', without needing to attribute it to women, and so that women can accede to the transcendental functions previously allotted to men. (The term 'sensible transcendental' serves to indicate the aim of this redistribution.) The 'natural' division into two sexes cannot be ignored, since it has provided the imaginary basis for the patriarchal division of roles. If Irigaray insists on the 'natural' division, it is because she believes that the weight of patriarchy is too heavy to shift in any other way. As in the martial arts, she is using the opponent's weight against itself, using the essentialism of patriarchy as a lever. The attempts of male philosophers to go beyond 'nature', beyond sexual difference (as in deconstruction, for example), underestimate what they are up against. By default, they assign to the usual sex (women) the task of bearing the unwanted functions, even when they do not lack good will. Irigaray's recent comments on Levinas are illuminating in this respect. Although in general she is sympathetic to Levinas, because of his ethical stance, she feels that he fails to offer assistance:

> After having been so far – or so close – in the approach to the other sex, in my view to the other, to the mystery of the other, Levinas clings on once more to this rock of patriarchy in the very place of carnal love. Although he takes pleasure in caressing, he abandons the feminine other, leaves her to sink, in particular into the darkness of a pseudo-animality, in order to return to his responsibilities in the world of men-amongst-themselves. For him, the feminine does not stand for an other to be respected in her human freedom and identity. The feminine other is left without her own specific face. On this point his philosophy falls radically short of ethics. To go beyond the face of metaphysics would mean precisely to leave the woman her face, and even *to assist her to discover it and to keep it*. Levinas scarcely unveils the disfigurements brought about by onto-theology. (QEL 115–16; my emphasis)

Her comments on contemporary philosophers seem to me to indicate that she feels they are still primarily concerned with the world of 'men-amongst-themselves' and that women cannot expect very much help from them. In the terms we have just been discussing, one could say that she feels they are still caught in the dominant imaginary.

Irigaray's insistence on nature, then, is not at all a crude biologism. It is intended to expose the complicity of philosophy in maintaining a completely traditional symbolic division between the sexes. Her so-called essentialism is primarily a strategy for bringing to light the concealed essentialism of philosophy. I am arguing that Irigaray's central concern is with the symbolic, and with the place of both 'woman' and women in relation to the symbolic order. It is ironic that someone who is arguing for the *re*structuring and *re*symbolizing of male and female 'nature' should be seen as essentializing, i.e. as assigning a fixed nature to each sex.

Nature, then, can refer to:

1. The raw material for symbolization – biology, reproduction, the body, mortality, cycles of growth and decay, the cosmos;
2. The support of representation – the screen, backcloth, or mirror;
3. The residue of the symbolic order;
4. A symbolic function carried (out) by women (symbolizing the residue);
5. The Lacanian Real (this may also be death);
6. The maternal-feminine (i.e. woman for-man);
7. That which is referred to by the sign 'nature' in male discourse;
8. A universal (like death). (See e.g. SP: 126–7)

This multiple connotation indicates that 'nature' has a range of discursive functions; in addition, of course, the mimetic strategy makes it difficult to know to what extent Irigaray is endorsing any of the positions she occupies discursively, and to what extent she is consciously imitating them in order to expose the patriarchal symbolic distribution.

Irigaray's point, then, is that a process of 'naturalization' takes place. This point is made quite clearly in *Ethique* in a discussion of Hegel (E: 105). Women, symbolically, remain part of the in-itself (*en-soi*); only men are allowed to be for-themselves (*pour-soi*). In Hegelian terms, women belong to the plant world – they are *végétales*; only men have an animal life. Although Irigaray often refers to 'naturalization' as 'appropriation' by the 'proper' or by the paternal genealogy, thus bringing the concept within the conceptual domain of ownership, I have preferred to call it naturalization for several reasons: (a) this foregrounds the notion that what has been appropriated is symbolized as nature (as opposed to culture, or the symbolic); (b) the result of the process is presented as if it were natural and inevitable, rather than the product of symbolization; (c) the term thus links Irigaray more readily with other feminist debates about women and nature, and makes it possible to see clearly Irigaray's contribution to these debates in terms which are recognizable. This does not mean that the question of ownership is irrelevant.

It is significant that Irigaray stresses that nature (the natural world) is not respected. This is not simply a version of ecofeminism (though it is that too), but part of her argument about the symbolic distribution, and the allocation of the 'lower functions' to women. The symbolic distribution is hierarchical. What is being disrespected is those parts of himself that the male imaginary has split off and projected – into the world, on to women. In a kind of neo-Hegelian scenario, hi-tech in its thrusting, sacrificial modalities is valorized; nature, along with women, is downgraded as 'merely' fertile.

Symbolic division is also – and importantly – about the organization of the death drives (translated in the Standard Edition of Freud as 'death instincts').[15] The death drives have a problematic status in psychoanalytic theory. It is not so much a debate about clinical evidence – about (self-) destructive impulses, about the drive to repeat, to return to stasis and immobility, about sadism and masochism, and so on – but about the kind of explanatory framework they call for, and the kind of evidence therefore which should be offered. The term 'death drive' itself covers a range of different categories which cannot simply be assimilated to each other; it is not clear, for example, that the drive to repeat or to return to a state of non-tension is identical with primary masochism (see on this Laplanche 1970). What is important in this context is that the concept of the death drives complicates the question of the appropriate distribution of causality to social and psychic respectively (see Copjec 1989; Ragland–Sullivan 1989; Rose 1989). In its most basic form, it is Rousseau's question: what makes people unhappy? Is it the fault of society or is there something inherent in the human psyche which is an obstacle to happiness? Most people would probably say 'both', but it is hard to determine with any precision what is 'inside' and what is 'outside'. When

Irigaray is talking about symbolic division, she is also quite centrally putting into question the symbolic organization and distribution of the death drives. Women's so-called 'natural' constitution (and men's too) is not natural at all, but is connected to a particular economy of the death drives, as the following passage from *Speculum* spells out:

> The prohibition, the devaluing of their desire of the 'same' – with which women are in any case said to be complicit through their phallic, 'masculine'? superego? – in the evolution of female sexuality would account, to a considerable extent, for what is deplored as frigidity, lack of sexual appetite. And could serve as an interpretative tool for many other concurrent or related symptoms: lack of autonomy, narcissistic fragility or excessive narcissism; incapacity for sublimation, which does not exclude an 'ethereal' erotism; relations with the mother, and moreover with all women, that are difficult to say the least; lack of 'social' interests and more generally any sustained interest; depressions and chronic somatizations, etc. These are all manifestations of a lack of an auto-erotic, homo-sexual economy. Or again, and even more, of an economy *of the death drives*. Their 'active' mobilization is prohibited for/in female sexuality. A prohibition which does not, and cannot, organize their rechannelling, metaphorization or sublimation, since the dominant organization of the *specular* is inadequate for women's sexuality, leaving, though no doubt in different ways, the female sexual function and the maternal sexual function in suspension, amorphous, awaiting the economy of their drives and/or far too determined by a heteronomous economy. An 'economy' governed by the exigencies of drives – particularly sadistic or scopophilic – which only men will be allowed to enact. And, above all, by the necessity of maintaining the primacy of the Phallus. (SE: 102; SF: 126; my trans.)

Women's 'nature' has been constructed by a particular symbolic organization, in which they are 'used' for the representation and sublimation of men's death drives, but are unable to sublimate or represent their own.

Irigaray's argument about western philosophy in general – including the attempt to deconstruct phallogocentrism in the work of Derrida – is that it perpetuates this symbolic distribution, leaving women still as the guardians of men's unwanted functions. Her emphasis on the specificity of women naturally brings her into conflict not only with Lacanians, but also with deconstructive versions of feminism. For although she has drawn on the work of Derrida to examine and destabilize the economy of the *logos*, yet it might seem as though, despite her disclaimer – women should not be attempting to construct a logic of the feminine – this is exactly what she has ended up doing. However, it seems to me that it is crucially her interpretation of the death drives that leads her to take a distance from deconstructive philosophy.

In addition, if one sees social organization as binding the death drive, as Irigaray appears to, then social organization is a paramount consideration.[16] As we can see from her later work, particularly *Sexes et parentés* and *Le Temps de la différence*, she is preoccupied with the problem of social order and the effects on both men and women of what she describes in more than one place as a 'worldwide disorder' (*désordre mondial*), in which money and possessions and conflicts between men have swamped questions of respect for human life. She diagnoses the sickness or crisis of civilization (E: 13) as the ascendancy of the death drives, and if she looks to women for hope for the future, it is because women have less investment than men in the current economy of the death drive, and therefore more motivation to attempt a social and symbolic reorganization. She suggests that the link with the death drive also explains the often expressed and persistent fear that 'women's liberation' will mean the dissolution of the symbolic order or the end of the civilized world. What is feared is what has been repressed; there is a kind of cataclysmic end-of-the-world phantasy of total disintegration, dissolution, and loss of self.

The second half of this book attempts to demonstrate the centrality of the themes of symbolic division, scission, and splitting to Irigaray's analysis of the history of thought. On this analysis, philosophy and society alike share the imaginary and symbolic values of this economy of death. The task of philosophy – of thought – is ethical and symbolic: to resymbolize sexual difference at all levels from the most corporeal to the most abstract and 'divine', and to develop ways of making symbolically available the divisions *within* each sex or genre. This is the task to which Irigaray is devoting herself. Although she is primarily concerned with the 'other woman', this should lead to the 'other man' as well, since in the process of redistribution both sides would have to shift their position fundamentally.

Section II

Philosophy

Chapter 5

The same, the semblance, and the other

ce rêve qu'est *aussi* la vérité (*Speculum*)
truth is *also* [a] dream

For Irigaray, the gesture which excludes women from philosophy and the gesture which excludes women from the polis[1] are, seen from the point of view of the imaginary, one and the same. It follows that to bring women into philosophy (in the form of the 'feminine') while continuing to exclude *women* from full membership of the human community does not change anything very much. The following four chapters look at Irigaray's investigation of the gesture of exclusion in philosophy, and her exploration of the conditions of women's full accession to culture and society. This may seem asymmetrical; but, as we shall see, she argues that women cannot enter philosophy *as women*, and so the issue of sexual difference is primary and fundamental. Thus what she refers to as the thought of sexual difference is both philosophical and non-philosophical. It is non-philosophical in that philosophy – even in its modern 'end-of-philosophy' form – cannot encompass sexual difference. It is philosophical in that, by thinking sexual difference, it is attempting – heroically – to undo that founding gesture (located for example in Plato), and to rewrite the script of western civilization. This is what I call provisionally philosophy in the feminine; it is thought which attempts to confront the double gesture of exclusion, the dual complicity of philosophy and the polis, which have to be confronted simultaneously. So that any account of Irigaray which focuses on 'woman' and misses out *women* just goes on reduplicating that complicity.[2] In the next four chapters I want to argue this point across a complex network of interwoven Irigarayan themes, in particular:

1. The incorporation and sometimes obliteration of the feminine by the masculine, resulting in a hom(m)osexual world in which only men are subjects.
2. The downgrading of the body, allocated symbolically to women, and the effects of this: the split between ideal and material, sensible and intelligible, for example.
3. The relegation of women to the status of appearance, non-truth, or any

of the other forms of 'otherness' which 'woman' signifies in philosophy.
4.   The place of women in a society founded on 'sacrifice'.
5.   The domination of a scopic economy.
6.   The domination of a patriarchal economy of the death drives.

One of the difficulties of reading Irigaray arises from the fact that we are, in practice, accustomed to reading statements about 'woman' as though they were statements about 'women', even when the speaker denies that 'woman' is anything more than metaphor. So we are not quite sure what status to give to Irigaray's statements: are they empirical descriptions (women as they are within patriarchy), ideal descriptions (women as they might become), descriptions of the reigning imaginary (women as defined by men), prescriptions (what women ought to become), or perhaps simply metaphors again? Irigaray appears to move between 'woman' in western philosophy, 'women' in western society, and 'the feminine' with great fluidity – and in fact this mobility is quite difficult to avoid without extreme semantic precision. The maternal-feminine, for example, can be seen discursively as another term for what in Heideggerian terms might be called 'gift' or in Derridean terms 'différance' or 'espacement'. But it is not accidental that the maternal-feminine also has inescapable sexual and corporeal connotations and an insistent social and material reference. (Jane Gallop (1983) makes a similar point with reference to Irigaray's language of the body.)

It is partly because Irigaray is arguing that there is a connection between the status of woman in western thought and the status of women in western society; the two domains share the same imaginary, so the difference between the metaphorical and the social reality at a certain level becomes in any case blurred. But more importantly, I think, she is redrawing the topography of sexual difference, in an attempt to bring women as subjects into the symbolic. When women attempt to speak in their own name, to speak *as women*, to speak their truth, as one might say, this is rejected in the name of truth; truth it is said, has a universal character, and women cannot speak for the universal. But as Irigaray sets out to show in *Speculum*, this is so *by definition*, and the economy of truth has been used to justify the exclusion of women (though also, as we shall see in Chapter 6, the economy of undecidability, i.e. the undecidability of truth and non-truth, can be used to perpetuate the exclusion of women too). In a sense, then, 'woman' has already been mapped on to 'women', and Irigaray regards it as more important to redraw the map – to reclaim 'woman' for women – than to throw away the maps altogether.

Irigaray's reinterpretations of classical mythology, of which we shall look at several examples, come from her belief that in mythology we can see a struggle taking place between the maternal and paternal genealogies, eventually ending in the installation of patriarchy. To 'undo' the gesture which puts patriarchy in place it is necessary to reveal the gesture in detail. But that in itself is not enough. It is clear from her method and from her interest in mythology that Irigaray does not regard the negative moment as sufficient. One has to prevent the patriarchal version from simply falling back into place again, by providing alternative versions, alternative readings, alternative mythologies and alternative imaginary configurations, however provisional. Unlike the philosophers, who can afford to argue that they are not essentialist, Irigaray in a sense has no option. From her point of view, the philosophers, of whatever persuasion, are comfortably installed in the male imaginary, so comfortably that they are completely unaware of the sexuate character of 'universal' thought. So Irigaray has a twofold task. The first is to reveal the imaginary body of philosophy, to show the sexual dynamics at work in the theoretical constructions of philosophy. The second is to show how the body of the maternal-feminine has been left out of the ideal and intelligible realm while continuing to nourish it and supply its sensible, material conditions. One cannot get 'beyond' essentialism at this point without passing through essentialism. As we saw in Chapter 3, the imaginary is a bodily imaginary. But the philosophers are not aware of this level of 'essentialism' which subsists in the most deconstructive thought. So this imaginary has to be *interpreted*, and at the same time, the female body has to be allowed its own imaginary existence in the form of symbolic difference. Unless one accepts Irigaray's premises that western thought is informed by an imaginary which in turn has the morphology of the male body, then one is bound to see her as metaphysically reactionary. But while philosophy may pride itself on its liberation from the shackles of essentialist thinking, it merely repeats the founding gesture of exclusion, because it has not analysed its own conditions of existence.

Irigaray's readings of mythology are partly interpretation (the negative moment), and partly alternatives which act as holding devices to prevent the immediate reinstallation of the male imaginary configuration. It is thus possible to accept her strategy without necessarily accepting her alternatives; other women could invent other alternatives. In this chapter, through a selective juxtaposition of Irigaray's readings of certain myths along with passages from different parts of *Speculum*, I want to show how she develops both a critique of the structure of patriarchal thought and a strategic restructuring which would allow, even if only discursively, a possible place for a different imaginary.

The final section of *Speculum*, 'Plato's *Hystera*', consists of a remarkable reading of the opening pages of Book 7 of Plato's *Republic* (which I shall be referring to here in the Loeb edition) and Plato's myth of the cavern. It is not a reading which can be simply summarized; it is dependent for its effects on word-play (often not reproducible in English), the free associations of an erudite mind trained in classics and philosophy, and the application of Freud's discoveries to an ancient philosophical text. The aspect of her reading to which I want to draw attention here is its presentation of the myth of the cavern as a figurative representation of the phallogocentric economy: the economy of truth, the metaphysics of presence and the dependence on the transcendental signifier. What follows is not an attempt to do justice to its complexity, but a focus on Irigaray's method, her project to 'psychoanalyse the philosophers' and her alternative imaginary topography. Against the threefold and patriarchal topography of Plato's myth (the cavern, the world and the Forms), she proposes an inverse topography (the Same, the 'other of the same' and the 'other of the other'). Originally produced as a reconceptualization of Plato's togography, these categories later come to remap the territory of western thought. They are not exactly offering a Hegelian schema, despite their Hegelian provenance (see SE: 90, note 93; SF: 109–10, note 123),[3] but provide the groundwork for the thought of sexual difference. Because it is easier to follow the argument if the terminology is familiar, I will anticipate slightly here, and outline this tripartite schema.

In her interpretation of Plato, the realm of the Idea or the Form is designated as the realm of the Same, or the Self-Identical. The world is described as the 'other of the same', i.e. otherness, but in the sense that it is a more or less adequate copy. The cavern then becomes the 'other of the other', i.e. it does not, in its materiality, figure in the other two worlds at all, it is not a copy or a semblance or a likeness of the Idea or the Same. This schema later becomes expanded in subsequent texts, as follows. The realm of the Same is the hom(m)osexual economy of men, in which women are simply objects of exchange. This is also called the realm of the Semblance (TS: 171; CS: 168), in that although relations between men are governed by love of the same, love between men is masked, and homosexuality as a *practice* is subject to prohibition. In the imaginary, woman is the material substratum for men's theories, their language, and their transactions. She is their 'house' or 'container'. The 'other of the same' now comes to refer to women in patriarchy. This too is the realm of the Semblance, of appearance, the realm of woman (or women) within the masculine economy, of woman (or women) as she is (or as they are) for men. The 'other of the other', finally, is an as yet non-existent female homosexual economy, women-amongst-themselves, love of self on the side of women. In so far as she exists already, woman as the 'other of the other' exists in the interstices of the realm of the Semblance. Her accession to language, to the imaginary and symbolic processes of culture and society, is the condition for the coming-to-be of sexual difference. The term itself, the 'other of the other', is a direct challenge to Lacan's lapidary pronouncement: 'there is no Other of the Other' (Lacan 1977: 311; 1966: 813).

The first chapter of section II is about the scene of representation. The scene of representation, as it is often called in French, and as Irigaray herself sometimes refers to it, is only partly to do with who portrays what or whom, and in what medium (for example the representation of women by male artists). It is also, and perhaps more centrally, to do with the economy of truth, that is, the conditions under which a representation, or re-presentation is said to be a true (or false) representation. This is a question which Derrida's dissection of the metaphysics of presence has brought to the fore in recent French philosophy, particularly since the problematization of language as a medium of representation has become a major critical issue.[4] Irigaray argues that, whatever the avatars of the history of 'truth', whether in its deeply influential Platonic version, or whether in the anti-Platonic critiques and the 'postmodernist' pluralism that they have ushered in, the scene of representation allows only the 'same' and the 'other of the same' to take the stage. Plato and his critics have that much in common. For that reason, women do not simply oppose a female truth to a male truth (AM: 92). First, it is necessary to tackle the scene of representation itself, to look at its props, its 'scenery', and its backcloth.

The Platonic myth is a working of the themes of loss of origin, identity, and death. However, it offers a solution which, while permitting men to deal with separation and loss, with their fears of death and extinction, allows no similar sublimation for women. In Plato's problematic economy, women bear the costs of truth; truth is achieved *at their expense*, since it offers no possible symbolization of their own death drives. Although Irigaray's overall project may be controversial, there is nothing in her analysis of Plato that will be radically unfamiliar to feminist analyses of patriarchy.

The myth of the cavern

Although she by no means shares all its presuppositions, Irigaray stands in the anti-Platonic tradition which runs from Kant to Derrida, via Hegel, Heidegger, and Nietzsche, and which recasts the question of truth as it is formulated in Plato. Three features in particular of Plato's mythical account are rejected. The first is the idea that objects might be looked on as they are in themselves, at least a certain sort of object – the Forms or Ideas: 'And so finally, I suppose, he would be able to look upon the sun itself and see its true nature, not by reflections in water or phantasms of it in an alien setting, but in and by itself in its own place', Socrates remarks (516). The sun here stands for the Idea of the Good (517). The second feature to be rejected is the possibility of Forms as origin, as: 'cause for all things of all that is right and beautiful, giving birth in the visible world to light, and the author of light and itself in the intelligible world being the authentic source of truth and reason' (517). The third feature to be rejected is that Plato puts the Ideas outside the world of becoming; they belong in the realm of pure unchanging Being. Mortal being and becoming, according to this account, weigh down the soul and pull it downwards to the Sensible world (509).

The strength of Irigaray's reading comes from her (psychoanalytic) attention to the words and details of Plato's analogy. Whereas the translator of the Loeb Plato, Paul Shorey, comments that: 'It is probably a mistake to look for a definite symbolism in all the details of the description' (Shorey, vol. 2 1980:

126), Irigaray in contrast focuses precisely on the details, the discrepancies and contingencies of Plato's account, seeing them from a psychoanalytically inspired perspective as fully significant in her reinterpretation of the history of philosophy. From a psychoanalytic point of view, the small, unimportant detail, the thing that is passed over unnoticed, the detail that is casually relegated as insignificant or accidental, can usually be reckoned to be significant and revelatory. It is obvious, even banal, that the cavern represents the womb; this is not a reflex, stereotypical Freudian reading – in the Platonic dialogues themselves Socrates is described as a midwife, his method as a maieutic method, and his role to assist the birth into knowledge of the truth. What Irigaray finds in the myth is an imaginary primal scene (i.e. a phantasied copulation between mother and father) which has attempted to remove the mother. Underlying the economy of truth is an imaginary phantasy of the primal scene in which the mother's role has been elided. Irigaray argues that the Idea in Plato is a male engenderer. The fact that the woman also engenders has been obliterated from the scene of representation by cutting off the Sensible from the Intelligible. The effect is that the male function takes over and incorporates all the female function, leaving women outside the scene, but supporting it, a condition of representation. The picture of the cavern *represents*, while concealing, the process. And in addition, the metaphoricity of light and vision, governed by the metaphysics of presence, is a function of the defective imaginary primal scene, so that the metaphoricity which has been so dominant in western philosophy, the spectator theory of representation, is inseparable from the exclusion of women. As a result, Plato's ideal republic, despite appearances, is not at all egalitarian; his city is homosexual, his women are all 'men' – they accede to all the civic functions in so far as they resemble men and renounce their specificity.

Plato's stringent and uncompromising account is an attempt to make the Intelligible realm invulnerable to harm. His presupposition – that which the whole scene of the cavern is designed to show – is the assumption that there is an original model (Idea/Form/Being/God, perhaps also Light and Eternal Father) which spawns an indefinite number of copies of itself.[5] The Idea, then, is the original *measure* of which things in the world are more or less adequate copies.[6] The Idea is Reality itself, compared to which the world is only appearance. Paradoxically, the measure is outside human experience – our knowledge of it appears to depend on the recollection of a time before we were born and a progressive recognition of it in life which will not be confirmed until after death. The adequacy of the copies or reflections depends upon the criterion of their closeness to the Original. But given that the Original is outside experience, this is a difficult criterion to apply; it is not surprising that Plato was deeply concerned with the problem of distinguishing between 'true' and 'false' representations. The myth of the cavern itself, we are to suppose, is an 'adequate' representation.

Plato's argument for the existence of a pure Intelligible realm works by analogy. Plato supposes (a) the symmetry between the cavern and the world and (b) a similar relationship between the world and the world of Ideas:

> This image, then, dear Glaucon, we must apply as a whole to all that has been said, likening the region revealed through sight to the habitation of the prison, and the light of the fire in it to the power of the sun. And if you assume that the ascent and the contemplation of the things above is the soul's ascension to the intelligible region, you will not miss my surmise. (517)

Although Plato begins, chronologically, with the cavern, in fact logically his argument depends upon a series of analogies between an Origin – the self-identical Idea – and the copies or more or less adequate shadows or reflections which are images of it. But the Origin is outside our experience. Thus the argument for the Idea – the intelligible realm as the highest Good, and our ability to grasp or 'see' it – depends upon an analogy (or two analogies) which it is the purpose of the myth to establish. And one might say that analogy itself is a copy or semblance, and belongs itself to the economy of truth, as will become evident, so that the analogy 'proves' that which guarantees the analogy. At all events, having concluded in the first part of *Speculum* that Freud's 'analogy' between the development of the little boy and the development of the little girl is a form of 'anal logic', Irigaray is alert to the possible phantasmatic implications of analogy as a mode of argumentation.

There are thus three scenes: the mythological scene of the cavern; the world we live in; and the world of Ideas, where the One Self-Identical Idea is pure self-presence. And as one might expect, given that each scene is an analogy or semblance of the higher one, the descriptions are marked by a proliferation of likenesses, in fact a dizzying profusion of appearances, shadows, reflections, doubles, mirror effects, inversions, and reversibilities. However, as the analogy progresses, as we move from the scene of the cavern to the scene of the world, which becomes in its turn the womb/cavern from which we must painfully ascend into the world of Ideas, certain features of the original picture begin to disappear. Irigaray notes in particular that they are features corresponding to the morphology of the female body: for example the difficult passage or ascent through which the reluctant prisoner is dragged into the light (the 'forgotten vagina' – SE: 247; SF: 306), the little wall, ' "like" a curtain' (SE: 249; SF: 308) (a hymen) which conceals the men carrying the stone or wooden images.

It is not irrelevant to notice some of the doublings that occur; their disappearance is all the more striking. For example, within the cavern there is a threefold semblance: the 'magicians', as Irigaray refers to them, who are responsible for staging the shadowscope by holding up the images of men and animals which are then reflected by the fire on to the wall of the cavern; the statues or images themselves; and finally, the shadows – both of the images and perhaps also of the prisoners – cast on to the wall. Then there is a further doubling: the little wall/curtain doubles the larger wall of the cavern (they are both a kind of screen, one which hides, one used for projection); the passage through the cave doubles the passage out of the cave. And in the world itself there are (real) shadows, reflections in water of men and other things, while the fire in the cave giving light is doubled by the light of the stars and the moon before being doubled by the light of the sun (and in the third scene, the light of the Idea). So the notion of multiple copies/reflections/shadows/images/likenesses of an original is reflected multiply within the myth itself.

The whole scene in the cavern is staged according to the needs of Plato's analogy: the reflections (shadows or copies of the original Idea); the fire (sun/Idea); the passage (the process of education or coming to learn about the Ideas); the veil (the oblivion in which the world surrounds the Ideas). It is therefore important to register that the cavern acts as a reflector/echo-chamber, and that this element has disappeared by the time we get to the third scene, the Intelligible realm itself. As we move from one equivalence to another, what becomes harder and harder to focus on until gradually it is lost sight of by a 'dialectical sleight of hand', is the fact that all the copies and images depend upon a material support – the screen or wall of the cavern, the water in which men and other things are reflected, and so on. This material support is the Sensible world which has to be set aside if the Intelligible world in all its purity is to be attained. Since the origin for Plato is the Light, attaining the truth depends upon leaving behind the darkness of the 'empirical origin', the cavern/womb. What Irigaray points to is the fact that in Plato's scenario the truth appears to have no material support. An analogy is made between the sun (still visible, still a part of the visible, Sensible world) and the idea (the Intelligible world). But the idea of *seeing* (a Sensible activity) is carried over with the analogy, though seeing of course is dependent on the body. The eyes are attributed to the soul – but in the process of transition from one stage of the analogy to another the Sensible *condition* of seeing is progressively abstracted from the picture. One eventually looks upon Truth itself as in the story the prisoner finally gazes on the sun: 'And so, finally, I suppose, he would be able to look upon the sun itself and see its true nature' (516). What has been abstracted from the scene of the cavern is the cavern as screen, which becomes first the 'ocular *membrane-screen*' of the body (SE: 317; SF: 397), and then the '*specular screen*' (SE: 318; SF: 398) of the soul. The cavity of the cavern becomes first the eye socket – that which limits any human gaze – and then disappears altogether. The soul is a mirror without the glass or the tain. The condition of human seeing has gone, and the seeing in the realm of the Intelligible is vision without any corporeal support, since this belongs to the sphere of the Sensible from which the seeker after Truth attempts to free himself.[7]

In Irigaray's reinterpretation, the roles of imaginary mother and father are attributed to the cavern and the Idea respectively. In progressively moving away from the shadows towards the light, the prisoner is moving away from the mother: 'the mother's child is engaged in stripping away the membranes, the inheritances that he finds too material, too physical' (SE: 318; SF: 398). The metaphoricity of vision is a scene in which the role of the mother as co-engenderer is progressively stripped away: 'Eclipse of the mother, of the place (of) becoming, whose non-representation or even disavowal upholds the absolute being attributed to the father. He no longer has any foundation, he is beyond all beginnings' (SE: 307; SF: 383).

In the light of 'Plato's *Hystera*', one can see clearly why Irigaray argues that the terms 'imagining', 'conceiving', or 'representing' are inadequate to speak of the representation of women. The terms themselves depend on an implicit division of labour between the Intelligible and its material and Sensible conditions of existence: language and the body. How can the cavern represent itself, since it is the *screen*, in a system which is *uni-directional*. The metaphoricity of vision amounts to the refusal of the thinker to admit embodiment and, more especially, the fact that embodiment means belonging to one sex or the other. The division of labour could perhaps be overcome if one could bring into relation, in Platonic terms, the cavern and the Idea (show that the *transcendental* is also *sensible*, that it is mortal, subject to becoming, dependent on its material conditions, and thus vulnerable, fragile, embodied, and therefore sexuate (*sexué*)). But Irigaray shows how, in the Platonic scenario, this is impossible; the scenes are laid out in such a way that imaginary intercourse between mother and father can never take place.

The fact that there are three scenes – the cavern, the world and the Ideas – means that there is no conjunction between the first and the third, between the realm of Ideas (Idea/Origin/Father) and the underworld of the cavern (the Mother); the scene of the world occupies a middle space between them and prevents them touching, prevents their intercourse. In this scenario, conception is a 'blind spot' (SE: 353; SF: 443): 'A whole system of kinship – that is, in this case, of analogy – makes contact between them [leur contigüité] impracticable. *The economy of metaphor that is in control keeps them apart [écarte leur conjonction]*' (SE: 346; SF: 434).

Of the two elements involved in reproduction, the seed of the Father (the Idea) and the womb of the Mother (the cavern itself), only the paternal element remains in the final scene. Of the primitive scene of giving birth, the paternal Idea has incorporated both elements, and engenders, alone, copies, replicas, and shadows without any material aid.[8] In the scene of the Intelligible, the woman's genealogy has completely disappeared. The contact between mother and father 'is lost in the analogy' (SE: 351; SF: 439–40). For Plato, the condition of ultimate Truth is the *absence* of any reflection; the Idea is pure presence to itself. In the world of appearances we see copies or approximations, but these reflections are 'sham offspring' (SE: 225; SF: 316) for Irigaray, not because they are lesser versions of the Real, but because (sexual) relations between Mother and Father have been rendered impossible by the metaphor (SE: 346; SF: 434). Truth has come to mean leaving behind the Mother (the cavern) and her role in reproduction. Truth becomes linked to the paternal metaphor, the Idea/Father engendering copies and reflections without apparent need for the other partner normally required in processes of reproduction. The Platonic myth stages a primal scene in which Plato gradually manages to turn his back, like the pupil/prisoner, on the role of the Mother altogether. From Irigaray's point of view, the consequences of this are not only philosophical but also social, as I shall explain later.

If we took seriously the other element, the 'other of the other', we would have to abandon the Platonic idea that Truth is a question of measurement against a single standard (the One) and allow for an incommensurable other: 'But how does one reproduce, *analogically*, what is not represented or representable?' (SE: 285; SF: 355). It is incommensurable because it is the condition of the reproduction of all the other models, copies, reflections, and so on, and therefore cannot itself be a copy of the original Idea. The analogy (and of course the recourse to analogy as a method, it is by now clear, presupposes that analogy is one of the 'authorized' copies, presupposes, therefore, its own demonstrandum) turns the cave/womb into a projection screen:

> The maternal, the feminine, serve (only) to maintain the reproduction-production of doubles, copies, semblances, fakes, while any hint of their material elements, of the womb, is turned into scenery to make the show more realistic. (SE: 265; SF: 329–30)

The mother, then, is outside the proliferation of copies and reflections. The one question that must not be asked is that of women's relation to the (re)production of images and copies: 'Similarly it seems to have been resolved that *the mother's relation to the specular* is an issue that cannot be raised' (SE: 308; SF: 384). For if the mother has a relation to the specular, then it would have to be admitted that: 'Truth would lose its *univocal* and universal character' (SE: 308; SF: 385). But the mother's role, by the 'sleight of hand' again, has been 'naturalized' in the following way, through another redistributive twist in the inter-relation of the three scenes.

When the pedagogue releases the prisoner and turns him round, he does not point to the machinery, the tricks of the magicians; he only points to the 'real' objects of which the prisoner has up to now seen only reflections, and tells him that, contrary to appearances, these things are more real. Similarly the voices of the men passing through the cave hide the fact that all of the scenography of the cave is a mechanism, set up by a stage manager, that the repetitions and reproductions – as also the obliterations – have been *staged by someone*. But the voice appears to be an immediate presence, guaranteeing to the prisoners the reality (for them) of what they see. It replaces/obliterates the conditions of truth, leaving only its *apparent presence*. In the second scene, the world above, the artifices have gone, and have been replaced by 'natural' screens and reflectors – the water which reflects, the body which casts a shadow. But Plato does not suggest that God is a magician/seducer/artificer, producing the conditions of apparent presence. He supposes that the reflections on earth are 'more' adequate, more real, than the reflections or phantasms of the cavern. In a sense, 'nature' has become a mirror/screen. The copies, images and so on are 'natural'. Just as the gaze was naturalized in the third scene, even though its condition of existence, the body and the eyes, has effectively disappeared, here the screens and reflectors have been naturalized by removing the stage manager. Irigaray suggests that what has happened is that the semblances or appearances have been incorporated into the definition of the proper (have been 'appropriated'):

> *The fact that the semblance has passed into the definition of the proper will have gone unnoticed.* (SE: 297; SF: 371)

And just as the solar shadows are 'natural' and thus have imperceptibly introduced the simulacrum into the economy of property, so gazing upon the sun will have served to subordinate the gaze, which is still mortal, to the intelligible order. The fiction at work in the tale has achieved this piece of dialectical sleight of hand. (SE: 299; SF: 373)

In other words, in the division set up between Intelligible and Sensible, Reality and Appearance, the screens of nature (water, the body casting shadows) which, according to the analogy ought to belong to the domain of appearance, simulacrum, copy, have been appropriated by the paternal regime of Reality; they are 'more real' than the cavern, although analogically they serve exactly the same function. From the point of view of the third scene, the world is the simulacrum; there should be nothing 'real' or 'natural' about it. But they are engendered not by the scene of the cavern, but by the Father/Sun, and are therefore 'legitimate', 'authorized'. In both cases what has happened is a surreptitious incorporation of the body or nature (the maternal) which at the same time obliterates the traces of the maternal role in reproduction. In the process, the maternal genealogy is written out of the scene of representation, leaving only the paternal line. Thus the pure Idea/Intelligible has no need of a vehicle or receptacle:

> The Idea of Ideas, alone, is itself in itself. Confusing signified, signifier, referent, *Idea holds nothing outside itself*. It neither indicates nor indexes anything *other* than itself, however akin. And needs no heterogeneous *vehicle*, no foreign *receptacle*, in order to signify and represent itself. . . . Like unto self, unaided by any re-presentation or figuration. Certainty of self-identity unassisted by any mirror. (SE: 298–9; SF: 372–3)

The result of this process of splitting the Sensible from the Intelligible is that: 'the mother-matter gives birth only to images, the Father-God only to the real' (SE: 301; SF: 373). Or, in other words, the shadows in the world are at least 'real' shadows, guaranteed by 'nature' as opposed to the shadows of the cave which are produced by artificial means. Everything in this scenario encourages the pedagogue's young pupil to turn away from the maternal to the paternal. The paternal is more 'real'. And thus maternal engendering becomes a less adequate imitation of the original than paternal engendering. It is but a short step from this to push out altogether the role of the mother in conception and birth: 'Engendering the real is the father's task, engendering the fictive is the task of the mother – that "receptacle" for turning out more or less good copies of reality' (SE: 300; SF: 375).

The character of patriarchy is written into this metaphysics, in this 'chiasma of family benefits' (SE: 301; SF: 375); 'the father is given all rights and powers over "his children"' (SE: 301; SF: 375) while the conditions of reproduction are denied. But what Irigaray insists on is that the maternal has not really been excluded; the father cannot really engender alone. It has been subordinated to the paternal, to the economy of the 'proper' to which it then 'belongs'. The patriarchal fiction of the 'other of the same' is in fact an appropriation of the maternal.

I do not think there is any evidence to suppose that Irigaray is positing the maternal metaphor as alternative origin. What she returns to again and again is that it is the relationship between the two parents that has been forgotten: 'Obliteration of the passage between outside and inside, up and down, intelligible and sensible . . . the "father" and the "mother" ' (SE: 344; SF: 431).

I think she is rather attempting to show that if you produce an account of truth which includes, or is derivative of, an imaginary primal scene in which the role of the mother is written out, leaving engenderment entirely to the father, then your whole theory and its consequences will be marked by that forgetting. It will have its effect on the evaluation of women who will then not be seen as having any different role to play, or as having any specific role at all – as indeed in Plato's ideal republic women are allowed as equals only by assimilation to men as far as possible. In so far as women are women, they will stand for the Sensible, that on which in Plato's account one has to turn one's back in the pursuit of truth, and therefore, as Nietzsche so clearly states, natural enemies of the truth. For Nietzsche's account is exemplary; he draws all the consequences.[9]

In Plato, the reason for the obliteration is clear: he wishes to obliterate becoming. For Plato, the highest truth – Being, the Good, the Idea – is that which has never been born (SE: 319; SF: 399), never been mortal, never been subjected to the vagaries of time and change, never been incarnate, never been *indebted* to an act of intercourse (SE: 312; SF: 390) or to a period of dependence on the maternal body:

If the process of the Idea's inscription is to be lost to consciousness, if the mirror that has always already reflected it is to be covered over, then it is obligatory to forget that the Idea once came into being. (SE: 310; SF: 387)

The Father, for his part, is eternal, because he has always refused to be born. (SE: 319; SF: 399)

An ideal copula at last, freed from the avatars of becoming. (SE: 332; SF: 415)

But becoming cannot be reduced to a single measure; it is too diverse:

But father and son, at least on the level of the purity of the intelligible, should . . . be related to the *form of the unit* [*unité*]. This is not the case, however, for the 'sensible' – the maternal, the feminine – for their diversity, discontinuity, and process cannot be reduced to a single model. (SE: 359; SF: 450)

Irigaray's response to this scenario is to attempt to put the Intelligible and Sensible back into contact via the *sensible transcendental* which can now be seen to represent or stand for an imaginary parental couple in intercourse together. But first this means coming to terms with the anxiety which leads to the split between Intelligible and Sensible in the first place, i.e. castration anxiety. In Plato's scenario, and in metaphysics more generally, woman (and women) bears the weight of men's castration fears and, by extension, their refusal to face mortality and death.

The myth of Athena

What is at stake in the obliteration of the maternal is only mentioned explicitly once in 'Plato's *Hystera*' (SE: 353; SF: 443): the threat of castration.[10] One needs to distinguish here between two terms, real castration where the organs of reproduction (in either sex) have been removed or mutilated, and 'castration' as a complex of phantasies, a kind of psychoanalytic shorthand for referring to the castration complex, in which the fear felt by little boys at threatened loss leads to the resolution of the Oedipus complex, the renunciation of their instinctual desires for the mother, and identification with the father. In *Amante marine* and *Speculum*, Irigaray keeps the term 'castration' to refer to men's phantasmatic anxieties, and uses the words *châtrage* or *châtrée* to refer to women who did not have a male organ in the first place. (Of course it is not *women's* organs of reproduction which are missing; either way, we are dealing with the structure of male phantasy.) For clarity's sake, I will keep *châtrée* in French. The central section of *Amante marine*, 'Veiled Lips' (*Lèvres voilées*) is concerned with the economy of truth, and suggests that it is an economy of castration; the problematic of truth in its western guise is essentially related to the male imaginary.

For Irigaray, it is Nietzsche's critique of truth which displays most clearly its sexual economy. 'Veiled Lips' is a response to certain passages from Nietzsche.[11] I won't give all of them here, but here are two central ones:

> From the beginning, nothing has been more alien, repugnant, and hostile to woman than truth – her great art is the lie, her highest concern is mere appearance and beauty. (*Beyond Good and Evil* § 232)

> Finally, *women*. Reflect on the whole history of women: do they not *have* to be first of all and above all actresses? Listen to physicians who have hypnotized women; finally, love them – let yourself be 'hypnotized by them'! What is always the end result? That they 'put on something' even when they take off everything. [Dass sie 'sich geben', selbst noch, wenn sie – sich geben. Literally: that they give themselves (that is, act or play a part) even when they – give themselves.] (*The Gay Science* § 361)

Irigaray points out, in a move now familiar to us from *Speculum*, that Nietzsche provides an accurate description of the place of woman in the economy of truth. Truth depends upon the 'other of the same', on the 'naturalization', and therefore surreptitious incorporation of what is supposed to be excluded: 'The lie is not, any more than appearance and beauty, "alien to truth". They belong to it [lui sont propres]. . . . And the opposite remains caught in the same' (AM: 83).

Femininity is systematically connected with the patriarchal order (AM: 102). Nietzsche's woman, the appearance or semblance, corresponds to the place of woman in patriarchy; she is not the 'other of the other', the non-representable other of the cavern, but the 'other of the same', the world of appearances which is supposed to be transcended in the final vision of truth. Femininity, then, *qua* appearance, is thus an integral if unacknowledged part of the economy of truth. For Irigaray, it is exemplified in the myth of Athena, daughter of Zeus, born through her father's head, and not through her mother's womb, since Zeus had already incorporated, literally, her mother.[12] Obliterating the female genealogy once again, Athena is an alibi for patriarchy, the father's daughter. In the Orestes myth, it is on her advice that Apollo, against the chorus of women, instals patriarchy by decreeing that Orestes's matricide was justifiable. In Irigaray's account of the myth, patriarchy covers its tracks by attributing the justification of matricide to a woman.

Athena carries the head of the Medusa on her shield. Any man who looked on the Medusa was turned to stone. Freud comments that Athena is thus also the sexually unapproachable woman; being turned to stone is equated with castration (SE XIX: 144, note 3). We need to look here at a complex of ideas which link death and castration, and which link the 'naturalization' of Plato's account and the 'naturalization' of Freud's account. In *Speculum*, Irigaray links castration with the death drives,[13] thus presenting castration – and philosophy – as a way of dealing with the death drives which continues

to leave women without adequate symbolization, while women continue to
represent for men the spectre of total dissolution and disintegration. Death
is a kind of 'hole' in being; as Laplanche puts it, it is even 'absent from
any unconscious' (1970: 193). That hole or *néant* (nothingness) cannot be
mastered; it is literally unthinkable. But if woman can stand for that hole
in representation (SE: 71; SF: 85), a kind of 'dark continent', then there is
at least the illusion of mastery – for men at any rate. The unthinkable has
been represented; woman *represents* death or the unthinkable for/by men.

What Irigaray does is to link the differential development of the little girl
and the little boy in this respect to the structure of the castration complex.
The aggression which both boy and girl are said to exhibit at the anal
stage is turned, in the case of girls, into masochism; their aggression,
that is, is turned against themselves, while men protect themselves against
self-aggression through castration and the 'normal' structure of masculinity:

> You will have realised also that the 'sexual function' requires aggres-
> siveness from the male, and that this authorizes *an economy of death drives
> disengaging and protecting the 'subject'* by exercising itself on the 'object'.
> And, by continuing to be the 'object' pole in the sexual act, the woman
> *will provide man with an outlet for his 'primary masochism', dangerous not only
> for the 'psychical' but also for the 'organic', threatening to 'life'.* Now, Freud
> states that *this 'primary' or 'erogenous' masochism will be reserved to woman,*
> and that both her 'constitution' and 'social conventions' will forbid her
> any sadistic way to work out these masochistic death drives. She can only
> 'turn them round' or 'turn them inward'. (SE: 54; SF: 62; trans. adapted;
> my emphasis)

In this scenario, so long as it functions effectively, the 'subject' (male) is then
protected from his own self-destructive masochism at the expense of woman
who cannot sublimate her own death drives. (These violent unsymbolized
drives can then be turned against herself; they become, for example, the
traditional self-sacrifice of the woman.) By connecting the trajectory of the
death drives with the castration complex, Irigaray makes a link between the
naturalization of castration and the naturalization of female masochism (it
is her 'constitution'), and can therefore claim that castration apotropaically
functions to ward off death. Athena, the patriarchal woman, shields man from
the confrontation with death/castration. Hence the image of the Medusa on
the shield and why he fears to look; it is his own fears that he turns away from
and projects on to 'woman'. The 'other of the other' for man is that which is
unthinkable. By making death (instead of woman) the 'other of the other',
and by making women the representatives of death, men attempt to master
and contain the unthinkable:

> In this proliferating desire of the same, death will be the only
> representative of an outside, of a heterogeneity, of an other; woman will
> assume the function of representing death (of sex/organ), castration, and

man will be sure as far as possible of achieving mastery, subjugation. . . .
(SE: 27; SF: 27. See also SE: 53 ff., 72, 94, 102; SF: 61 ff., 86, 115, 126)

But both sexes have to effect 'symbolic castration' in order to enter the symbolic. In this economy, no system of representation is provided for women to deal with their death drives, their 'castration', and this has an effect on their possibilities for sublimation, for becoming 'subjects', whether subjects of representation or subjects in the social world. It is in this light that we can see Irigaray's interpretation of truth in philosophy: as a function of the castration complex, it is an endlessly repetitive gesture of blocking women's subjectivity in order to protect an endlessly threatened economy which is a fragile barrier against an unthinkable death and dissolution.

In the economy of truth, then, castration is equated with death, and the split between Sensible and Intelligible (or between men and gods – AM: 100) is an attempt to ward off castration as loss of identity and the fear of death. In psychoanalytic accounts, someone or something has to go on carrying the split-off fears, and women appear 'naturally' suited to this role because they are already *châtrées*. In the Platonic account, the attempt is made to split off the Intelligible realm from any contact with the Sensible world, but the apparatus of the 'natural' world and the body has been used without any acknowledgement, because something or somebody is needed to carry or contain what has been split off. As Irigaray explains it:

> Castration? Was it not, in a precise gesture of repetition, to provide the key to the scenography of the same? (AM: 86)

> Castrated [châtrée], she threatens with castration [castration]. (AM: 89)

> Predicable *qua* object 'in general', the/a woman remains exterior to the objective. From this exterior, she supports its economy – castrated [châtrée], she threatens with castration. To glimpse that she might subtend the logic of predication without that logic's functioning being in any way her own [lui soit propre] is to fear that her intervention will disturb its order; the death of the subject would not be anything other than this. A ground rises, a heap [montage] of forms collapses. The horror of the abyss, attributed to woman. The loss of identity – death. (AM: 97)

But in the slippage that has taken place, to equate castration with death means that 'the other still comes to the same' (AM: 97), so long as it is woman who is *châtrée*, so long, that is, as the symbolic (and symbolic castration) is supported by women. So that the emergence of the woman as subject appears to threaten the male subject with 'loss of identity – death': 'the other . . . threatens only with the reminder of that with which she has been surreptitiously entrusted: death' (AM: 85–6).

The male subject fears that to recognize the debt to woman, to recognize all she bears *for* him, would be to lose mastery; it would mean to recognize that from the point of view of woman as subject, man might be 'other'. It would mean facing castration anxiety instead of splitting it off and projecting it, and it might also involve confronting what it might mean to 'contain' women's anxieties, to be a container for women in the way that woman has traditionally been a container for men.[14]

The dominance of the economy of truth means that women cannot appear in this economy without losing themselves as such (AM: 90). The economy of truth is an economy with a single measure, as in the Platonic scene. Irigaray calls it the *étalon*, or standard (as in *étalon or*, gold standard) and sometimes by extension, *gold*. (Gold is one of the substitutes Freud gives in the imaginary equation penis–faeces–baby, and is thus one of the markers of the anal economy.) In this economy women cannot be other than appearance. Since there is but one measure, and women are inadequate or lesser in relation to it, they are bound to be seen (in Platonic terms) as semblances, inferior copies of the truth. As a result, if a woman wishes to enter the scene of truth, she has to do so in disguise:

> For she can only be known and recognised under disguises that denature her; she borrows forms that are never her own and that she must yet mimic if she is to enter even a little way into knowledge. And when she does this, she will no doubt be stigmatized, after the fact, for owing her power of seduction to *deceptive* appearances. . . . Whereas the logos, in order to preserve the purity of its conception, so veils her in the truth of his word that it is no longer clear what she is hiding in her store and all the desires and delirium of potency denied by the measure of Reason can be projected on to her. (SE: 344; SF: 431)

> To speak of herself, to try to speak of herself, comes to exposing herself – if, that is, a woman can – to being merely the object, the stake, of a repetition of negation, of disavowal. To lending herself to a reexclusion, a repression, outside of representation in general. (AM: 90)

Man 'as master . . . cannot hear her' (AM: 90). In order to be in a position where he could hear her, he would have to face his own castration anxiety, instead of projecting lack and *châtrage* on to woman. The insistence that the economy of truth is not 'proper/appropriate' to woman underlines this; the 'proper' can incorporate the woman only in so far as she has been naturalized, like the scene of the world, in a way that does not disturb the functioning of the system. The fear is of the 'death of the subject'.

In this sense, then, Irigaray can say that 'truth is *also* a dream' (SE: 346; SF: 433).[15] Whatever desires are excluded by the *logos* or the 'measure of Reason' are seen as the irrational – whether phantasy, hallucination, dream, or hysteria. But the *logos* itself has a phantasmatic structure; the *logos* too is implicated in phantasies that it has to repress: 'Socrates is dreaming . . . but he does not know it, does not want to know it . . . he no longer sees what he no longer sees (nature). This double negation founds the order of philosophy as such' (AM: 106). And what is made clear again is that the symbolic is completely inadequate for representing women.

The myth of Antigone

Socrates was dreaming and, many centuries later, Hegel is dreaming too.

Like Athena, but in a different way, Antigone too represents the 'other of the same' (SP: 125). One can see why the Antigone myth interests Irigaray:[16]

1. It represents a moment of transition from the genealogy of the maternal to that of the paternal.
2. Antigone's mother, Jocasta, was both *mother* and *wife* to Oedipus. The difference between the two generations is blurred, making a maternal genealogy impossible. The woman simply takes the place of the mother.
3. Antigone and her brother have the same mother; they are linked by the blood tie which Antigone puts before the claims of the polis.
4. Identification with the *mother* in this kind of situation means obliteration of the *woman*, or her 'death'. Antigone identifies with her mother to the extent that she repeats her mother's self-destructive gesture (SE: 219; SF: 272).
5. Antigone is the guardian of the dead.
6. Antigone in the tomb, walled up alive, is an image of woman in patriarchy, walled up, unable to be heard, but also a guilt-producing phantasy. The threat represented by women's refusal to be 'unconscious earth, nurturing nature' (SE: 225; SF: 280) is the threat of the phantasy/phantasm returning, and the guilt it brings with it for what has been done to Antigone/the woman.

Here again I want to make a short detour to explain Irigaray's terminology. In her reworking of the Hegelian version of the Antigone myth Irigaray introduces a term for the maternal genealogy, which she calls the realm of the *sang rouge*, (red blood). Despite its 'natural' referent (the child in the womb is fed by the mother's blood), it is in fact a play on words – the *sang rouge* is opposed to the *semblant*, or the 'other of the same', which is a homophone for *sang blanc* (white blood). So red blood is opposed to white blood, the maternal genealogy to the economy of the semblance.[17]

Sang rouge is also referred to as a 'proximity without distinction' (AM: 101), a 'natural contiguity' (AM: 104), the child's original dependence on the mother in the womb. What Irigaray is suggesting is that there is a sense in which men have not yet effected symbolic castration. So long as women *support* castration anxiety, men retain an unsymbolized and unconscious nostalgia for that original proximity, which means that they block women's attempts to emerge as subjects, i.e. as women who are not just for-men. The mother 'belongs' to men in the economy of the 'proper'; the *sang rouge* has been incorporated. We saw in Chapter 4 that women cannot, according to Irigaray, symbolize their own loss of origin in the categories available to them. For men, the case is rather different; men use women (and in particular the evidence of their 'naturally' castrated bodies) to symbolize loss of origin, but this is a kind of evasion, a non-acknowledgement of the original debt (to the mother) and a non-acknowledgement of the continuing debt to women, still the maternal-feminine. This non-acknowledgement is transformed into 'femininity', what Irigaray sometimes calls a 'value-envelope/container of exchange' (AM: 121), i.e. the values women have for men. In *This Sex*, these are threefold: (1) *mother*, who is a 'natural value' (TS: 185; CS: 180) in the sense that we looked at in 'Plato's *Hystera*', where the world is 'naturalized' as the screen or semblance incorporated into the proper: 'the mother . . . will be private property' (ibid.); (2) *virgin*, the semblance, woman as sign, who is 'coin of exchange' (TS: 186; CS: 181); (3) *prostitute*, who is 'for-men': 'nature' has become simply a 'vehicle for relations between men' (ibid.). I shall have more to say about exchange in Chapter 8. Here I am more concerned with the aspect of woman as *support* or *screen* for the projection of the male phantasy, and the values that 'woman' has in this system. What Irigaray is trying to do is to symbolize and bring to consciousness the continued unconscious dependence on the maternal body and its consequences for women.

Sang rouge indicates the maternal genealogy, the relation that women might have to their mothers and to/for themselves. In Irigaray's rereading of Hegel she argues that the woman who respects the *sang rouge*, the blood tie with the mother, has to be excluded from the polis:

In these analyses devoted to the relation of family to State, Hegel explains that the daughter who remains faithful to the laws regarding her mother must be excluded from the polis [cité], from society. She may not be put to death by violence, but she must be imprisoned, deprived of liberty, of air, of light, of love, of marriage, of children. . . . The figure of this daughter is represented by Antigone. Hegel's analysis draws on the content of Sophocles's tragedies. (SP: 14)

The transition to patriarchy 'forbids the daughter to respect the blood ties *with her mother*' (SP: 14):

> With the installation of patriarchy, the daughter is separated from her mother and more generally from her family. She is transplanted into the genealogy of the husband, she has to live with him, she has to bear his name, likewise his children. (SP: 14)

The situation we looked at in Chapter 4 – the struggle to occupy the place of the mother – is the regime of the semblance. It is related both to the absence of a maternal genealogy and to the absence of the sexual relationship in the imaginary, the two being more or less equivalent, since the woman, for the man, is a *substitute* for his mother. The man does not sublimate the relation to his mother, he merely transfers it, if there is no maternal genealogy (SP: 15–16; see also SE: 31, 110; SF: 33, 136–7). This both prevents the heterosexual relationship and, since the woman is never for-herself, blocks her access to the ethical.

Hegel is aware, according to Irigaray, that women support the community (of men). From guilt, he tries to construct the relationship between Antigone and Polynices, between brother and sister, as a relationship of genuinely reciprocal recognition; neither a master/slave relationship, nor an asymmetrical relationship like that between husband and wife. Significantly it is also non-sexual, without desire. This 'recognition' is Hegel's phantasy, a '*Hegelian dream*':

> It is a consoling fancy, a truce in the struggle between uneven foes, a denial of the guilt already weighing heavily upon the development of the subject; it is the delusion of a *bisexuality* assured for each in the connection and passage, one into the other, of each sex. Yet both sexes, male and female, have already yielded to a destiny that is different for each. (SE: 217; SF: 269)

In fact the relation is not reciprocal, because:

> Woman is the guardian of the blood. But as both she and it have had to use their substance to nourish the universal consciousness of self, it is in the form of *bloodless shadows* – of unconscious fantasies – that they maintain an underground subsistence. (SE: 225; SF: 280)

Antigone is placed outside the dialectic (E: 115). Hegel recognizes that women are essential – as it were the lifeblood of the community – but that they are suppressed by civil society. So Irigaray suggests that the guilt of that suppression, in which Hegel too is implicated, comes back to him as the phantasy of Antigone walled up in her prison. To absolve himself of the guilt he posits a moment of genuine reciprocity between man and woman, in the form of brother and sister. But Irigaray points out that whereas the brother *acts*, using the sister as a 'living mirror' for his actions while alive, and leaving her to be the guardian of his burial rites, the action is not reciprocated; there is no one to recognize Antigone's act. The law of the polis is founded over her suppression; she is confined to family relations and to burying the dead; she does not, like her brother, act in the universal. She signifies for Hegel the limited ethical sphere of the family. She does not accede to the public sphere to which the man has access *because* his particular needs are looked after in the family. So Antigone is not acting for-herself; she is still the 'other of the same', fulfilling a function for the State: 'Antigone is already serving the State, in that she tries to efface the blood that the latter causes to flow in order to assure its power, its human rights erected on a sacrifice' (SP: 125).

*

The Antigone myth is a resonant one for Irigaray; we shall have occasion to return to it in three further contexts: identity, ethics, and citizenship. For now, I want simply to draw together the threads of this chapter. The move that Irigaray identifies is what I have called 'naturalization'. The polis, from Plato's ideal republic to Hegel's universal sphere, is founded upon a gesture of exclusion which constitutes the social as such; what is left outside is 'nature'. But in that gesture of exclusion 'nature' has been incorporated in order to bear or carry what has been excluded – but tacitly, unconsciously. The social is constructed against men's fears of death and mortality. In the process it is women, the living reminders of birth, and therefore transience and death, to whom the sign of 'nature' has been attached. 'Woman' (a naturalized version of women) has been mapped on to 'women', as though women were not, like men, in society, and as though men were not, like women, embodied and 'natural' too. And to make doubly sure, to avoid any confusion, 'women', the bearers of that which must not be acknowledged, have been excluded from the polis. This is perhaps not so easy to see in Plato, where apparently the ideal republic admits women. But Plato's myth, for Irigaray, shows clearly that the gesture of exclusion is in operation. The qualification for civic leadership is the love of truth, and the pursuit of truth splits off the Sensible from the Intelligible. In addition, the Platonic myth, with its three scenes, shows the insufficiency of simply 'adding' the feminine to philosophy, where it has in any case been all along, 'naturalized'. The 'feminine' in philosophy is the 'other of the same', but the cavern and the Idea remain separated by the intervening scene which prevents them from meeting; the 'scene of the world', as one might say, or, extrapolating, the patriarchal organization of society. The 'feminine' screens from the male philosopher the absence of women in the polis and 'naturalizes' it. The women who are there can only be there 'in disguise', not *as women*. 'Bisexuality' is a 'delusion', a phantasy, so long as the 'destiny' of each sex is different.

Similarly, the process of naturalization conceals the absence of the woman in the symbolic order. In both cases the exclusion is achieved by 'nature'. Although the symbolic is supposed to cut off the subject definitively from nature (according to the Lacanian account of symbolic castration), the 'naturalness' of women's *châtrage* still supports the symbolic that Lacan describes. From this point of view, Lacan is providing the psychoanalytic basis for Platonic theory. To bring women into the symbolic, then, so far from being an 'essentialist' gesture (as essentialism is commonly understood), is in fact completely the opposite; it is only by *de*naturalizing this picture of women as *châtrées* that they will accede to the symbolic order at all. It is the social/symbolic organization and distribution of the death drives which 'castrates' women; it is the logos which presents them as *châtrées* (SE: 142; SF: 176). In psychoanalytic terms, one could say that women suffer from imaginary castration (i.e. the phantasies projected on to them by men);

what they need is symbolic castration (their own relation to origin and loss).

This leads Irigaray to challenge the Hegelian definition of transcendence.[18] It is a definition which perpetuates and gives fresh life to the Platonic split between Sensible and Intelligible, for it still leaves *someone* or *something* to be transcended, and the sexual division of labour is completely predictable. In the concept of the sensible transcendental, Irigaray is positing that the oppositions might come into relation – the mother and father, the Sensible and the Intelligible, the immediate and the transcendent, the material and the ideal – in imaginary and symbolic processes, that is, that each sex might be able to assume its own divisions, its own negativity, and its own death. The problem is that of the conditions under which women might be able to assume their own death. In the following chapter I shall suggest that, for Irigaray, the deconstruction of metaphysical oppositions is only part of the story for women, and corresponds only to the negative moment. What is also needed is a framework which 'allows access to life and to death to two' (PN: 303), and this has to be a construction, the construction of an identity which allows each sex its own life and its own mobility.

Chapter 6

Identity and violence

La philosophie s'intéresse beaucoup à la déconstruction de l'ontologie, à l'anti- au post-, mais peu à la constitution d'une nouvelle identité rationnellement fondée. (*Sexes et parentés*)
Philosophy is very interested in the deconstruction of ontology, in the anti-, in the post-, but not much in the constitution of a new, rationally founded identity.

In preceding chapters, I have discussed two issues which are central preoccupations for Irigaray: the question of woman's identity in the symbolic order, and the question of the organization and violence of the death drives. In this chapter I want to suggest that it is illuminating to see these two issues as essentially interconnected in Irigaray's thought, enmeshed in each other; in other words, that the possibility of woman's identity is linked to the possibility of a resymbolization and reorganization of the death drives in the imaginary.

The question of identity is perhaps the issue which divides Irigaray most decisively from other versions of deconstructionist-inspired feminism. Although Irigaray has made full use of the perspectives opened up by deconstruction and the critique of phallogocentrism, and her debt to Derrida's destabilization of metaphysics is obvious, I suggest that we can find in Irigaray's work an implicit (and at moments briefly explicit) critique of Derrida as a philosophical exemplar of the patriarchal organization of the death drives, which works by separating women from each other (E: 103). On this account, the deconstruction of identity continues to leave women in a state of fragmentation and dissemination which reproduces and perpetuates the patriarchal violence that separates women. Although both Derrida and Irigaray point to the violence of patriarchal metaphysics, for Irigaray, deconstruction seen from women's point of view has not been able to imagine any way of addressing its own theoretical death drive, its own 'nihilism'. Her theorization of identity is not a simple regression to patriarchal metaphysics, but an attempt to resymbolize, which at certain critical moments employs methods and strategies quite different from those of Derrida.

As in the case of Lacan, there is some disagreement on Derrida's potential value for feminist politics, and the issue is in many ways even more complex, because while Lacan's theory is aggressively phallocentric (in that the phallus is the signifier which guarantees the symbolic), Derrida, despite his overtly unsympathetic remarks about feminism, sets out to deconstruct phallogocentrism. The feminist reception of Derrida has been characterized by ambivalence and in some cases has led to a 'post-feminist' position. Feminists who want to make use of his elegant and devastating reading strategies often identify a contradiction between Derridean theory and feminist politics. In practice, feminists have often tended to read the deconstruction of metaphysical identity as a deconstruction of feminism too (which is how Derrida himself appears to view it). This leads either to the rejection of deconstruction *in toto*, or to the rejection of feminism. Neither of these positions does justice to the complexity of the issue. A more sophisticated version of the contradiction has been to see it as a feature of our contemporary historical location, in which the current necessity for affirmative political action appears to be undercut by the necessity for theoretical negativity. The theoretical negation, although essential, appears to take away the ground for political action or solidarity, since 'woman', like 'man', is revealed to be a metaphysical construct, whereas political action would seem to depend upon the (patriarchal and metaphysical) positing of the woman that simultaneously and theoretically you are exposing as a construct. A deconstructionist feminist, then, may often feel that she is cutting the ground from under her own feet.[1]

This is the larger issue with which Irigaray has been grappling since *Speculum*. While she is prepared to adopt – mimetically – Derrida's terms, concepts, and reading strategies so long as they suit her purposes, nevertheless she does not have precisely the same aims. As she points out briefly in *This Sex*, her position in relation to deconstruction, as in relation to metaphysics, is different from that of a male philosopher:

> It is not correct to say that I have 'entered into' the 'theory of woman', or even simply into its deconstruction. For, in that particular marketplace, I have nothing to say. I am only supposed to keep commerce going by being an object of consumption or exchange. (TS: 158; CS: 153)

Irigaray's issue is that of creating a place from which women can speak *as women*. Her argument with the philosophers is that they continue to take 'speaking as men' as if it were 'speaking universal'. She deliberately attempts to speak as a woman, from a non-existent place, which has to be created or invented as she goes along, and at the same time to show that philosophers have a locatable, sexual place of enunciation. Of course she runs the risk of falling back into the oppositions that she is exposing, but we should not think that she is unaware of the risk, any more than Derrida is, when he deconstructs the processes at work in metaphysics. But as Irigaray points out herself, there is no position outside phallogocentrism that one could simply step into and occupy: 'There is no simple manageable way to leap to the outside of phallogocentrism, *nor any possible way to situate oneself there, that would result from the simple fact of being a woman*' (TS: 162; CS: 157). So one could suggest that whereas Derrida tends to set up deconstruction and feminism as an opposition to be deconstructed (see pp. 130ff.), Irigaray refuses that particular opposition and adopts the position of the both/and: she is both a woman/feminist and a deconstructor.

In terms of what has already been discussed, one could put her position like this. In imaginary and symbolic terms, theory, like language, constitutes a house or a home for men: 'men continually seek, construct, create for themselves houses everywhere: grottoes, huts, women, towns, language, concepts, theory, etc.' (E: 133). We could say, then, that the theory of the male philosophers is equivalent to the maternal body, the body-matter of woman which forms the imaginary infrastructure of metaphysics. But this still leaves woman 'homeless' in the symbolic order, and it is this homelessness and dereliction with which Irigaray is concerned. Thus Irigaray's project is different from Derrida's project, and requires different methods and strategies. For unlike Derrida, she is dealing with 'the politics of self-representation'[2] in a situation in which the very existence of that self is problematic. Another way of putting the question is this. If theory, as Irigaray suggests, is the body of the mother, over which men fight (see SE: 81 note 67; SF: 98, note 88), what is women's relation to theory? If women have (or could have) a different relation to the mother, might they have a different relation to theory?

Although Irigaray does not often speak of Derrida directly, one can frequently discern an indirect reference (when she is discussing Nietzsche or Kant, for instance).[3] In the first section, therefore, I am going to try to reconstruct an Irigarayan critique of Derrida, keeping in mind certain questions: What is Derrida's place of enunciation? From where does he speak and what 'interests' are involved (see SE: 270; SF: 335)? Do they coincide with the interests of women? What is the nature of 'woman' as an object in Derrida's discourse? What is the status of Derrida's remarks about feminism? What is the nature of the deconstructive imaginary? In the second section I shall go on to consider more directly the function of the concepts of essence and identity for Irigaray, and to suggest the kinds of reason why Irigaray might be using them, and the reasons why she might still regard them as indispensable. Again, I shall suggest that the question of the economy of the death drives is the key to understanding Irigaray's analysis. In the third section I shall look at her notion of the divine, attempting to show that it fulfils a function in her thought, specifically in relation to questions of identity and the death drives.

From the point of view of feminism, Irigaray is sometimes seen as an exemplar of hysterocentrism, a kind of reversal of phallocentrism in which the womb, the maternal function, is privileged instead of the phallus. It is then argued, for example, that Irigaray regresses to a metaphysics of presence (Berg 1982: 18), or that Irigaray privileges the feminine, which is the devalued term in 'phallologic', but that 'the system of binary oppositions remains the same' (Stanton 1986: 170). In either case, it is sometimes thought that Irigaray falls into all the problems that are created by the appeal to feminine specificity: essentialism, reinforcement of already existing gender ideologies, absence of the historical dimension, ignoring differences between women, and so on. I shall suggest here that the reception of Derrida, whatever its ambivalences, has been characterized by a relative openness and readiness to engage that has been lacking in the reception of Irigaray. He has been given a more extended philosophical credit. While the most sophisticated deconstructionist feminists recognize that, from a feminist point of view, deconstruction has certain limitations,[4] none the less it is thought to provide an illuminating and even unarguable critique of patriarchal metaphysics. Many of Irigaray's readers, on the other hand, fail to appreciate her complex relationship with philosophy, and are therefore unable to identify what is specific to her critique of metaphysics, or to evaluate her aims as anything other than inferior versions of Derridean deconstruction. The argument underlying the first section – fairly schematically – is that Derrida and Irigaray interpret differently the articulation of identity and death/violence, and that it is Irigaray's interpretation of their interrelationship which motivates her stance vis-à-vis deconstruction. (This argument is not intended to preclude other versions of the relation between the work of Derrida and Irigaray, but to throw into relief the Irigarayan themes discussed in the final two sections of this chapter.)

The deconstructive imaginary[5]

Derrida shows that metaphysics is constructed upon a system of differences. These differences are not positivities, but positions, *effects* of a play of difference which may be called *différance*. One of the two poles is always privileged at the expense of the other, the intelligible over the sensible, for example, or man over woman. The main point is that metaphysics is based upon a process of exclusion and hierarchies. The practice of deconstruction then begins by privileging the subordinate term, with a view to disrupting the hierarchy. The strength of this account is that it recognizes that the hierarchy is held in place by force:

> In a classical philosophical opposition, we do not find a peaceful coexistence between the two sides, but a violent hierarchy. One of the two terms dominates the other (axiologically, logically, etc.), occupies the higher place. To deconstruct the opposition one must first of all, at a given moment, reverse the hierarchy. (Derrida 1972: 56–7, trans. in Wood 1979: 24)

At a second stage, one attempts to prevent the opposition from merely reasserting itself by introducing some term or mechanism which prevents the field from simply returning to its original state. One can call these terms *indécidables*, undecidables, that is to say, terms which cannot be said to be one or other of the previous terms, either because they are referring to the conditions under which the pair of terms is possible at all, or else because it is not possible to say that they are, or are not, one or other of the two terms. The most familiar of these undecidables is of course *différance*, which can mean both difference (spatial) and deferment (temporal). However, to prevent the movement or the play which continually displaces metaphysical oppositions from solidifying or ossifying by its attachment to a single term, Derrida uses a large number of different names or 'nicknames' for *différance*. With each text that he discusses, a different term is used: this could be arche-writing, dissemination, supplement, parergon, hymen, trace, iterability, and so on, so that he is never trapped into the fixation of meaning by the semantic field of any one particular term. Each has a different semantic field which makes them all, strictly speaking, non-substitutable; they are generated by the semantic and rhetorical field of the text. This is one way of pointing out that deconstruction is not an operation that can ever be completed, but a continual, no doubt an infinite process (Derrida 1972: 57).[6] One never stands outside the metaphysical enclosure; one can only deconstruct it, show its ground to be undecidable. So Derrida wrote in *Of Grammatology*:

> The movements of deconstruction do not destroy structures from the outside. They are not possible and effective, nor can they take accurate aim, except by inhabiting those structures. Inhabiting them *in a certain way*, because one always inhabits, and all the more when one does not suspect it. Operating necessarily from the inside, borrowing all the strategic and economic resources of subversion from the old structure, borrowing them structurally, that is to say without being able to isolate their elements and atoms, the enterprise of deconstruction always in a certain way falls prey to its own work. (Derrida 1974: 24; 1967: 39)

Now, taking 'woman' as one of the names of *différance* can be a deconstructive device for looking at the history of philosophy, as Derrida explains in 'Women in the Beehive'. ('Women in the Beehive' is a transcript in English of a seminar with Derrida; the transcript, authorized, but not 'authored' by Derrida, appears in Jardine and Smith 1987). The following remarks are attributed to Derrida. What could be more feminist than this?

> What we could call the neutralization of sexual marks, has as you know, the effect of giving power to man. When you say, 'well you are in a neuter field, no difference', we all know that in this case the subject will be man. So, this is a classical ruse of man to neutralize the sexual mark. In philosophy we have such signs all the time: when we say that the ego, the 'I think', is neither man nor woman, we can in fact verify that it's

already a man and not a woman. It's always the case. So, to the extent which universality implies neutralization, you can be sure that it's only a hidden way of confirming the man in his power. That's why we have to be very cautious about neutrality and neutralization, and universality as neutralization. (Derrida in Jardine and Smith 1987: 194)

Both Derrida and Irigaray agree, then, that the transcendental subject, traditionally thought to be non-gendered, is in fact gendered male. At that point, they part company. Irigaray, focusing on sexual difference, privileges the subordinate term, and argues for women's accession to subjectivity, while Derrida sees this demand as phallocentric (ibid.: 193) and takes 'woman' provisionally as an undecidable, 'a good trope for writing' (p.194) (or a trope for the non-truth of truth or for man's 'random drift'). But once you have deconstructed the opposition, you do not need the name/trope 'woman' any more. This leads to his vision of a kind of post-gendered sexual multiplicity, 'one sex for each time' which we looked at briefly in Chapter 4. As we will see, there is an asymmetry here, between the stress on women (Irigaray) and woman (Derrida).

Initially, Derrida's account seems an attractive vision for feminism; it looks as though deconstruction might be a means for approaching a desirable state beyond gender difference, where the evils of sexual stereotyping and gender differentiation might be transcended. By seeing the female pole of the opposition as a metaphysical construct, imbricated with the male pole in the maintenance of a phallocentric order, it seems to avoid all the problems inherent in the appeal to a feminine specificity. What we have instead is a 'differential' in which the 'line of cleavage' between the sexes is shifting. 'Men' and 'women' may still remain as effects of the play of difference, but these effects are no longer fixed or immobile, mapped on to nature or biology.

However, from an Irigarayan point of view, Derrida is colonizing women's potential space, and this emerges when one looks at their respective assessments of and positions in relation to feminism. Because of the slippage between speaking 'like' and speaking 'as' a man or a woman, Derrida is in the position where he can speak 'like' a woman (this is clearly very important to him) but, since he has deconstructed the opposition male/female, he can glide over the fact that he is speaking 'as a man'. He particularly does not want feminists 'distributing sexual identity cards' (Derrida and McDonald 1982: 69). So he is then able to point out that feminists are phallocentric in that they speak 'like men' (1985: 32) while at the same time refusing them the possibility of speaking 'as women', which would be a phallocentric stance too. In both cases, women lose out. But the distinction between the 'as' and the 'like' is one which Irigaray never loses sight of. She points out that speaking like a woman is not the same as being (socially positioned as) a woman: 'And what man today is prepared to divest himself of his social power to share the social destiny of womankind that has been theirs for centuries?' (SP: 137).

By dismissing feminists who speak 'like men' – despite acknowledging a tactical necessity – Derrida is trivializing feminism and, by extension, women's agency. The implication is that deconstruction is a *superior* activity (from what point of view? in whose interests?). He assumes that it is equivalent for men to speak 'like men' and for women to speak 'like men'. But to speak mimetically like a man is not to be a man speaking like a man; it does not elicit the same reactions or produce the same effects. Derrida appears to minimize the larger scene in which both deconstruction and feminism exist. He makes it possible to address the question of the *maleness* of the speaking subject/the subject of philosophy; what he does not do is make it possible to address the question of how one might be a woman speaking subject/philosopher. One of the points of feminism is that it attempts to create a space where women can be speakers/agents *as women*. Derrida's deconstruction of metaphysical identity has had the effect of disconnecting the deconstructor from embodiment. If masculine and feminine positions are not connected to social positions in the world, to embodiment and the social effects of that embodiment then, whatever his intentions, the effect of his stance is to make it seem as though one could enter the intellectual arena – deconstruction, say – as a disembodied and non-social intellect. Either sex could adopt 'masculine' or 'feminine' positions, and women – bearing all that it means to be a woman in patriarchy – are once again elided. In this sense, at any rate, the philosopher repeats the familiar gesture of exclusion; to enter philosophy as a woman, one must leave behind embodiment.

Although Derrida does distinguish between two kinds of feminism, a reactive kind (being like men) and a more 'maverick' kind (Derrida and McDonald 1982),[7] there is an unusual reductiveness about his use of the term 'feminism' which is quite uncharacteristic of Derrida. Whereas his work is normally completely text-specific, he never as far as I know refers to any specific feminist texts (and presumably if he did, he would find in them the ubiquitous phallogocentrism). While deconstruction is indulgently allowed to be 'finally [essentially?][8] . . . a rather heterogeneous movement' which is a 'multiplicity of gestures of movements, of operations' (1985: 6), the heterogeneity of feminist gestures, movements, and operations is reduced in his account to a kind of spurious simplicity. (Only two kinds of feminism? Good and bad feminism? With Derrida as the arbiter?) Unlike those phallogocentric feminists who speak like men, he aspires to write like a woman. His whole deconstructive stance is to take apart the structures of meaning, to show their metaphysical underpinnings. For him, to write like a man would be to fall back unreflectively into metaphysics; that is why he wants to write like a woman, where 'woman' is understood as the trope that makes meaning undecidable. *Spurs* is a case in point. It is the text where he speaks most specifically of woman, and one in which what writing like a woman means is made absolutely clear. At the end of *Spurs* there is a section entitled: 'I have forgotten my umbrella'. As Derrida points out, this contextless fragment from Nietzsche's writings is both completely transparent and completely opaque. Without a context, we can never know exactly how to interpret it and why Nietzsche wrote it down or what he was going to do with it. The fragment then becomes an example of the infinite possible contexts of all writing and the ultimate elusiveness of any definitive meaning. Derrida then comments: 'The whole of Nietzsche's text is, perhaps, overwhelmingly, of the kind "I have forgotten my umbrella"' (Derrida 1978: 112). As he says explicitly (p.115), one could substitute the name 'Derrida' here for that of Nietzsche. The implications of this are the elusiveness of the name 'Derrida' in relation to anything he writes. As he says, 'moreover, I never speak about woman – I mean, assuming that discourse as my own. When I say "la femme", I'm quoting someone else' (1985: 31). Discourse is citation; meaning is ultimately elusive (feminine). Where is Derrida's place of enunciation if he is always quoting someone else? In a sense, he wants to make his position impregnable, ultimately undecidable, ultimately 'feminine'. Deconstruction enables him to speak indefinitely, to hold the floor. As has often been pointed out, he 'masters' feminist discourse by speaking about it. In a sense it is useless to try and prove him wrong (where is he?), and to agree with him changes nothing. It is, as Rosi Braidotti once put it cogently, a 'passage à vide' – that is to say, it is a mechanism like an engine turning over, but not in gear, so that the motor is not driving anything.

I would suggest that there is in practice a 'violent hierarchy' at work in which deconstruction is the privileged term. In the opposition which he sets up between deconstruction and feminism, there is no question for Derrida of privileging the subordinate term, since it could leave him without a place to speak. It is fairly well known that Derrida's attitude towards feminism has been somewhat uncommitted, not to say defensive or hostile at times, and this follows from his theoretical position. For deconstruction, as practised by Derrida himself, and feminism, are heterogeneous. Derrida remarks in an interview as follows:

> [F]or me deconstruction is certainly not feminist. At least as I have tried to practice it. I believe it naturally supposes a radical deconstruction of phallogocentrism, and certainly an absolutely other and new interest in women's questions. But if there is one thing it must not come to, it's feminism. So I would say that deconstruction is deconstruction of feminism, from the start, insofar as feminism is a form – no doubt necessary at a certain moment – but a form of phallogocentrism among others. . . . So let's just say that the most insistent and the most organized motif in my texts is neither feminist nor phallocentric. And that at a certain point I try to show that the two are tantamount to the same thing. (Derrida 1985: 30–1)

> I am not against feminism, but I am not simply for feminism. (Derrida 1986b: 71)

Derrida recognizes the violent hierarchy in metaphysics, but the social violence of the opposition which gives him his privileged speaking position cannot, it seems, be addressed directly by deconstruction. And yet, when in *Spurs*, we see the enactment of a paternal genealogy, the figure of woman mediating the relationship between Nietzsche, Heidegger, and Derrida, the arrangements of men disputing the possession of the body of woman/philosophy, what is he doing here but repeating that familiar gesture of hom(m)osexual exchange which Irigaray exposes in *This Sex*? Perhaps because violence is a *general* structure, ubiquitous in all binary opposition, Derrida does not find it necessary to address the specificity of violence, why men are the hierarchically superior term, for example, and what is to be done about it. Or in other terms again, the economy of the death drive is not connected up to the feminist analysis of society and the links made between patriarchy and the *social* organization of violence. And here, perhaps, lies the difference between Irigaray and Derrida.

The question one needs to ask of Derrida (in the light of Irigaray's stress on the patriarchal economy of the death drives) is: where has the violence gone when the deconstructor deconstructs? Is deconstruction itself violent? Or does it merely allow another violence to continue unchecked? It is difficult to avoid the conclusion that deconstruction avoids addressing its own implication in violence, by simply locating the violence elsewhere: in metaphysics, in phallogocentrism and, in so far as feminism is, according to Derrida, phallogocentric, in feminism. This means that Derrida cannot deal with the feminist analysis of violence at all, or with his own complicity in the patriarchal economy. His response to feminism, from an Irigarayan point of view, can be seen as an equally violent and cannibalistic attempt at incorporation.

After reading Christine Battersby's book *Gender and Genius* (1989), I am tempted to conclude that Derrida, for all his alertness, is simply recycling the enunciative positions of Romantic aesthetics, in which the man incorporates femininity while excluding women. This is certainly how Irigaray interprets it:

> As soon as something valuable appears to be coming from the side of women, men want to become women. (CAC: 61)

> There's nothing new about man wanting to be both man and woman. . . . But in this desire to master the whole, he becomes a slave both of discourse and of nature/the mother. (E: 94).

> [A] person who is in a position of mastery does not let go of it easily, does not even imagine any other position, which would already amount to 'getting out of it'. *In other words, the 'masculine' is not prepared to share the initiative of discourse. It prefers to experiment with speaking, writing, enjoying* 'woman' rather than leaving to that other any right to intervene, to 'act' in her own interests. (TS: 157; CS: 152)

What I am able to say without any hesitation is that when male theoreticians today employ women's discourse instead of using male discourse, that seems to me a very phallocratic gesture. It means: 'We will become and we will speak a feminine discourse in order to remain the master of discourse.' What I would want from men is that, finally, they would speak a masculine discourse and affirm that they are doing so. (WWT: 243)

By this Irigaray does not mean that men should speak phallocratically, but that they should acknowledge the false universality of their discourse. Derrida, for example, is able to acknowledge that the transcendental subject is male, but is less willing to acknowledge that his own place of enunciation is male; he insists on his feminine voice. But Irigaray comments in *Amante marine* that undecidability still belongs to the economy of truth: 'the general economy of truth – and therefore also of appearance, simulacrum, suspense between, and even more [voire] of that reserve: the undecidable' (AM: 94). From Irigaray's perspective, Derrida's attempt to write like a woman appears more like an incorporation of, or at least an attempt to incorporate, women's discourse. There is a kind of 'metaphysical cannibalism' involved, she says, in depriving women of their status as actors in the social world (SP: 134–5, quoting Ti-Grace Atkinson). When Derrida tries to write like a woman, it is still from his position as a man, and for Irigaray men and women are non-substituable: 'They cannot be substituted for each other. Never will I be in a man's place, never will a man be in my place. Whatever the possible identifications, never will either occupy exactly the place of the other – they are irreducible' (E: 19–20). So when Irigaray appears to fall back into the metaphysics of presence, when she appears to stop at Derrida's first stage – reversing the opposition and privileging the subordinate term, woman, but not destabilizing the field – it is in order to stop the opposition from reasserting itself. Destabilizing the field allows sexual hierarchy to continue unchecked, even as the deconstructor deconstructs. Hers is not a strategy based on a limited understanding of Derrida, but a deliberate and feminist intervention.

It is not difficult to see that, if deconstruction can 'deconstruct' feminism, feminism offers a standpoint from which to contextualize or interpret deconstruction.[9] An early article on Derrida suggests that Derrida is still using the materiality of language as his mirror (PN: 149–68), exploiting the 'silent plasticity' of the spaces and the letters in alphabetic writing to 'ensure the cohesion, the articulation,, the coherent expansion of established forms' (SE: 142; SF: 176). This is confirmed later by what he says about woman as a trope for writing. As Irigaray had already pointed out in *Speculum*, woman is so 'cathected by tropes' that it is difficult for her to 'articulate any sound from beneath this cheap chivalric finery' (SE: 143; SF: 177). The question one needs to ask from an Irigarayan point of view is: what is the imaginary of Derrida's discourse? Is there any reason to suppose that when the name 'woman' becomes one of the names of *différance*, any significant shift has taken place in the imaginary? Irigaray argues that it repeats the gesture of territorialization, in which men use the *substance* of women, the maternal-feminine body as language, to build their own theoretical edifice:

> That pleasure which perhaps constitutes a discovery for men, a supplement to enjoyment, in a fantasmatic 'becoming-woman' . . . has long been familiar to women . . . don't we run the risk once more of taking back from woman those/her as yet unterritorialized spaces where her desire might come into being? (TS: 141; CS: 138–9)

Derrida's woman is still the 'other of the same'. The *drift* which woman signifies is woman as she is for-men, but not woman as she is for-herself.

This point needs to be recontextualized in the light of Irigaray's analysis of the social and symbolic distribution of the death drives. There is evidence, I think, that Irigaray sees deconstruction as a product of the symbolic division, and a symptom of the cultural economy of the death drives, in relation to which, as we saw in Chapter 5, she argues that men and women are positioned differently. The juxtaposition in *Sexes et parentés* (pp.220–1) of the manifestations of the 'constitution of the male subject' (SP: 42) in philosophy, and in the human, social, and physical sciences, put side by side the big bang theory of the origin of the universe, catastrophe theory, the pessimistic stress on the death drive in Freud and Marcuse, and deconstruction, among other examples. Everywhere, she writes, we find the language of disintegration, bursting apart, splitting, multiplicity, loss of bodily identity. This reinforces what she had already said in *Ethique* on the 'end of philosophy' as a kind of nihilism, one of the 'multiple forms of destruction of the universe' (E: 13). It is clear that she sees these symptomatic breakdowns (in philosophy, in health, in communication, in the social order and so on) as connected with the symbolic division, and that the basic split, for her, is that between man and woman in the imaginary. If that split were to be healed, then regeneration might be possible. In terms which will be discussed further in Chapter 7, one might say that, in reducing feminism and phallogocentrism to 'the same thing', Derrida immobilizes feminism, cannot allow it to have an independent existence or a life of its own, encloses woman in a trope and thus 'buries her alive'. From Irigaray's point of view, the imaginary of Derrida's discourse is still in thrall to a particular economy of the death drive, in which women still occupy the same position.[10] As *Spurs* enacts, woman is still the object of exchanges (and potentially violent conflict) between men. The male gesture which simultaneously claims femininity while asserting superiority to feminism is an equivocal one.[11] Deconstruction offers the spectacle of a postmodernist version of the paternal genealogy deployed in Plato, and its incorporation of woman.

The different reception accorded Derrida and Irigaray indicates the difficulties of taking the maternal genealogy seriously. Why is it that Derrida is 'borrowing all the strategic and economic resources of subversion from the old structure' while Irigaray is simply being essentialist? (As we saw in Chapters 4 and 5, she is quite well aware that she is obliged to use existing concepts – 'representation' and 'conception', and so on, and including 'woman' – while contesting their foundation.) Why is that Derrida allowed to make 'contradictory gestures' (1985: 6–7), whereas Irigaray is merely logocentric? Why is Derrida able to be 'paleonymic' (using the old terms while contesting their meanings), and not Irigaray? Why is it that Derrida's issue – the relation of the son to the father (the history of philosophy) and later of the son to the mother (deconstruction)[12] – is perceived as more significant than the daughter's relation to father or mother (particularly mother)? These questions highlight the difference between Derrida's relation to philosophy and Irigaray's, and indicate why, when Irigaray turns to philosophy, she looks for the trace of the mother, for the maternal genealogy, for any evidence that the philosopher has had a relation with an imaginary or symbolic woman, a mother or a bride. Why is it that the son's relation to the woman (Lacan's 'the woman does not exist' or Derrida's 'woman has no essence') is a serious theoretical issue, while the daughter's relation with the woman can only be investigated *somewhere else*, on some different terrain, 'in' feminism? The opposition that Derrida sets up between deconstruction and feminism is clearly a territorial demarcation; only the philosopher's woman, the 'other of the same', is allowed in.

One can understand why Irigaray writes that deconstruction is not her concern. And yet she is not satisfied with the exclusion. She does not simply want to be relegated to another space, outside culture, on the margins. She wants to *think* sexual difference, to bring the maternal genealogy into *thought*. But where the 'interminability' of the operations of deconstruction is put forward as a philosophical operation, the insistent repetition of feminist questions is readily reduced to a cultural stereotype ('nagging'). One is forced to register the virtual impossibility, within the dominant culture, of addressing the question of the maternal genealogy without aggression, stridency, insistence, idealization, hysteria, surfeit, loss of credibility, or any one or other of the failures of sophistication and poise ('charging about like a bull perhaps' – Derrida 1985: 30) that have been located by men and women alike in feminist discourse. What Irigaray does is to reconceptualize feminism, giving it a respect and a value that Derrida is reluctant to accord it (which does not of course mean that she always agrees with what other women say). While for Derrida the feminist is caught within the 'same', destined to repeat the phallogocentric gesture, at best to be a maverick, undecidable, elusive like meaning, not to be pinned down, for Irigaray feminist discourse is an indication of a possible 'other of the other'. By seeing the 'inadequacies' of feminism as the 'symptoms' of a process of change, the struggle of the 'other woman' to achieve a position of enunciation in discourse, she is attempting to make a cultural space, within thought, for something that would not simply repeat the past, but might usher in a different future. She *assumes* the utopian position that Derrida is reluctant to risk. When looking at Irigaray's 'contradictory gestures', we should bear this context in mind. Mimesis is a 'strategic and economic resource of subversion'.

Essence and identity

When Irigaray is called essentialist by Anglo-American critics, she looks puzzled, and no wonder. In the French context, essence – the ontological question – is the question of the proper (*propre*), and Irigaray has always insisted that the proper is phallocentric, that woman can only be defined, essentialized, from the point of view of *man*. When Irigaray then goes on to talk of woman's identity, we may well feel puzzled in turn. But I would argue that, rather than resorting to the immediate assumption that Irigaray has fallen back into phallogocentrism, we should regard it as a problem of interpretation. It is not a question of the empirical discovery of some previously unknown object, but the discursive articulation of an ontological category. Woman's identity, then, should be seen in terms of the construction of a 'house of language'.

It is not difficult to locate in Irigaray's work a number of other apparent (or real) contradictions. For example, she writes in *Amante marine* that truth is not woman's concern: 'She does not oppose a feminine truth to a masculine truth' (AM: 92). At the same time, she also argues that women are seeking to become subjects in their own right, 'producers of cultural, political and religious truth' (E: 130).[13] Or she writes that women are the support of representation, that one cannot speak of representation where women are concerned, and yet also that they need images and representations of their own. Or that in a woman's language, the concept has no place (TS: 122–3; CS: 122), while offering what appear to be new possibilities of conceptualization. Or that she is not trying to provide an alternative onto-theology, but also that women need a religion of their own. And she hovers between a referential and a non-referential discourse, between discursive strategy (the 'two lips') and apparently essentialist ontological strategy (the sexuation of nature – see e.g. SP: 121 ff.),[14] between mimeticism and prophetic vision. She is caught between the negative and the positive. She is not trying to provide a theory of/for woman; that is men's affair. But, on the other hand, women need their own religion, their own language, their own economy, their own imaginary and symbolic representations, in short a 'generic identity' (SP: 149). To provide definitions or theories would be to fall back into the metaphysics of the same, to define 'woman' as the 'other of the same'. Yet to remain on the negative side (always saying 'woman is *not* this') is to leave women 'homeless' in the symbolic order. There is a tension between the negative moment and the utopian future moment in which women will be for-themselves. Virtually nothing corresponds to the second moment, and yet one has to suppose it as a horizon in order to act and avoid complete negativity. The problem that Irigaray is dealing with, then, is: how to give women an imaginary and symbolic home, how to introduce sexual difference into the symbolic economy, by giving women an identity so that there are *two* interrelating economies, without falling back into identity as sameness. How to bring into existence an 'other woman'? How to mobilize the 'double syntax'? Even to state the problem at all, Irigaray is obliged to use the language of onto-theology, the language of essentialism. Without a meta-language, how can the 'other woman' speak about herself? And the danger she runs is that: 'To speak of herself, to try to speak of herself, comes to exposing herself – if, that is, a woman can – to being the object, the stake, of a repetition of negation, of disavowal' (AM: 90).

The aim of the mimetic strategy, and of all the strategies, has become quite specific in Irigaray's recent work: first of all discursive change: 'to bring about a change in discourse [faire muter un discours]' (SP: 191), to shift the position of the subject of enunciation. Second, to state the conditions for women's 'generic identity'; (sometimes she says: for women to become a *peuple*, a people).

In the wake of Derrida's exposure of the logic of identity as a logic of exclusion, it is tempting to conclude that the politics of identity has been rendered illegitimate.[15] And in the light of Irigaray's exposure of the logic of identity as phallomorphic, one might infer that for Irigaray too, a politics of identity should be a contradiction in terms for women. However, current forms of 'identity politics' tend to be based upon elements in the social/symbolic order as it already exists, whereas Irigaray is positing an identity that still has to be created. The social order in its present form offers women no adequate mirror: 'Women lack a mirror for becoming women' (SP: 79). From the man's side it seems to be assumed that identity is 'the same' for women as previously it had been for men, that is, there is an assumption that a social identity for women will not change anything very much, but simply *add* to the existing state of affairs. I see this assumption, in practice, as being rather close to the liberal assumption, the idea that feminism is merely the extension to women of men's rights, so that women will be 'like men' (and the feminine will perhaps disappear). This is not at all what Irigaray has in mind. She argues that to give women an identity (however problematic the concept) will change our notion of what identity means. The existence of two 'kinds' would have an effect on *man*kind. If identity is formed by identification with elements in the social/symbolic order, then it means that social/symbolic formations will have to change for womankind to come into existence at all, and this will not leave mankind unaffected. (It means too that speaking (as) woman is something which still has to be created. If woman is a future identity rather than a biological or metaphysical determination, then we cannot yet give the phrase a clearly defined content. The condition of speaking (as) woman in Irigaray's sense, it has become clear, is the social and symbolic existence of a maternal genealogy.)

In so far as it revolves around the *son's* place in the genealogy, deconstruction does not offer any strategies for dealing with the kinds of problem that feminists are concerned with, which are centrally to do with love of self on the woman's side; for example, how to deal with the problem of female subjectivity in a heterogeneous social field; the differences between women and the complicated heterogeneity of race/class/sex and other differences which are criss-crossing and multi-determinant; the ways in which feminists themselves construct an 'other' (for example racism) because they have not been able to symbolize their own negativity; the problem of violence *between women*. Deconstruction does not offer women any ways of dealing with the horizontal or vertical relations between women, the conflictual position of the female speaking subject, because it is not concerned with relations between women at all. The problem for deconstruction appears to be: how can the (male) speaking subject continue to speak once his position has been demonstrated to depend on an illusory wholeness? How can he remain within philosophy? The problem for Irigaray is: how to locate the means by which the female speaking subject has been excluded from philosophy/discourse/culture, and to work out the conditions for her accession to speech and social existence. 'Identity' may be illusory, but men are still speaking, and speaking *for and in the place of women*. Deconstruction is so concerned to see itself as a radical critique of tradition that it misses the extent to which it is still determined by tradition; the attempt to neutralize feminists – women speaking *as women* – as merely phallogocentric, merely a repetition of the same – is a rather familiar move. It assumes that for women to speak, they must be men of some sort: 'like men', pseudo-men, or whatever. The possibility of women's difference has not entered the deconstructive imagination.

But the point is that if you assume a reorganization of the economy of the death drives as one of the conditions for women's collective accession to subjectivity,[16] then identity will no longer be exactly a repetition of the same. The symbolic economy *binds* the death drives in a particular way, preventing total disintegration, and providing some cohesion (albeit partial and threatened) but with different effects for each sex. Both Derrida and Irigaray would see male identity – the construction of the male subject – as 'violent' and hierarchical. But for Irigaray it is not just a question of deconstructing, but also of reorganizing the economy. An 'undecidable' will not prevent the economy from reasserting itself (and she is not alone in thinking that this is what happens in Derrida's work). It is also a question of constructing the fragmentary feminine, binding together the scraps into a cohesion that is less destructive for them. As I suggested in Chapter 3 (see especially note 15), there is a tension between mobility and immobility here. Phallomorphic identity has become rigid and destructive to men and women alike; but its deconstruction may be equally destructive if it does not allow mobility to women. However we conceive identity, it must be thought of in terms of the female imaginary, an imaginary that will bind or attach the scraps and debris together into something which gives women a 'home' but which does not prevent their mobility, their becoming, and their growth. Identity is feared – rightly – because of its immobilizing and blocking tendencies; but without it there is paralysis. Multiplicity in the male imaginary means that women remain dispersed, separated, and scattered, unable to move.

The condition of gendered subjectivity is a relation to the death drives that does not *use* the other sex to deflect or otherwise mediate them. *Each* sex must have an economy of the death drives. (Thus I think that Irigaray would probably disagree with radical feminism in so far as it attributes all the aggression to men. Her argument would be, rather, that this is an effect of the symbolic distribution.) So the question of the death drives is central to feminist thought, and is related to the question of identity. Can we do without a notion of identity? On the other hand, are its problems insoluble? To see this question in terms of the economy of the death drives, it seems to me, prevents the too speedy abandonment of the notion before its problems have been fully explored. The problems do not indicate its bankruptcy, but rather the scale and importance of the question, linked to the enormous conceptual problem of theorizing the death drives. There is no identity without violence, perhaps. But to reject identity could be another way of failing to challenge the symbolic division, an attempt to locate violence in the 'other'. If you take the death drives seriously as constitutive of the *human* (and not just of men), then it is possible to approach the question of identity and violence, and their relation, as problems to be negotiated – symbolized and thought – by women too – and not simply as male or patriarchal issues. Patriarchy handled them in one way; we are invited by Irigaray to think of other ways of handling them. (In this perspective, one might well argue that the crisis of confidence being displayed by some Anglo-American feminists in the notion of identity – under the dual pressure (a) of what is loosely called postmodernism, and (b) of the women who are marginalized by feminist politics itself – means that feminism is finding it difficult to resist the disintegrative force of the patriarchal order. One would not, after all, expect the 'fragments' and the 'debris' to magically reconstruct woman anew in two brief decades.) For in fact, Derrida's deconstruction is that of the identity of the male subject. The identity of the woman-as-subject, as Irigaray insists on several occasions, should *not* mean a reversal which amounts to the same. She has not solved the problem. What she has done is to offer a possible framework in which its implications can be thought.[17]

When Irigaray talks about identity, she is asking the daughter's question. Irigaray's response to Derrida's woman-as-trope is to say that *woman does not yet exist*. Against the endless play of differences, she argues that not only do we still need woman, but that woman has not yet arrived. Essence is not a given, behind us, but a collective creation, ahead of us, a horizon: 'To become, it is necessary to have a genre or an essence (belonging to one sex or the other) as a horizon' (SP: 73). The problematic concepts – woman, women, femininity, woman's identity, women's bodies, women's subjectivity and so on – though they provide an impetus, are not a cause, ground or foundation of Woman. Since Woman does not exist, she cannot be the ground. Bringing the maternal-feminine into discourse does not imply that this is what women's generic *identity* will consist of. On the contrary, it is the condition for distinguishing between mother and woman, so that *woman* can come to be. But women cannot have a generic identity if there is nothing, or nothing adequate, for them to identify with. The choice between a phallic mother and a castrated mother offers women no satisfactory choice of subject-position. But if the mother were separable from the woman, then the daughter could identify with a woman instead. So Irigaray sees it as a feminist priority to create a socially valorized identity that would make possible love between women, love of the same on the woman's side (see E: 100 ff.). What the daughter wants is to be able to love *another woman*, and not simply a phallic or castrated mother.

At the same time, Irigaray is arguing that woman is not self-identical, that she is already self-divided. As in the figure of the 'two lips', she is neither one nor two. What this figure expresses, on the woman's side, is the internal self-division of the split subject. Irigaray argues that the divisions which are internal to any human being, and by extension to the genre, have been divided into two functions, and that one genre takes over for the other the unwanted functions: '*Human kind has divided itself into two functions, two tasks, and not two kinds*. Woman has given up her kind under threat of death. Man has too, but in a different way' (SP: 135).

Thus the 'double syntax' is split between the genres, rather than being a part of the identity of each genre. Communication between the sexes is then difficult, since women represent the split-off functions, and repression intervenes to prevent what has happened emerging into consciousness. The only way to allow each sex its freedom, its life, and its mobility is for *each* sex or *each* genre to assume its own 'negative' (E: 116), its own 'schize' and its own otherness (its own death drive, one could also say). For women to achieve the level of the ethical as 'singular universals' (SP: 126) they must have the possibility of contradiction and opposition *internal* to their genre: 'The feminine would then learn to oppose itself by and for itself in a specific [propre] ethical consciousness' (SP: 134).[18] Women would then no longer be the guardians of the (Hegelian) male genre, taking the family as their universal in order for the man to be a particular individual within the family: their identity 'resides in the systematic non-scission of nature and the spirit in the re-touching [retouche][19] of these two universals' (SP: 126). The condition of this, on the woman's side, is, as far as Irigaray is concerned, a generic identity.

The figure of Antigone appears again in this context. Antigone illustrates here the paralysing effects of a social order founded on the generic split (E: 115). The decision of Creon to bury her alive: 'condemned society to a "schize" in the order of reason which leaves nature without gods, without grace; the family without any future except the work of the State; procreation without joy, love without ethics' (E: 115).

The phrase 'nature without gods' indicates the violent separation of the sensible from the ideal. So when Irigaray comes to talk about the ideal on the woman's side, she employs the vocabulary of the divine. The divine is one of the most controversial aspects of Irigaray's latest work, and yet within the context I have outlined it makes sense, as I shall go on to explain in the next section.

The divine, identity and the death drives

I want to approach the question of identity first via the sensible trans-cendental, in its double aspect of divine and language, before going on to look at the phenomenology of space and time (Chapter 7) and the social contract (Chapter 8). I shall suggest that 'God', like other terms in Irigaray's discourse, is a symbolic category – like *sang rouge*, or semblance, or gold – although it is perhaps rather more difficult to handle, because of the enormous weight of symbolic meaning it already bears. As we saw in Chapter 2, the divine and language are related:

> We lack, we women with a sex of our own, a God in which to share, a word/language to share and to become. Defined as the often obscure, not to say hidden, mother-substance of the word/language of men, we lack our *subject*, our *noun*, our *verb*, our *predicates*: our elementary sentence, our basic rhythm, our morphological identity, our generic incarnation, our genealogy. (SP: 83)

Whatever one's personal beliefs about the reference of transcendental statements, there is no doubt that the discourse of religion is an extremely powerful discourse or symbolic structure, in almost all parts of the world, even if western Europe has become, relatively speaking, secular. The discursive and representational systems of religion, like those of philosophy, are part of the domain of representation on which Irigaray's work focuses. For Irigaray, religion is a 'dimension of social organization' (SP: 205). She points out that at a social level, if not at an individual level, the phenomenon of religion appears inescapable:

> To exclude or suppress the phenomenon of religion seems impossible. It re-emerges in different, often degenerate forms: sectarianism, theoretical or political dogmatism, religiosity. . . . So it is important to rethink it, particularly in its structures, its categories, its initiations, its rules, and its utopias, all of which have been male for centuries. Not forgetting

that these are often nowadays called science and technology. (SP: 89; cf. (WSM: 6)

In *Ethique*, she links religiosity to other forms of nihilism and 'destruction of the universe' (E: 13).

Yet later, she writes that: 'Patriarchy has deprived women of the divine' (SP: 205). Like Kristeva, she feels that it is necessary 'to take transcendence seriously' (Kristeva, quoted in Weed (ed.) 1989: 32). The hypothesis she is making is that the projection of a woman divinity could introduce sexual difference into the symbolic. Even to entertain the idea and to consider its implications can reveal how far-reaching symbolic changes would have to be to accommodate women:

> [A]re the peoples of monotheism ready to assert that their God is a woman? How will they realign their entire socio-religious economy if this substitution is made? What upheaval in the symbolic order will be a necessary prerequisite to achieve such a substitution? (QEL: 117)

What she is trying to think through is the implication of supposing women to be persons to whom the function of mediating the divine could be entrusted, i.e. to suppose that women could represent the most celestial as well as the most terrestrial.

We might approach her discussion of the divine through two of the writers whose work she uses, Feuerbach and Girard.[20] Her use of, and discussion of, these two theorists of religion indicates what she sees as positive and what she sees as negative. What I shall suggest is that Irigaray's approach to the divine can be understood in terms of the link she makes between identity and violence. The divine has the dual function of providing a non-restrictive horizon for identity, and at the same time binding the violence of the social body. The first of these functions informs Irigaray's reading of Feuerbach, the second her reading of Girard.

Irigaray follows to a certain extent Feuerbach's analysis of religion in *The Essence of Christianity*. For Feuerbach, God is a projection of the human; the essence of religion is that it 'conceives and affirms a profoundly human relation as a divine relation' (1893: xi). In a mirroring process similar to that which Irigaray describes in the relation between the sexes, Feuerbach describes the relation between man and God thus: 'In the religious systole man propels his own nature from himself, he throws himself outward; in the religious diastole, he receives the rejected nature into his heart again' (p.31). Interestingly, Feuerbach points to the anomaly that in Protestantism the Holy Family excludes the mother, although Mary fulfils that function in Catholicism; it does not occur to him, though, to notice the absence of the daughter. Feuerbach, as Irigaray interprets him, argued that a God/divine principle/transcendent principle was necessary in order to establish a genre (mankind as distinct from animals, say). Mankind with a capital M exists as a genre (a kind) because a divine principle has been posited as a *guarantee*; as

Irigaray puts it, men ensure their self-love with reference to a God (E: 99). The 'death of God', so much talked about in the twentieth century, is the end of an epoch, but, says Irigaray, it is only the male God that is dead (E: 133); read: it is male subjectivity, the male self-image that is in crisis. Women have yet to become a genre. Irigaray emphasizes that when she refers to God: 'The capital letter designates the horizon of the accomplishment of a genre, and not a transcendent entity which is not subject to becoming' (SP: 75). But for women to become, 'it is necessary to have a genre or essence (belonging to one sex or the other) as a horizon' (SP: 73), otherwise women are just an additive collection of units (1+1+1+ – Lacan's 'not all'). The additive does not constitute woman as a genre, as womankind. An ideal/transcendent/divine is needed at the horizon to avoid the purely additive. But if women alone continue to represent the body, the sensible, then they are excluded from the ideal or transcendent. Hence the concept of the sensible transcendental – apparently a contradiction in terms – but in fact a recognition that the body should be recognized and symbolized in such a way that women are no longer sole guardians of the corporeal, so that men can incorporate their own corporeality into their sublimations, so that women can sublimate as women. (So that philosophy does not depend on the split between intelligible and sensible.)

In the Christian tradition of the west, the highest place to which women can aspire is to the status of the Mother of God – still the Mother of God, still the mother–son relationship: 'For centuries we've been living in the mother–son relationship.'[21] What about the Bride or the Daughter? What of her transcendent status? Men have refused to confront their limits. By creating a male God (Father/Son/Holy Spirit) they have given infinite extension to the male principle, while assigning women the role of guardians of death (sex and death are then fused in a deathly equation). They *incorporate* the feminine rather than recognizing women. If they had confronted Woman as another kind/genre, they would have been obliged to confront their own finitude and their own limits; the fact that Mankind is not universal (SP: 73).

What has to be imagined is that the divine horizon could be female, that 'the perfection of our subjectivity' (SP: 75), as Feuerbach describes it, could be a woman. 'There is nothing more spiritual than female sexuality', Irigaray writes in *Ethique* (p.57), and yet it has been deprived of its spiritual dimension (QEL: 117–18). Women need a mirror too; not the one in which they check their appearance-for-others, but a mirror that will send back to them an image that confirms them in their autonomous subjectivity, for-themselves, and not just in their exteriority, for-others (the 'other of the same') (SP: 77–8). Given Irigaray's stress on imaginary equivalents – gold, faeces, phallus, children etc. – I think there is a good case for seeing her use of 'God' as another discursive representation of the monosexual economy. God would then figure in this economy as a mirror for the male imaginary[22], reinterpreting Feuerbach's claim that God is the mirror of Man, while '[w]omen lack a mirror for becoming women' (SP: 79).

Women's goals have always been proposed to them by others: they should want a man, a child, the good of the polis. Women have never loved and wanted themselves: 'That project can only be divine' (SP: 80). Self-love[23] is not the traditional narcissism of the female (clothes, make-up, jewellery etc.) which Irigaray sees rather as women's attempt to give themselves an envelope, a protective 'house' which discourse and the symbolic deprive them of. Self-love, as Irigaray conceives it, depends on creating a symbolic among/between women (E: 103), on a divine word/language which mediates the conflicts and divisions *within* the genre, creates an interval of exchange and spiritualizes the female body: 'Only a God can constitute a place where we can meet, which will leave us free' (SP: 80), and:

> If women lack a God, there is no possible communication or communion between them. One needs, they need, the infinite in order to share *a little*. Otherwise, the distribution [partage] leads to fusion–confusion, division and conflict in (each of) them, between them. If I cannot be in relation to some sort of horizon where my genre is accomplished, I cannot share while protecting my becoming. (SP: 74).

In the language of *This Sex*, and linking God with auto-affection (see Chapter 2, note 25), we could say that the problem of women's auto-affection – the two lips – is that one cannot distinguish between them: 'there is no possibility of distinguishing what is touching from what is touched' (TS: 26; CS: 26); woman '*is neither one nor two*' (ibid.). So '[h]ow can the relationship between these two [i.e. mother and daughter] be articulated?' (TS: 143; CS: 141). God, then, that is, the divine in the feminine, stands for the place where women can meet without (con)fusion – a place in the symbolic order. However, within the dominant symbolic, the assertion of female specificity is inevitably seen as retrograde, so there is a desire to get beyond sexual difference, beyond the polarities. Women are afraid that asserting Womankind will turn to their disadvantage, and put them back into all the old traps. But Irigaray is well aware of this danger. She thinks it is bound to happen unless for women there is an ideal or essence as a *horizon*.

Given the symbolic distribution of functions, in which the body is allotted to woman, it is only by defending – symbolizing – the value of what has been placed outside the transcendental that some redistribution can take place. If that is interpreted as essentialism or phallogocentrism, it is because what has been lost sight of is the horizon. It is to fix a moment of becoming as if it were the goal. In the perspective of the sensible transcendental, feminism itself is no longer a repetition of the same, but the possibility of the other. It is a movement which can operate in two ways, first to break up the imaginary formations that have become too constraining, and provide an interlocutor to enable the male subject to shift his position; second, to function symbolically as a 'home' for women while they seek to build and create a different place for themselves in the social order. The sensible transcendental is offered, I think, as a horizon in which we are all implicated: 'bringing the god to life through us, between us' (E: 124).

There might appear to be dangers in the attempt to reclaim the divine for women. The traditional connotations of the divine are not promising, particularly if, as Irigaray hypothesizes with Feuerbach, God was created in the image of man. However, Irigaray's concept of God as a sensible transcendental attempts to avoid the dangers by conceptualizing the divine as (1) corporeal; (2) sexuate, either male or female; (3) subject to becoming; (4) multiple; (5) incarnated in us here and now:

> a *sensible transcendental* coming into being [advenant] through us, of which *we would be* the mediators and the bridges. Not only in mourning for the dead God of Nietzsche, nor awaiting the god passively, but bringing the god to life through us, in a resurrection or transfiguration of blood and flesh through their language and their ethic. (E: 124)[24]

The point to be stressed here is that the realization of the divine is *in language and ethics*, i.e. it is firmly within the symbolic order, in its possibilities for becoming.

Through the concept of the sensible transcendental, it is possible to link together the different parts of Irigaray's work – the imaginary and the symbolic, language, the body, ethics and so on – and in particular to see the context in which her stress on women's multiplicity should be placed. Woman is not One but multiple. Or, woman's identity is multiple (*in-fini* – both infinite and unfinished). Multiplicity should not be linked with dissemination of identity, but understood within the framework of the genre, of womankind. We saw earlier that Irigaray wrote in *This Sex*: 'isn't a multiplicity that does not entail a rearticulation of the difference between the sexes bound to block or take away something of woman's pleasure?' (TS: 140; CS: 138). Her work on the sensible transcendental and on the genre can be seen as undertaking this process of rearticulation.

The implications of this concept for feminist politics are on the whole non-prescriptive (apart from ruling out integration into the current economy as a long-term strategy). It allows for differences between women as aspects of their multiple identity. It allows for exploration, failures, and mistakes, since Woman is becoming, perfectibility and not static perfection. It allows for ethics and for responsibilities, a symbolic home for women in the genre which does not limit their capacities arbitrarily. It provides a framework for thinking further the problems of identity and negativity (violence). And it also allows for the possibility of dialogue with Irigaray herself; since part of the definition is its becoming, this makes the definition itself part of a process: not a theory placed outside time or history, but the enunciation of an 'I' calling for an interlocutor, a 'you', in a collective process of self-definition. It allows for the possibility of seeing her as *another woman*, instead of as an ideal or bad mother, and therefore of relating *to* her work rather than simply swallowing it whole or rejecting it altogether.

If identity is one side of the coin, violence is the other. The second aspect of Irigaray's discussion of religion is its role in mediating conflict in the social order. Irigaray uses here the work of René Girard and follows his line that religion is a way of regulating social violence and creating social cohesion. In *La Violence et le sacré* [*Violence and the Sacred*], Girard makes a direct connection between violence and the role of religion. He argues that society is perpetually threatened by self-destructive violence, that all society is based on a founding sacrifice, and that through the sacrifice, the violence that threatens the community is ritually cast out, turned outwards rather than inwards on to the members of the community. (It is clear that for Girard, society is an affair of men – he says this explicitly, 1972: 198.) Girard relates the phenomenon of sacrifice to religion; he claims that the function of religion is to keep violence out of the community by means of the mechanism of the scapegoat, or a ritual which substitutes for it. For Girard, brotherhood, the pact between the brothers, does not lead to harmony; the regime of the Same produces conflict, because the brothers have the same desires,[25] which they are unable to negotiate, except through the medium of a third party, a scapegoat, who ensures their unanimity. Violence, then, can be temporarily expelled from the community, but only at the price of another violence, a sacrificial victim.

For Irigaray, however, this account of sacrifice and its function corresponds to the model of male sexuality described by Freud – the model of tension/dis-charge/homeostasis (SP: 90). There is a more fundamental sacrifice that Girard does not mention: mothers, who are 'a *totem prior to any designated totem*' (WSM: 13; SP: 97). Relations between men and women are paralysed because society does not recognize this initial sacrifice, does not acknowledge the debt which it owes to mothers. Irigaray argues that in Christianity the body and blood that are ritually consumed are the body and blood of women. To the symbol of *sacrifice*, she opposes the value of *fertility* (which I shall discuss further in Chapter 8). The suppression and incorporation of the maternal genealogy by the paternal genealogy leads to a non-respect for fertility (SP: 15). She does not suppose that women are essentially non-violent. Women too are subject to the violence of unsymbolized affects (SP: 84), although their relation to the death drive is likely to be structured differently from that of men, and they are likely to turn the violence on themselves. But she suggests that violence could be mediated in ways different from the tension/discharge/homeostasis mechanism characteristic of male violence as described by Girard for example. She insists on the need for rites and for *paroles* – words or symbolization. The *parole* can ideally mediate the unsymbolized affect. The link is made here between the divine, exchange, and language. God is the place *between*, what mediates and negotiates conflict (SP: 94). Without an order of exchange, women, without rites or sacraments, devour each other, or men, or become over-possessive of their children (see WSM; SP: 89–102). She suggests a possible source for these rites in the rhythms of nature, the cycles of fertility, partly as a different mode of temporalization more adequate to the female imaginary, partly because what in particular needs to be symbolized is women's fertility, their body and blood on which, as she puts it, society lives for free, assuming that the supply of mothers will never run out.[26] In what seems to me another echo of the psychoanalytic model – in which the symbolization of affect through words in the here and now of the psychoanalytic session enables the violence of immediate, powerful, and inarticulate unconscious feelings to be symbolized rather than acted out – she stresses first the *word*, and second *attentiveness to the present* (WSM: 8; SP: 91). I think there is a plea here not to imitate the sacrificial violence of men by making other women scapegoats to ensure unanimity within communities of women, but to find other ways of resolving conflicts. And it is essential that rites be public, social, symbolic – not private, individual, and hidden. Without symbolic mediation, violence always threatens.[27]

God as mediating language is to take the place of the God who demands sacrifices. One can make conceptual links here both with linguistic theory and with theology, and they need to be brought into relation. In linguistics, Benveniste explains that the condition of dialogue is constitutive of the person (1966: 260). The 'here and now' is related to discourse, to instances of 'I' and 'you' (p.253). We saw in Chapter 2 that for Irigaray the 'I' and the 'you' subtend third-person discourse, even when they are absent from the *énoncé*. So attentiveness to the present is a question of the assumption of the subject of enunciation, the 'I' and the 'you' of discourse, and the sexuate identity of the subject. At the same time, the 'here and now' is linked to theology, specifically to parousia, or the Second Coming (E: 139):

> Does parousia correspond to the expectation of a future not only as a *utopia* or *destiny*, but as an act *here and now*, the willed construction of a bridge in the present between the past and the future? . . . Must God always remain inaccessible transcendence and not a realization – here and now – in and through the body? (E: 139)

There seems, then, to be a good case for seeing the divine in terms of the symbolic, and of the subject of enunciation underpinning the symbolic *énoncé*, while parousia would be an ideal enunciative moment in which two subjects were addressing *each other* (the other sex rather than a transcendent God), and not using the body of the other for their own temporality and their own becoming. The theme of the divine would then be a reworking of the themes of imaginary, subjectivity, and language in terms of the conceptual framework of theology, in addition to secularized philosophy. It could be seen as addressing the question of the transcendental signifier in more traditionally theological terms than it is usually addressed in the discourse of a would-be secular culture, but in this way linking the feminist issue to questions of the role of religion in maintaining the fabric of patriarchy.

In the light of her stress on the cultural possibilities for women to be subjects of culture, seeing religion as one of the discourses/institutions which allow or inhibit this, we might understand the main points of Irigaray's discussion of religion as follows:

1. The religions of the west offer a purely male genealogy, in which relations between mothers and daughters have been effaced. Although we can find in classical mythology examples of mother–daughter couples: Demeter and Persephone (the latter often called simply Kore, the daughter), Jocasta and Antigone, Clytemnestra and Iphigenia/ Electra, we cannot simply return to those goddesses in contemporary times (WSM: 11; SP: 95). We have to invent a divine for our own times.
2. The absence of the maternal genealogy leads to ethical error, to believing that substitution is possible. The man takes the woman/wife as a substitute for his mother, and she is subsumed within the paternal genealogy. But ethics requires the radical non-substitutability of one for the other (QEL: 114). Whether cause or effect, this ethical error has the backing of religion (QEL: 114–15).
3. It should not be assumed that the sacrificial is inevitable; it corresponds too closely to the male imaginary. An exploration of symbolic alternatives to sacrifice should be made. In its exclusion and 'sacrifice' of women, the sacrificial also brings about ethical error. Christianity for example has made the sacrifice central, although Irigaray argues that sacrifice is pre-Christian and a much older phenomenon – it is a pre-Christian 'accident' in Christianity (WSM: 8; SP: 92).
4. Because of the division of functions (man = mind, woman = body), only relations between men have been spiritualized. It is then impossible to spiritualize the sexual relation which historically has been seen by Christianity as less spiritual than chastity. The spiritualization of the sexual relation is essential in order to avoid the reduction of the woman to animality and dependence (QEL: 117–18), and in order to allow for the possibility of women's ethical responsibility.
5. The Other has always been seen by men as God, but never as the other sex. The 'You' is always addressed to the transcendental, never to women. With a sensible transcendental, the exchange between the 'you' and the 'I' could take place in the here and now, with each sex assuming its own 'I' and addressing its 'you' to a transcendent other.[28]

Irigaray concludes that in order for society to have a foundation other than the sacrificial, it will be necessary to modify our understanding of space and time (SP: 97, 148; WSM: 12), which at present is based on the imaginary male body. It is to this issue that we turn in the next chapter.

Chapter 7

Ethics, sexuality, and embodiment

La révolution copernicienne n'a pas encore produit tous ses effets dans l'imaginaire masculin. (*Speculum*)
The Copernican revolution has not yet produced all its effects in the male imaginary.

The transcendental subject

Irigaray wants to restore the link between epistemology and ethics. I don't think it would be putting it too strongly to say that, for Irigaray, epistemology without ethics is deadly – destructive to women, destructive to men, destructive to the earth. The danger of our times is that the subject as knower has become split off from the embodied and social subject. It is essential to think through again the implications of the fact that the Other is constitutive of subjectivity, whether the Other is the unconscious – that which the subject cannot master or control, or even know in himself – or whether the Other is embodied in other people who likewise constitute that which is irreducible to the subject, or whether the Other is the Lacanian Other, whose desire is located in the symbolic order.

An ethics of sexual difference, that is, an ethics which recognizes the subjectivity of each sex, would have to address the symbolic division which allocates the material, corporeal, sensible, 'natural' to the feminine, and the spiritual, ideal, intelligible, transcendental to the masculine. A sensible transcendental is the condition of an ethics of sexual difference, necessary if the fate of Antigone is not to go on repeating itself (E: 106). If women are cut off from their own becoming, then they are 'buried alive' in our culture. Because of the split, women, as the body, represent sexuality, which is then cut off from the ideal or spiritual, and becomes a 'lower' function, that which is to be transcended in the pursuit of the good. To end the cultural schizophrenia (which does not seem too strong a term in this context), and for women to be able to love themselves, and be for-themselves, women need to be able to move freely from the most 'subterranean' and the most 'celestial', between the depths and the heights. Similarly, if men continue to allow women to represent the carnal for them, they collude in keeping women in a kind of pseudo-childhood, which is both 'perverse' and 'animal' (QEL: 118), i.e. pre-ethical, unsymbolized, outside the sphere of the so-called 'higher' human activities.

So the issue of the body and of sexuality is central to ethics, not in the limited sense of a set of taboos and prohibitions, but in the sense that the symbolic division of labour prevents women from becoming-for-themselves. However, it is not an issue that is easy to address without falling back into male parameters: 'Female sexuality has always been conceptualized on the basis of masculine parameters' (TS: 23; CS: 23). As Foucault has argued, though in quite different terms, the discourse of sex is the locus of the (male) subject's subjection.[1] So however we understand parler-femme, whatever it means for women to 'speak (of) their sex [parler leur sexe]' (PN: 272), it does not mean to begin simply turning the tables, speaking of men as sex objects in a kind of imitation or revenge, or treating men as they might be for-women. Similarly it is not focused around the orgasm, which is a kind of technical criterion, a quantitative measure of 'success',[2] more to do with the requirements of male sexuality than with a possible different sexuality. Nor is it organized around the scopophilic imagination, the pleasure of dominating with the look. It is not even primarily a question of the 'truth' or unarguability of sexual pleasure, since for Irigaray sexuality is not a raw, primitive, and untouched territory which is somehow private, 'outside' conceptualization, uncontaminated by patriarchy and unstructured by the paternal genealogy. On the contrary, the links between sexuality, conceptualization, 'knowledge', and social organization are intrinsic. Women are 'in exile', or 'unhoused' in male sexuality, male discourse, and male society.

We saw in Chapter 3 the role of the imaginary in conceptualization. The imaginary works in images that are much simpler than the abstractions of philosophy; it has the morphology of the body, and this corporeal morphology informs the symbolic and the social at all levels. So when Irigaray 'interprets' philosophy, what she finds is the shape of the male body and the rhythms of male sexuality (as sacrifice, for example, is said to correspond to the model of tension/discharge/homeostasis). Earlier we saw that man needed a mirror, but Irigaray also writes that he needs a base (sol or socle), a ground on which to stand upright. On Heidegger, for example, she comments that: 'As long as Heidegger does not leave the "earth", he does not leave metaphysics' for metaphysics 'always supposes, in one way or another, a solid crust on which a construction can be elevated' (OA: 10). Here is a passage from Speculum on the morphology of the male subject:

If there is no more 'earth' to press down/repress, to work, to represent, but also and always to desire (for one's own), no opaque matter which in theory does not know itself, then what pedestal [socle] remains for the ek-sistence of the 'subject'? If the earth turned and more especially turned upon herself/itself, the erection of the subject might thereby be disconcerted and risk losing its elevation and penetration. For what would there be to rise up from and exercise power over? (SE: 133; SF: 165)

In the male imaginary, the transcendental, the ec-stasy (*ek-stase, hors-de-soi*) of ek-sistence, corresponds to the projection of erection, male narcissism extrapolated to the transcendental (TS: 151; CS: 147).

In addition to the ec-static structure, we find oculocentrism (or, in terms of the structure of desire, scopophilia). Irigaray links this with castration. Whatever the subject cannot dominate, or overlook and perceive from his transcendental elevation, threatens the subject with castration (SE: 138; SF: 171) – the cavern, the womb, the inside of the mother's body is a dangerous place (whose dangers are represented by the phantasy of the *vagina dentata*). In myth, this phantasy is embodied in the tale of Ouranos, castrated by his son Kronos who was hiding in his mother's body, waiting for his father to penetrate her (see Chapter 5, note 12 for a fuller version). This castration phantasy is alluded to in *Amante marine* and discussed specifically in *Le Temps de la différence* (in 'Le Mystère oublié des généalogies féminines') as an example of the primitive phantasies underlying the male view of sexuality as 'chaos, night, bestiality, error, annihilation' (TD: 103). The castration phantasies of the transcendental subject are linked to the symbolic split which assigns women to the carnal, excluding them from the spiritual and relegating them to a domain of lesser (and despised) being. The split operates as a defence against the terror evoked by the phantasies. Even Levinas – whom Irigaray otherwise admires for his ethical approach to the Other – is included among the philosophers who perpetuate the split.

One can discern phenomenology in the background here, and at the same time a critique of it. A relation between the lived body and the concept can be found in the work of Merleau-Ponty and Simone de Beauvoir in particular, and it is probably true that the 'second-wave' feminist appeal to lived experience is predominantly indebted to Simone de Beauvoir's account of the phenomenology of the female body.[3] But, as Alison Jaggar points out, experience is not self-authenticating:

> Because feelings and emotions are socially constructed, however, radical feminists are wrong if they suppose, as some do, that the feelings and emotions of feminists should always be accepted as appropriate to the situation or even that those who experience them always identify them correctly . . . a theory may require that we revise even the descriptions of the world on which the theory itself is based. (1983: 380–1)

Feminist philosophers have become wary of the concept of experience.
The categories with which we describe our experience are derived from
a collective and shared discourse which we have inherited, and it is
essential to understand our inheritance critically. Even such apparently
basic understandings as those of space and time may be masculine in
their construction. Categories *construct* the symbolic division between male
and female. The phenomenological account of the lived body and the
lived world needs to be complemented by the awareness that there is an
interaction between the lived experience, the imaginary, and the discursive
and social construction of both. Although Irigaray is sympathetic to certain
phenomenologists (particularly Heidegger, Merleau-Ponty and Levinas),
because they *do* stress language, the body, and ethics, she points out that in
each case, their philosophy reproduces in one form or another the morphology
or imperatives of the male body.[4]

So what of woman's sexuality and imaginary? Here, says Irigaray: 'The
Copernican revolution has not yet produced all its effects in the male
imaginary' (SE: 133; SF: 165). For what the male imaginary has difficulty
in conceiving, or fears to conceive, is that his base, the earth/woman, might
turn, and turn upon her own axis. He needs the illusion that 'the object
is inert' (SE: 134; SF: 166). But in fact, though he does not want to
see it, 'he is dealing here with a nature that is already self-referential
[qui se rapporte déjà à elle-même = which is already in relation with
itself]. Already fissured and open' (ibid.). So Irigaray offers a pair of
terms which refer to male and female sexuality respectively, indicating
a difference in their positioning relative to the mother, and a different
representation of their imaginary body: the *retour* (return) and the *retouche*
(touching again).

The *retour* can be interpreted in various ways, but what it comes down to is
that the male imaginary depends, for its transcendence/projection/flight/ek-
stasis, on the earth, the maternal-feminine, to which it must always return:
'On the side of man, men, it will always be necessary to seek the first dwelling
for auto-affection to be possible' (E: 64). To love himself, he needs that
unconditional first home which contained him: 'Love of self [on the man's
side] would present itself as a long *return* to and through (*par*) the other' (E:
64). The *retour* can also refer to the temporalization of male sexuality and
its return to homeostasis. It is quite a complicated picture; the forms which
the *retour* takes can vary considerably. So woman can serve as a mirror for
reflecting him back to himself (confirming him); or he can be nostalgic for a
container or a home (in language, in theory, in a woman) which is a substitute
for that first dwelling; or he can use the earth, the maternal-feminine, as a base
or launching pad for excursions into transcendence; or he can seek a route
via God, in order to avoid seeing woman/the maternal-feminine as Other;
or he can invest in the phallus, the erection of theories, buildings, and so on.
Irigaray summarizes:

Love of self, for the man, seems to oscillate between three poles:

–nostalgia for the matricial-maternal;
–the quest for God through the father;
–love of a part of the self (in conformity, particularly, with the dominant sexual model).
In this economy, the feminine [either] becomes the unique woman [the mother] or becomes the 1+1+1+ . . . parts of a shattered whole. (E: 64; my square brackets)

To sum up, it is called the *retour*, I think, because what it signifies is that the male imaginary has never completely accomplished symbolic castration. Everyone is born into dereliction through the loss of their original home (E: 122–3) but men palliate the loss at women's expense. One will always find in this imaginary a nostalgia for the original home, an attempt to keep it for himself, own it and control it, in order to be able to return to it in phantasy (by keeping women in the home, for example, or ensuring their social dependence). But this phantasy, in symbolic form, prevents woman from acceding to her own separate being; she must always be for-men, available for their transcendence. (This picture is extremely clear in Hegel's account of marriage.)

The *retouche*, symbolized by the 'two lips' (which I shall discuss further in Chapter 8) is an attempt to symbolize auto-affection on the woman's side, the idea that woman is not simply for-men, but that she has an existence of her own; the fact that she is not an inert object, passive 'nature', but that she 'also turns upon herself' and also 'knows how to re-turn (upon herself)' (SE: 134; SF: 166), although not how to 'seek outside for identity within the other: nature, sun, god . . . (woman)' (ibid.). Whereas the male imaginary seeks 'closure', the woman's imaginary corresponds to something more open, something *in-fini*, both infinite and unfinished. 'She' is not that immobilized maternal-feminine that the male imaginary would like to keep firmly within its possession.

We need to return here to the idea of the body-image. It is clear, I think, that if in fact the male imaginary is predominant, then women will experience particular difficulties in our society. The lived experience of their body-image, a body image of a different morphology from that of men, will be forced into a conceptualization and socialization to which it does not correspond. And in addition, if women, like men, attempt to retain the mother as their home, the dangers of fusion/confusion of identity are great. Given that there is only the one place of the mother, the woman can never come into separate existence. This leaves the choice of either being 'like men', making a masculine identification, or being for-men (a kind of living doll) with all the conflicts of identity and self-respect that this brings, or having to forge a tenuous identity against or in the margins of the symbolic (at the risk of being socially isolated, or branded as lesbian, feminist, man-hater, witch, virago, or any of the other insults reserved for 'eccentric' women). The one identity that the symbolic offers is that of maternity, but this is not an identity as a woman, only as a mother (and ideally as the mother of a son). It is not a sexual identity as *amante* – woman-as-lover – but an identity made to stave off dereliction which in practice makes it difficult for women to become *women* (PN: 298).

For Irigaray, sexual identity (whether heterosexual or homosexual) is conditional on generic identity. There has been some debate about whether Irigaray is primarily concerned with the 'politics of the couple' (Braidotti 1986a) or whether she is recommending lesbian separatism (discussed in Grosz 1988b). I think there are two conceptually distinct but mutually implicated strands here. The first is the question of the 'other woman', the woman 'for-herself'. The second is the issue of sexual difference and the question of the fertile couple: fertile according to the spirit. The first is the condition of the second. For exchange to take place between the two terms of sexual difference, there must first *be* two terms. Sometimes Irigaray foregrounds the one issue, sometimes the other. But whatever provisional strategy one adopts, one should keep in mind as a horizon that the sexual difference has to be rearticulated within the symbolic for any radical change to take place; this would be true whether one is homosexual or heterosexual. Irigaray does not think that lesbian women can create a private enclave in which a different order prevails. Lesbian women too are within a patriarchal symbolic order. Either way, there is no question of policing women's sexuality; compulsory homosexuality is no more satisfactory than compulsory heterosexuality.

The concept of the sensible transcendental is another way of formulating the question of the symbolic order, another way of approaching the problematics of rationality and the need for subjects of different sexes. 'Transcendental' is not a term which has a fixed meaning.[5] I think Irigaray understands it as the arena of the (philosophical) subject split off from its ground; in whatever terms rationality, epistemology, and ethics are addressed, they depend upon a process of splitting or division which constitutes a higher and a lower domain to which men and women are respectively assigned. Because the sensible transcendental is a concept intended to integrate these divisions (at least as a horizon), to overcome the sexual division, and because it is defined, in one of its multiple definitions, as a 'perpetual transvaluation', it has sometimes been taken to correspond to Derrida's space of multiple sexuality, beyond male and female. However, as I have already argued, the issue of 'beyond male and female' obscures the double question of (a) women's generic identity in the symbolic, and (b) the exploration of the sexual construction of the *male* subject who needs the maternal-feminine as his base. Because the body of woman serves as the base for the topography of the male subject, it is part of the structure of the transcendental subject, whether rational, ethical, or epistemological, and should be addressed within the transcendental field (in so far as the latter, for Irigaray, corresponds to the symbolic order itself).

Whether the topography of the male subject is conceptualized in terms of reflection (Hegel, Lacan), space and time (Kant), dwelling (Heidegger, Levinas) or *différance* and espacement (Derrida), in each case the maternal body is being used as building material; this exploitation prevents women's accession to subjectivity unless woman has a topology too: 'the maternal-feminine . . . necessarily exists, but as *a priori* condition (as Kant would put it) of the space-time, of the male subject . . . the maternal-feminine does not necessarily exist as woman' (E: 86).

One of the things that Irigaray has been consistently seeking to define, from *Speculum* to *Ethique*, and including *L'Oubli de l'air*, is the condition for the topology of the female subject, of *her* reflection (the speculum), of *her* space-time, of *her* dwelling, of *her* espacement:

> In order for [sexual] difference to be thought and lived, we have to reconsider the whole problematic of *space* and *time*. . . . A change of epoch requires a mutation in the perception and conception of *space-time*, the *inhabitation of place* and of the *envelopes of identity*. (E: 15)

The context in which the sensible transcendental must be seen is that of love of self on the woman's side. The 'sensible' would no longer be the body of woman as it figures in the male imaginary, but a reworked phantasy in which the body component of conceptualization was reclaimed by men, freeing women for their own subjectivity.

In the following discussion I shall juxtapose passages about the transcendental subject with passages from the essays about psychoanalysis and the imaginary. In this I follow Irigaray, who makes the same kind of juxtapositions, particularly in *Ethique* and in *Parler n'est jamais neutre*. She does not make a hard and fast methodological distinction between the two terminologies (although she makes it clear that she is not talking about 'psychology'). The discourse of psychoanalysis intertwines then with the discourse on ethics, space and time, and the divine. I would suggest that this is deliberate, and that what has been removed or blurred is the distinction between 'higher' and 'lower' which would risk perpetuating the split. In this context, too, one might venture a possible explanation for Irigaray's rejection of the concept ('In a woman('s) language, the concept as such would have no place' – TS: 123; CS: 122). As I suggested in Chapter 2, she is primarily concerned with the subject of enunciation which subtends epistemology, the identities of the 'I' and the 'you' which underlie the third-person statement. There are three problems with the concept, from this point of view. The first is that the *concept* of concept belongs to the symbolic division; the concept is situated on the transcendental side of the divide, while women are situated on the sensible side. So Irigaray is trying to invent terms (which I have sometimes, though misleadingly, called concepts, for want of a better word) which do not split women from the transcendental. The second is that the concept thematizes, refers to the *énoncé*, whereas in a situation of enunciation

– an ethical situation for example – the other person should be addressed directly, not spoken *about*. Enunciation has primacy over epistemology. The third problem is that the concept freezes, immobilizes what is or should be fluid and mobile. Like identity, the concept is linked with the stasis of death. But still, one has to invent a language for speaking to the other, and it is in those terms that Irigaray's language should ideally be addressed.[6] The aim of psychoanalysis – that situation of enunciation which I think Irigaray is using for her model – is to enable the analysand to structure his or her house of language (SP: 107). Similarly the aim of rethinking the conditions of the male subject and the modalities of space and time, and of dwelling, is to give women *their* house of language, a home in the symbolic order. The problem as before is that of fertility, and the symbolic distribution of roles, in which women are only allowed to be fertile in the body, while men are fertile intellectually and spiritually. Both sexes need to be 'fertile according to the spirit' (SP: 117). So while men need to take back and own their body, women need to accede to a symbolic representation of their own.

The house of language

I mentioned in an earlier chapter that Irigaray is diagnosing a cultural pathology, a sclerosis in thought and civilization, with effects on both men and women. For women, the effect is dereliction, symbolic homelessness, or imprisonment. For men, the morphology of the male body, enshrined in theory/philosophy, has become a 'sepulchre' (SE: 143,144; SF: 177,179), however decorative or comfortable; transcendence cut off from its conditions of existence paralyses and immobilizes (OA: 149). As she says in a paper on Schopenhauer, philosophy is all about death ('une affaire de mort'). We have already looked, in Chapter 5, at the link between truth and the economy of the death drives. The problem emerges again quite clearly in the discussion of dwelling and the topology of the male subject. In her discussion of Heidegger, the philosopher from whom she borrows the notion of 'dwelling', Irigaray writes that here too we find the familiar division of labour: 'Some [masculine] creators of worlds, constructors of temples, builders of houses; others [feminine], guardians of a *phuein* making its resources available, prior to any culture' (OA: 120). But *phuein* (meaning literally 'to grow, to engender, to come into the light',[7] and from which *phusis* – nature – is derived), in the symbolic code, means: 'as yet unthought and left in forgetfulness' (OA: 35) and also hatred and death:

> For, if she was not, and available to him, what would become of his language [langage]? . . . The dwelling of man is not built without hatred of nature; that is why she must be the one to safeguard it. (OA: 71)
>
> In order to impose [his] sexual destiny as the truth of the whole [du tout], as the advent of the all [du tout] in the same, man has taken from

nature her life and in exchange has given (back) to her death. (OA: 85)

So building and dwelling reveal hatred and destructiveness as intrinsic moments, yet unthought, so never confronted. The underside of male creativity is the deathlike immobilizing 'appropriation' of 'nature'.

Irigaray's question is: 'Where and how to dwell?'[8] How are women to live (in both senses – to dwell and to remain alive) in the edifices built by the male imaginary? Can other structures be built for them? Very schematically, the issues are: (1) the way in which philosophers have constructed dwellings for themselves; (2) the question of ownership, or 'appropriation' of space (nature, the cavern etc.) in the gesture of 'naturalization'; (3) a possible reconceptualization which would provide dwellings for women.

Irigaray's discussion is organized by a number of paired terms, which can be set out as follows: life/death; mobility/immobility; destruction/creation; movement/rigidity; (flowing) blood/sclerosis and so on. The argument her work sets forth is that the symbolic division in which woman represents nature, the body, sexuality, the unthought, the unthinkable, castration, and death, cut off from the transcendental, in facts prevents life, mobility, and fertility *on both sides*. Man may think he is active, dynamic, propelling himself upwards from earth to sky, but he is in a sepulchre, while woman, like Antigone, is imprisoned and buried alive. The house of language in which man dwells to protect himself from his original dereliction can become a prison for both sexes. In immobilizing, or attempting to immobilize, the mother, to keep her under his control, prevent her from being a woman and having a (sexual) life of her own, he has blocked not only women's fertility but his own. Thus although Irigaray tends to agree with the modern philosophers who announce the 'crisis' of the subject and of philosophy, she has a rather different diagnosis.

This diagnosis of modern philosophy can be seen to inform her discussion of Kant. Irigaray concludes that Kant's philosophy operates a particularly ruthless refusal to recognize its debt to the sensible, by seizing the imaginary (which is bodily in form) and reallocating it to the intelligible, the understanding:

This is the first instance of the passage from sensation to understanding whereby – not without *mystery* – a schematism arises that will never give back to the sensible world what it owes to it. For the imaginary, the most subtle faculty of the senses, will remain in the service of the understanding. What is conceded to nature is thus immediately and imperiously taken back and will have served only to ensure a more rigorous dominion over nature. Thus the function of the transcendental schema will be to negate something particular to the sensible world, a negation from which it will not recover. A closed fort/foreclosed in its primary empirical naïvety. And what in this process will have been set aside in all its sensible diversity in order to elaborate the concept of object, is the immediacy of *the relationship to the mother*. (SE: 204; SF: 254; trans. adapted)

The Kantian philosopher who allocates the imaginary to the intelligible is a philosopher who has repressed the relationship to the mother. It is a system designed to control that which the philosopher cannot dominate, to 'legislate the link to the empirical matrix/mother's womb' (SE: 204; SF: 254), and thereby to ward off the threat of castration/death, but also to immobilize that which is threatening. Irigaray goes on to write that Kant's categorical imperative could be otherwise interpreted as a '*noli tangere matrem*': do not touch the mother (SE: 210; SF: 261):

The prohibition on touching the mother comes from the fear and dread of an all-powerful nature; the courage of resistance to her attractions procures the right to judge oneself independent, while at the same time, not neglecting to make sure one is in a position to resist its/her recurrent dangers by developing one's culture. (SE: 210; SF: 261–2; trans. adapted)

But, as she goes on to say in *L'Oubli de l'air*: 'Something of the mechanism [dispositif] installed by man in order to confront the danger of death in his contact with nature remains unthought' (OA: 22). And, as a result of this unthought: 'Does this exploitation of nature by man not lead to the risk of his own death?' (OA: 23)

One might say, she suggests, that the mechanism (Kant's system, for example) has been designed *in order not to* acknowledge the mother. Nature appears of no inherent interest:

of course what matters is not the existence of the object – *as such it is indifferent* – but the simple effect of a representation upon the subject, its reflection, that is, in the imagination of man. (SE: 207; SF: 258; trans. adapted)

Or, as one might say, the earth does not turn; it is immobile, or immobilized in a theory: 'The relation to *phusis* [nature] being determined by a project of appropriation rather than by the desire for life or survival' (OA: 19). Or, if this point is put in terms of specularization, specula(riz)ation ensures that what will be reflected back will be nothing that has not already been put into nature, the possibility that the mirror might have a life of its own being too dangerous to contemplate. Irigaray comments, then, that Kant's 'two pure forms of sensible intuition, serving as principles of *a priori* knowledge, namely, space and time' (*Critique of Pure Reason* A22, B36), is a system which houses men as they were once housed in the womb: 'In this way, bit by bit/room by room, the subject will have constructed his dwelling' (SE: 212; SF: 265). The *a priori*, 'essential to his/the mind's foundation [is] the seduction of nature in its entirety' (ibid.). As in the Platonic picture where nature was surreptitiously incorporated, here nature has been subjugated by the categories of space and time, and rendered safe, immobile, cut off from thought and the transcendental. What is unthought, and unthinkable, is that these categories of space and time might not correspond to the imaginary morphology of the female body: 'Unthinkable through [the] absence from any possible economy, through the missing categories of *her* space-time' (OA: 32, loosely translated; my emphasis).

How then, to create a house, a possible space-time, for the woman-as-subject?[9] For this, we have to consider the morphology of the female body and *her* relationship to the ground, to the mirror, to space and time, and to dwelling. What Irigaray is putting forward here is inevitably tentative and, as she recognizes herself, it is not clear that there is any genre or style available to her to express the female imaginary; it is necessary to create a new style, as she frequently points out (see e.g. SP: 191). As a result, the analyses of *Ethique* cannot simply be summarized; they can evoke, stir the imagination (or the imaginary) but are not 'theories' as such, although they are trying to put into words the unthought and the unthinkable. So the categories I am going to discuss here: the threshold, espacement, mucosity, the passage between, the angel, air, singing, and dancing, are not in any sense a new *synthetic a priori*. They are a language, a way of talking about women which should keep open rather than close shut, and above all, allow women to be *mobile*, alive and turning on their own axis. As Catherine Chalier points out, women's access to subjectivity requires the *invention* of language: 'Words, which are resistant to the meaning that the other would give to them without even listening, are indispensable for her' (1982: 47).

The threshold   The house of the male subject is closed – Irigaray calls it in one place a 'maison close', literally a closed house, but also a brothel or house of ill fame (SE: 143; SF: 178) – whereas one characteristic of women's sexual bodies is that they are precisely not closed; they can be entered in the act of love, and when one is born one leaves them, passes across the threshold. (One might argue that men's bodies can be entered too, but no doubt Irigaray would argue that the massive cultural taboo on homosexuality is linked to men's fear of the open or penetrable body/house.) So the male imaginary needs to phantasise the maternal body as his property:

> that from which women suffer comes also from the fact that men cannot conceive that they [women] do not exist. It is so essential for men that they [women] exist. For men to have the possibility of thinking themselves or imagining themselves *causa sui* (self-caused), they have to think that the container 'belongs' to them. (Especially since the 'end of God' or the 'death of God' ...) For this ownership – without the guarantee of God – those who provide the container must necessarily exist. *Therefore* the maternal-feminine necessarily exists as cause of the

causa sui of man. But not for herself. She exists necessarily but as *a priori* condition (as Kant would put it) of the space-time of the male subject.[10] A cause never revealed under the threat that his identity would be torn apart, would plunge into the abyss. She does not necessarily exist as a woman because, insofar as she is a woman, his container is always open [entrouverte] . . . (E: 86)

For women, then, the crucial question is that of *territory*, and whether the enterer is a welcome guest, invited in, or an intruder. For this reason, Irigaray proposes to make *virginity*, the right to refuse entry, and abortion, the right to refuse the uninvited entrant, basic civil rights for women, the condition of women's being for-themselves (see TD: 74 ff., 87 ff.).

Traditionally, too, men have used the body of woman, representing space, as the material of their own temporality (see OA: 89, 95 and QEL: 112).[11] This claim needs to be put in the context of the *fort-da* (discussed in Chapter 2). For Irigaray, it is not accidental that in Freud's account of the *fort-da* and his interpretation of its meaning (that the little boy is coming to terms with the absence of his mother, so that language acquisition takes place in the situation of loss or absence), the child is a boy. The rhythm described in the *fort-da* is that of presence/absence: 'Men have to reject in order to grasp, abandon in order to keep, exclude in order to admit or choose. They come and go from the more to the less, from above to below. From excess to penury. From accumulation to loss. From tension to discharge? From erection to detumescence? From erection to ejaculation?' (FPE: 52). When the little boy says 'fort' (gone), he is 'rejecting in order to grasp', introjecting the mother in some sense. It is difficult for this imaginary to accomodate the thought of a 'becoming without breaks' (FPE: 53), continuity of jouissance rather than punctuation. The daughter, Irigaray suggests, reacts to the absence of her mother in a different way; she may play with a doll (rather than throwing away an object on a piece of string); she may relapse into anorexia and depression (if she is unable to symbolize what has 'gone' as just a part of her, rather than the whole of her); or she may, through dance, through gesture, attempt to create a symbolic territory around herself, like girls skipping in the school yard. The skipping rope defines a circle around them, and within that circle they can turn and twirl, as it were turn on their own axis:

> The girl-subject does not master anything, except perhaps her own silence, her becoming, her excesses. Unlike the boy, she has no objects. She is split differently in two and the object or the aim is to reunite the two by a gesture, to make the two touch again, perhaps to repeat the moment of birth, in order not to regress thoughtlessly, to remain whole, sometimes to stand upright. They do not want to master the other, but to create themselves. (GP: 133; SP: 114)

The acquisition of language is not by introjection, as with the boy, but *with* the mother: 'The woman always speaks *with* the mother, the man speaks in her absence' (GP: 134; SP: 113). The daughter, as subject, 'does not master anything'. In the terms which we discussed in the first section of this chapter, men's temporality, their *retour*, depends on woman as material support, whereas woman's space-time for herself is that of the *retouche*, the unpunctuated, more or less continuous contiguity of the 'two lips', the co-presence of mother and daughter.

In analysis between women, the end of the analysis should be to constitute a horizon for each woman, not through 'rejection, hatred or mastery', as in the male mode, or the female mode within the male symbolic (where the daughter has to reject her mother and turn towards her father), but 'moving and remaining open to the other' (PN: 304). This means that temporary merging or crossing of boundaries does not put identity into danger.

Men respond to the difficulty of coming to terms with birth, loss, and separation by constructing homes for themselves, either figuratively or literally. Women, with inadequate symbolic material, fall into fusion/confusion of identity. Men through the *fort-da* keep the mother at a distance (e.g. OA: 63); women cannot use the mechanism of the *fort-da* without detriment to themselves. If they are not to hate and reject the mother, they must identify with her. But this identification is dangerous for their identity: 'The lack of symbolic and imaginary territory [*sol* = ground or base] accorded or recognised "on the side of women" means that everything takes place in a potentially deadly immediacy . . .' (PN: 296). If the threshold is unsymbolized, the openness means that it is difficult to tell where one woman ends and another begins.

In fact, there are two different kinds of fusion operating. The mother–son relationship is one kind of merged relationship (*fusionnel*), 'because the son does not know how to situate himself vis-à-vis the one who has given birth to him without any possible reciprocity' (TD: 121). The central cultural relationship is in fact mother–son incest, the fusion that comes from non-recognition, in the symbolic, of the debt. The son *distances* the mother, but like the cotton reel in the *fort-da*, he never finally lets go of her; she is kept, as it were, on the end of a piece of string. The mother–daughter fusion also fails to recognize the debt, because mother and daughter have no possible separate identity within the symbolic. Both failures come to the same fault: the failure to 'allow the woman her face' (QEL: 116), to put it in Levinas's terms. Men use God, objects, Truth, the transcendental, to make the separation, but a certain incest meanwhile continues unremarked. To symbolize the threshold, then, is an essential move to open up the container to allow passage in and out, both to contest male ownership of the container, and also to give woman *her* space, where she can move freely.

Espacement   Because of the rhythms of male sexuality, men can establish limits, boundaries, punctuation in time. But woman as threshold knows nothing of temporal boundaries: 'The *thresholds* do not necessarily indicate a limit, the end of an act' (E: 67). Women have difficulty, for this reason, in being subjected to the discontinuity of the mother's absence, of the other's being or temporality (PN: 301). Separation is not easy for them: 'Traditionally, espacement is created, or occupied by a man, child, housework, preparing food. Not by the woman *for herself* (E: 72). Each act of intercourse for a woman is an act of (re)separation as she is subjected to the temporality of the man's sexuality. But it is not an espacement that she symbolizes in terms of her own body. She is involved in men's anal erotism, without the corresponding satisfactions and sublimations, since the symbolic division has obliged her to repress her sadistic drives, as we saw in Chapter 5 in the discussion of castration and the death drive:

> Thus she is apparently party to anal erotism. But except for her pregnancy
> ... woman's role seems to require only that she detach herself from the
> anal 'object': the gift-child, just as she is required to give up the 'fecal
> column' after coitus. Repeating, thus, her separation from the feces. But
> without pleasure. For the drives [pulsions] correlated with anal erotism,
> drives of aggression and narcissistic retention, are not allowed to her. (SE:
> 75; SF: 90; trans. adapted)

How to punctuate her relationship with another, in terms of her own space-time? At the very least, a symbolic redistribution of the death drives would be necessary.

Women need to perceive their limits 'which do not constitute those of a body or an envelope, but the living edges of flesh opening' (PN: 301). Irigaray offers the image of the two lips to conceptualize those limits. The lips can open for creation and generation, in touching each other they represent women's subjective identity (*with* the mother), and in closing (as the lips of the mouth close in silence or to say the 'm' of 'mama' or 'maman') they represent women's home in the mother's absence. 'To take a woman's lips would be like taking the *fort-da* away from a man' (GP: 136; SP: 116). The woman is not protected by the mechanism of the *fort-da*, 'by the way in which it is constituted by divisions of time and space, the other, the self, by its phonetic divisions' (ibid.). The *fort-da* takes away from woman her subjective relation to her mother, and submits her to the economy of the male imaginary, whereas the mouth – and speaking (opening and closing the mouth) – has a different meaning for women, because of the other two lips which open or close in invitation or refusal. Although the ownership of the container is important to men – the paternal genealogy – the woman loses in this genealogy her own relationship to space-time. Sexual pleasure, Irigaray suggests in 'Questions to Emmanuel Levinas' is time. But not yet for women.

The mucous or mucosity   The mucous is related to the threshold, but is never theorized (PN: 302); perhaps one could say that the mucous represents the non-theorized. It corresponds to 'what is to be thought today' (E: 107) or sexual difference itself: 'the question to be thought in our era' (E: 13). For a number of reasons, it lends itself to the representation of the unthought: (a) it cannot be seen in the flat mirror, it is *interior*; (b) therefore it is more accessible to touch than to sight; (c) it is essential to the act of love, i.e. to exchange between the sexes; (d) it is always partly open (*entrouvert*); (e)it cannot be reduced to the maternal-feminine and the production of children; (f) it is not a part object, like the penis; it cannot be separated from the body, and so eludes the male imaginary which is perhaps 'exclusively dependent on organs?' (PN: 270); (g) it is neither simply solid nor fluid; (h) it is not stable, it expands, it has no fixed form; it expands, but not in a shape; (i) it cannot be swallowed (incorporated) or spat out; (j) it corresponds both to sexuality and to speech (the two pairs of lips). So, suggests Irigaray, what is unthought, and what we need to think, is the relationship of the mucous to the divine, for: 'this mucous, in its touching, in its properties, would hinder the transcendence of a God foreign to the flesh, of a God of immutable and stable truth' (E: 107).

The mucous is also related to air, because of the mouth's links with breathing, speaking and singing (E: 108). Air corresponds closely to a possible female imaginary; it is both mobile and immobile, permanent and flowing, with multiple temporal punctuations possible (OA: 15), and yet it is that of which the philosopher may remain permanently unaware (ibid.). Specifically in relation to speaking, it is the condition of the *parole*, that which punctuates the mother–daughter fusion: 'This *with her* . . . must tend to put speech *between* (them), lest they remain woven together, in an indissociable fusion' (GP: 134; SP: 113). And the little girl may speak or sing to her doll.

The between and *the angel*   It is not simply that women represent space and men represent time. Women represent aspects of time too, for example duration. Man 'cannot establish a duration of his self-love' (E: 73), because of the rhythms of his sexuality, and because of the parts of men's self that have been given to women for safe keeping. This particular organization of space-time is another way of describing an incomplete symbolic castration on the side of men – they are still linked by a kind of umbilical cord in an incestuous union with the mother, which in fact prevents real mobility for either men or women. The *between* is a way of rethinking this space-time organization which detaches it from the spatio-temporality of the phallus.

One way of seeing the angel is to see it as an alternative to the phallus. In psychoanalytic terms, the phallus has sometimes been thought of as that which 'goes between', creates a bridge between the two lovers (therefore women have penis envy). Irigaray comments that for men, since the woman has been incorporated, she is no longer separate, and so the phallus is suspended (OA: 86), not effecting the conjunction. In Heidegger's question of Being as copula, the ex-tase is erection or ejaculation (OA: 84), but women's space-time has been used for building the house of Being. In Heidegger's copula, as a result, there is no copulation. But this 'bridge', in Heideggerian terms (see OA: 33), organizes space; therefore, we could say, if it is imagined as a phallus, then space is organized in terms of the male body; the phallus punctuates the female space. Irigaray, in contrast, describes the 'between' as an 'interval', a 'process', 'becoming', 'mediation' and, crucially, 'love'. Love is the vehicle (E: 33) which permits the passage between, the passage to and fro between sensible and intelligible, mortal and immortal, above and below, immanent and transcendent. Instead of an abyss, or an enclosure which defines an inside and an outside, there should be a threshold, and the possibility of permanent passage in and out, to and fro, from the highest to the lowest, and back again. Men, as we saw, are said to achieve this through the rhythm of the *fort-da*. Women too need to move freely, they need an axis which grounds them in the earth and connects them to the heavens:

> What [women] do need is to stand centred about their own axis, an axis which passes microcosmically from their feet to the top of their head, macrocosmically from the centre of the earth to the centre of the sky. This axis is present in the iconographic traces left by traditions in which women are visible. It is on this axis that women find the condition of their territory, of the autonomy of their body and their flesh, and the possibility of an expanding jouissance. (GP: 134; SP:114)

'Penis envy' naturalizes what could be expressed in a different way, for example by the concept of the angel (E: 22–3), the messenger between earth and heaven, passing through boundaries (*clôtures*), always in movement.

The figure of Antigone appears again in this context. What paralyses Antigone in her becoming, in her act, is the law of the *one*:

> Antigone too needs to emerge from the domination, the empire of *one* law – in order to move in herself and in the universe as in a living house. It is important that life, blood, air, water and fire should be given back to her for her share, and not simply that she should be there to serve the cult of something which is already dead: individuals or laws. (E: 105–6)

Hegel's brother–sister couple, which we looked at in Chapter 5, replaces the 'amorous fertility' with a relationship in which the blood (the life, the passions) (the sexuality) have been left out, and in which *both* die. This couple, suggests Irigaray, is the 'substratum' of the family as it is conceptualized and put into practice even now (E: 113–14).

Women are nomadic; their 'living house' should move with them; they need to escape from the properties in which they have been legally confined by the paternal genealogy (PN: 266). But love, instead of being a space between, an angel, a vehicle, has been delegated to women (E: 73), and men, fearing their own dereliction, confine them – in the house, in the law, in their genealogy, cutting them off from access to their own space-time. Because men deal with their loss and dereliction by using the elements of 'nature' to build houses for themselves, they do not come to terms with their loss (OA: 72), and then they obscurely hate women for the unspoken and unacknowledged dependence, the shield that women provide against the confrontation with mortality. Men resist, therefore, being a container or envelope for women in the way that women represent a container for men:

> The taking place of the enjoyment [jouissance] of her, of *her* jouissance, which he could never assimilate to himself but in which he could only participate, that is the mourning which the thinker could not accomplish, unless he renounced the ownership of thought. Proposing himself, then, himself too, as the being in which she might find a space where what she might have to say could deploy itself. (OA: 83; see also OA: 38)

But this seems to them like the gulf of non-identity and death. So they block women's access to subjectivity for fear of what it might mean to them, and as a result, women are immobilized in their becoming, while men continue to reside comfortably in their sepulchre:

> The woman who enveloped man before his birth, until he could live outside her, finds herself encircled by a [langage] of places that she cannot conceive, and from which she cannot exit. (E: 94)

The mediator, the bridge, must either pass through generation (two sexes) or through God (E: 94), in order to ensure a 'reciprocal limitation' of container, so that one is not swallowed up for ever in the other.

The amorous exchange

The amorous exchange is not the exchange of commodities but a mode of ethical being. The horizon opened up by the woman's accession to her own space-time is that of fertility and creation. In speaking of the amorous exchange, Irigaray is at her most visionary and her most utopian. In order to become a woman, it seems, it is first necessary to rethink *all* the categories which structure our thought and experience. It is not just a question of inventing some new terms, but of a total symbolic redistribution. However, the imaginary intercourse she describes does not mean a kind of pre-established harmony between the sexes, and the end of conflict and aggression. Rather it is a new organization of the economy of the death drives. The division within the split self means that there will always be conflict to be negotiated, both internally and externally. In addition, each sex has its own interests, needs, and desires, and therefore represents limits to the interests, needs, and desires of the other sex. For example, the need of men to own the container, and their anxiety and fear of castration/death which this ownership palliates, conflicts with the need of women to move freely, or determine who enters their space or not. Women's needs for autonomy, freedom of movement, sexual self-determination, contraception, and abortion clash with male desire for their containment, enclosure, or control. What it does mean is that the other sex – the other woman – has an imaginary and symbolic existence, so that she cannot be incorporated any longer without awareness or acknowledgement. It means that each sex is alive, mobile, and fertile, and can grow/become, as in the passage we looked at in Chapter 3 from *Passions élémentaires:*

> [L]ove may be the motor of becoming which allows each its own growth ... each one must keep its body autonomous. Neither should be the source of the other. Two lives should embrace and fertilize each other, without the other being a preconceived goal for either. (PE: 32–3)

Although some of Irigaray's formulations seem to imply a kind of belief in a utopian future of peace and harmony, she is too aware of the death drives (women's as well as men's) not to underestimate the need for their symbolic organization, and its sometimes inevitable failure. So I think we cannot take her visions as literal accounts of an imagined ideal future. But on the other hand, psychoanalysis also recognizes moments of integration between different parts of the psyche; the unconscious may be a resource, and crossing boundaries in phantasy may have real and tangible results in the world. If the 'object' (the mother or woman) is living and engaging in intrapsychic intercourse, that means that the desire for mastery may be temporarily in abeyance, and the destructive or immobilizing phantasy has relaxed its grip. The language of amorous exchange is the language of phantasy; it offers an imaginary account of a different unconscious 'scene'. It should no doubt be seen as an ideal, a touchstone or horizon.

The following passage from 'Questions to Emmanuel Levinas' indicates, in sexual imagery, such a scene in which the woman will have come to be in her own right, with her own space and time. It is a vision of the 'fertility of the caress':

> He knows nothing of communion in pleasure [volupté]. Levinas does not ever seem to have experienced the transcendence of the other which becomes an immanent ecstasy [extase instante] in me and with him – or her. For Levinas, the distance is always maintained with the other in the experience of love. The other is 'close' to him in 'duality'. This autistic, egological, solitary love does not correspond to the shared outpouring, to the loss of boundaries which takes place for both lovers when they cross the boundary of the skin into the mucous membranes of the body, leaving the circle which encloses my solitude to meet in a shared space, a shared breath, abandoning the relatively dry and precise outlines of each body's solid exterior to enter a fluid universe where the perception

of being two persons [de la dualité] becomes indistinct, and above all, acceding to another energy, neither that of the one nor that of the other, but an energy produced together and as a result of the irreducible difference of sex. Pleasure between the same sex does not result in that immanent ecstasy between the other and myself. It may be more or less intense, quantitatively or qualitatively different, it does not produce in us that ecstasy which is our child, prior to any child. In this relation we are at least three, each of which is irreducible to any of the others: you, me and our creation [oeuvre], that ecstasy of ourself in us [de nous en nous], that transcendence of the flesh of one to that of the other, become ourself in us [devenue nous en nous], at any rate 'in me' as a woman, prior to any child. (QEL: 112–13)

In the light of the preceding discussion, we can now interpret, to a certain extent, this enigmatic passage. It seems to me to reproduce a divine trinity: 'we are at least three'. 'We' includes both sex and generation, but the child is 'according to the spirit' and does not have to be embodied in a real child for the exchange to be fertile. The 'immanent esctasy' is another formulation of the 'sensible transcendental'; it is both transcendent (ec-static – as in the structure of the male subject) and immanent (in-stante). The one does not exclude or incorporate the other; transcendence is represented by the 'flesh of the other', but each has an other, so each is transcendent and transcended, each is flesh. At the same time, each is immanent or present: crossing the boundary of the skin 'into the mucous membranes of the body', entering a 'fluid universe' where the divine is not 'foreign to the flesh'. The universe of the mucous is fluid: the stable universe of 'truth' becomes unstable. Love of the same, on the man's side, or on the woman's side, does not have the same quality as love of the other. It does not produce a child. The woman exists in her own right here, not through her children, since the children produced by this exchange are 'of the spirit'. Each is a 'subject' in love; each is transcendent to the other (each is divine for the other); each can confront the other with *admiration* (E: 75–84). (This does not, I think, imply that heterosexuality is superior to homosexuality as a practice, since the fertility Irigaray is describing is symbolic, 'of the spirit'; women or men together could merge in this creative way.) *Love*, the mediator, is a 'shared outpouring', a 'loss of boundaries', 'a shared space', 'a shared breath', bridging the space between two persons, two sexes; it does not *use* the body of the other for its *jouissance*; each is irreducible to the other or to the child. The loss of boundaries does not lead to a fusion in which one or the other disappears, but to a mutual crossing of boundaries which is creative, and yet where identity is not swallowed up.

The sensible transcendental, as we saw, the mediator in this exchange, can be called God (E: 94) or love (E: 33) or language: 'the feminine, in and through her language [langage] may, today, raise questions whose fertility is as yet unheard (of)' (E: 121). Stereotyped or dead language (E: 127) is opposed to living language, the dead God to a living God: 'resurrection or transfiguration of blood and flesh through their language and their ethic' (E: 124).

The amorous exchange represents in the most corporeal and the most intimate terms Irigaray's vision of the new world, deploying the erotico-transcendental vocabulary of mysticism, and the language of the imaginary body. It recasts the questions of Chapter 6 – identity, sacrifice, fertility, the god – in terms *both* of the sexual and sexuate body, *and* of the parousia or advent of the divine (the third era of the Spirit and the Bride), linking together the carnal (sensible) and the transcendental. It attempts to emerge from the immobility and stasis (death) of the solipsistic male subject to the mobility and fertility (life) of the couple. In the final chapter I want to take this sexuate corporeal vocabulary as a starting point, and make the links back to the social world again. The amorous exchange, it will be argued, is a phantasy of exchange in general, the basis of human society.

Chapter 8

Women and/in the social contract

The society we know, our own culture, is based upon the exchange of women. Without the exchange of women, we are told, we would fall back into the anarchy (?) of the natural world, the randomness (?) of the animal kingdom. The passage into the social order, into the symbolic order, into order as such, is assured by the fact that men, or groups of men, circulate women among themselves, according to a rule known as the incest taboo. (TS: 170; CS: 167)

If women are to accede to a different sort of social organization, they need a religion, a language, and either a currency of their own or a non-market economy. These three conditions go hand in hand. (WSM: 9; SP: 93)

A women's sociality is necessary for love and its cultural fertility to take place. This does not signify that women should enter the current systems of power as if they were men, but that women should establish new values corresponding to *their* creative capacities. (E: 70)

A world for women themselves. Which has both never existed and at the same time is already there, repressed, latent, potential. (E: 106)

[The availability of contraception and abortion] imply the possibility of *modifying women's social status*, and thus of modifying the modes of social relations between men and women. (TS: 84; CS: 80)

These gains [contraception and abortion] make it possible to raise again, differently, the question of what the social status of women might be – in particular through its differentiation from a simple reproductive-maternal function. But these contributions may always just as easily be turned against women. In other words, we cannot yet speak, in this connection, of a feminine politics, but only of certain conditions under which it may be possible. The first being an end to silence concerning the exploitation experienced by women: the systematic refusal to 'keep quiet' practiced by the liberation movements. (TS: 128; CS: 126)

> Patriarchal culture is a culture founded on sacrifice, crime, war. (SP: 200)
>
> 'Only a god can save us', writes Heidegger. (E: 123)

We have seen that, according to Irigaray, women are, in Hegelian terms, 'like plants' or in-itself (*en-soi*). However, one could also recontextualize the argument of the preceding three chapters in Rousseauistic terms by saying that for Irigaray, women are still, symbolically, in the 'state of nature' and need to be brought into the social contract.[1] (We can see from the remarks just quoted that the social order and the symbolic order are assimilated; structurally they are seen as equivalent.) In this concluding chapter, therefore, I want to make the case again, in yet another set of terms, for interpreting Irigaray's most apparently biological remarks about the female body as statements about the adequacy or inadequacy of the symbolic/social order and the place allotted to woman/women. My argument will be that for Irigaray, the social contract – that which transforms 'nature' into 'culture' – systematically excludes women, who are then left representing nature. Thus I will frame Irigaray with Rousseau, an author whom she hardly ever mentions, and yet who casts a long shadow over his descendants. I shall begin each section with an Irigarayan 'fiction': in the first section, the 'two lips', in the second and third sections, examples of Irigaray's mini-utopias, linking each of them to the social contract. Irigaray's position is that the fictions or myths of a society indicate representationally how that society is structured and organized at other levels.[2] I will suggest at the end that Irigaray's myths or utopias are attempts to construct new fictions, to anticipate and perhaps assist the birth of a new social order, or the parousia mentioned at the end of Chapter 6.

What we have seen throughout this study is that Irigaray is dealing with a single problem, in its multiple aspects: the absence of and exclusion of woman/women from the symbolic/social order, and their representation as nature. This problem is reworked and restated over and over again, in a variety of discursive formulations, in terms borrowed from a variety of philosophers, and in relation to a wide range of different conceptual systems. In each case, Irigaray elaborates sets of interweaving terms: the realm of the semblance, the gold standard, hom(m)osexuality, sacrifice and fertility, the god, the sensible transcendental and so on, all of them borrowed and put to new purposes. In this concluding chapter I want to make a link between the corporeal/sexual vocabulary and the vocabulary of the social and economic domains, thus connecting representationally what might otherwise be seen as different levels of explanation.

The patriarchal contract

The discussion of female sexuality in *This Sex* is often taken as a naturalistic account of female sexuality, an essentialist picture of what women's sexuality is really, or could really be, like. Irigaray is thought to be positing a real body, unmediated by the symbolic order, which women might recognize as their own. The essentialist picture has been sharply criticized, and the critique has often focused on the image of the two lips, and the inference that language, or women's language, should be a direct expression of the non-symbolized body. For example, Janet Sayers claims that for Irigaray, 'femininity . . . is essentially constituted by female biology, by the "two lips" of the female sex' (1982: 131). The problem of the literalist reading is exemplified by Kate McCluskie, who stands Irigaray on her head and suggests that Irigaray is putting forward an 'anatomical determinism' which rules out the need for language (in fact the *reverse* of Irigaray's main thesis): '[Irigaray] is able to deny the need for language . . . there is no need for the symbolic substitution which language provides'; and she expostulates that 'to relinquish that function of language would be to return to the ghetto of inarticulate female intuition' (McCluskie 1983: 57–8). Like Sayers, McCluskie focuses on the 'two lips' which seem to prove a stumbling block for many readers. Kaja Silverman, for example, whose analyses elsewhere are both subtle and original, falls back on this literalist reading of Irigaray and concludes:

> What Irigaray advances here . . . is the notion of a language which would be 'adequate for the [female] body', a language capable of coexisting with that body as closely as the two lips of the vulva coexist. This is the obverse of the linguistic model proposed by Lacan, which stresses the incommensurability of signifier and body, the loss of the latter constituting the price which must be paid for access to the former. It is also, to my way of thinking, an impossible paradigm, one which attempts to deny the fundamentally arbitrary relation of language to the referent. (Silverman 1988: 144)

This reading too depends upon the literal extrapolation of the two lips to female language. Counter-readings of the 'two lips' can be found elsewhere, and I will give a range of examples to illustrate how the 'two lips' can be read as representation of whatever interpretation of Irigaray the interpreter wishes to highlight (as I shall myself read them in this chapter; what is interesting is the range of different interpretations which the image supports).

There is an obvious flaw in the literalist reading, as Jan Montefiore points out: 'this metaphor of the "two lips" is *not* a definition of women's identity in biological terms; the statement that they are "continually interchanging" must make it clear that Irigaray is not talking about literal biology' (Montefiore 1987: 149). So several interpreters insist that the 'two lips' should be seen as a discursive strategy. Carolyn Burke explains clearly that: 'The lips of "When Our Lips Speak Together", for example, should not be reduced to a literally anatomical specification, for the figure suggests another mode, rather than another model. It implies plurality, multiplicity, and a mode of being "in touch" that differs from the phallic mode of discourse' (Burke 1981: 303). For Jane Gallop and Elizabeth Grosz, it is a question of a poetics of the body, devices of writing and representation, 'whose function is *inter-discursive* rather than referential. In short, Irigaray is not outlining the *truth* of female sexuality or the makeup of the world. She is creating a discourse to contest or combat other prevailing discourses' (Grosz 1986c: 9). Gallop points out that despite the referential illusion, anatomical reference is never an unmediated reflection, even in phallomorphic discourse, and that one might perhaps see the 'two lips' as a healing metaphor (Gallop 1983: 81), loosening the rigidity of phallomorphic logic.

Other interpreters see the 'two lips' as more of a 'struggle concept', produced specifically to combat Lacanian theory. Rosi Braidotti suggests that the image of the two lips is 'chosen for its value of metaphorical subversion, in response to the Lacanian image of the black hole' (Braidotti 1981: 373, quoted in Morris 1988: 49). Diana Fuss makes a similar point: 'Irigaray's production of an apparently essentializing notion of female sexuality functions strategically as a reversal and displacement of Lacan's phallomorphism' (Fuss 1989: 66). The two lips, by shifting the focus from sight to touch, challenge Lacan's obsession with veiling (ibid.: 67). So Fuss sees it as a question of the symbolization of the imaginary, rather than a question of biology: 'The symbolization of the female imaginary is precisely what Irigaray seeks to elaborate through her conceptualization of the two lips' (ibid.). A further interpretative possibility is to see the 'two lips' as a deconstructive concept, perhaps as an undecidable. This move is made in another article by Elizabeth Grosz:

> The two lips can be seen as the third movement in the process of deconstruction – the creation of a third term occupying an *impossible middle ground* of binary oppositions. This third term simultaneously participates in both categories of the opposition, defying the demand for one *or* other. Such an image demonstrates that what had been conceived oppositionally – the distinction between clitoris and vagina, one and two, inside and outside, visible and invisible – need not be regarded oppositionally. Rather, such oppositions may be seen as, for example, poles within a continuum. (Grosz 1986d: 76)

Anna Munster appears to take a similar line when she writes that the two lips are 'a strategic representation defying the logic of definition and identity' (Munster 1986: 121). It is also possible to see the 'two lips' in terms of feminist politics, as well as deconstruction. This is Mary Jacobus's interpretation: 'The lips that speak together (the lips of female lovers) are here imagined as initiating a dialogue, not of conflict or reunion ... but of mutuality, lack of boundaries, continuity' (Jacobus 1986: 78; see also 281, 282). This interpretation also allows for the possibility that one pair of lips (the labia) can stand for the other pair (the mouth) and vice versa, as Irigaray often suggests.

Irigaray herself, in 1977, insists that it is a question of discourse and representation, not of nature:

> To seek to discover-rediscover a possible imaginary for women through the movement of two lips re-touching . . . does not mean a regressive recourse to anatomy or to a concept of 'nature', nor a recall to genital order – women have more than one pair of two lips! Rather it means to open up the autological and tautological circle of systems of representation and their discourse so that women may speak (of) their sex [parler leur sexe]. (PN: 272)

So rather than focusing on biology, I think we need to look at how the 'two lips' work within Irigaray's discursive system. To put it as succinctly as possible: biology (or nature) must receive a symbolic mediation which is more adequate for women. We saw in the last chapter that the imaginary representation and phenomenology or lived experience of a woman's body will be different from that of a man's body. This difference needs to be *represented* so that women exist as such in systems of representation, and *a fortiori* so that women have a distinct legal, civil, and ethical status. But while rejecting the literalist reading of the 'two lips', I also find the postmodernist reading limited. Although I would accept the point that a discursive representation can support any number of interpretations, at the same time however, I think that the context of Irigaray's writing does not allow us to see the 'two lips' simply as a representation of postmodernist plurality. There is nothing automatically feminist about postmodernism, which as often as not continues to confuse women with the 'feminine'. By linking the 'two lips' to the aim of transforming the social contract, I want to offer an interpretative 'closure' which reclaims the image for a specifically feminist reading.

For many modern thinkers, the symbolic contract (that is, the possibility of exchange in general, in whatever register: linguistic, interpersonal, mercantile and so on) and the social contract (the passage from 'nature' to 'culture') are inseparable, although the theoretical accounts vary. The two orders may be thought to be in a relation of mutual causality, or of structural isomorphism; or it may be argued that one presupposes the other, or even that one *is* in some sense the other.[3] Jean-Joseph Goux, who argues for structural isomorphism, suggests that it is possible to see the symbolic function as the condition of symbolic exchange in general, while the process of symbolization is the consequence of socialization (1973: 26). What is generally agreed, however, whether this is seen as reprehensible or as inevitable, is the patriarchal nature of the contract. This is the framework, then, within which I shall situate Irigaray in this chapter; I shall interpret the 'two lips' as an image for what has been left out of the social/symbolic contact. The modern interpretations of the social contract which I shall look at briefly here, whether defending the contract or exposing it, appeal both to political and to psychoanalytic theory, in order to show its patriarchal nature. (I am following here Irigaray's definition of patriarchy: 'an exclusive respect for the genealogy of sons and fathers, and the competition between brothers' (SP: 202).) They bring into focus the sexual division of labour upon which the contract depends.

In Rousseau's theory, we are first (in the *Discourse on the Origins of Inequality*) shown human beings in an original state of complete (natural) freedom in which they are isolated, atomistic, unrelated, radically asocial individuals who are none the less autonomous, self-sufficient, independent, and happy. They have no needs that cannot be satisfied, and those needs are very few. At some point, however, the state of nature gives way to a kind of primitive society. As Rousseau outlines the stages of development or degeneration, first there is a kind of pastoral golden age, based on the family and a primitive division of labour in which individuals give up some of their early independence and autonomy for the pleasures of human companionship; then there is an inevitable process of degeneration, in which the strong and powerful take advantage of their strength to become successively wealthy, then politically powerful; finally there is a stage of complete despotism. (The familial – patriarchal – division of labour has been smuggled in at a very early stage; it is neither to be found in the original state of nature, nor is it instituted by the social contract; the social contract merely subsumes it, so that it is surreptitiously included without ever being put into question.) In *The Social Contract*, Rousseau suggests a way out of the despotic 'second state of nature', by means of a contract whereby we all give up some of our freedom for the benefits conferred on us by a community. This leads to the apparent reversal of his earlier position, and the statement that freedom consists in obedience to the law that one has prescribed for oneself: 'for to be driven by appetite alone is slavery, and obedience to the law that one has prescribed for oneself is freedom' (*The Social Contract*, 1_9). This reversal of the earlier definition of freedom marks the passage from nature to culture which is necessarily fictional.

In her book, *The Sexual Contract* (1988), Carole Pateman sets out to show that the social contract, that fiction which inaugurated liberal theory and the notion of civil society, is a patriarchal construct. Peopled by individuals who freely enter into contractual arrangements with each other, it conceals, beneath the civil contractual order, a patriarchal sexual contract which gives men access to women: 'contract is far from being opposed to patriarchy; contract is the means through which modern patriarchy is constituted' (1988: 2). The concept of the 'individual' itself is a patriarchal construct; the individual is in fact male: women are not among the individuals party to the contract. The contract which founds civil society depends upon the separation between the public (male) realm, and the private realm to which women are relegated. The construction of sexual difference is thus essential to this form of civil society. Pateman argues that sexual difference is politically relevant: 'To argue that patriarchy is best confronted by endeavouring to render sexual difference politically irrelevant is to accept the view that the civil (public) realm and the "individual" are uncontaminated by patriarchal subordination' (p.17). To understand the other side of the story, the side that has been left out, the sexual contract which the social contract conceals, Pateman argues that we need to turn to another fiction, the account in Freud's *Moses and Monotheism* of the pact made by the brothers after the murder of the father. According to Pateman, this pact is also a sort of fictional contract, which could more appropriately be termed a sexual contract. Freud's 'state of nature' is the primal horde; what his pact institutes is a society of brothers based on the incest taboo (rather than on a contract per se); what it ensures is men's *access to women.*

Pateman's account is helpful here because it is situating itself more explicitly than Irigaray's with reference to social contract theory. I'm not sure if Irigaray ever mentions the term 'social contract'; and in fact she draws much more readily on Hegel, an anti-contract theorist,[4] than on the theory of social contract. What Pateman's account shows is that the conclusions which both Irigaray and Pateman draw – that the citizen is always in fact male; that women have to become 'men' in order to become citizens; that the social pact is a pact between brothers (or a hom(m)osexual pact) – can usefully and illuminatingly be interpreted in the light of the social contract and its modern variations.

This becomes even clearer when we look at a political interpretation of Lacan (who *is* important to Irigaray) as a modern incarnation of social contract theory, however unlikely that may appear initially. An extended interpretation along these lines can be found in Juliet Flower MacCannell's book *Figuring Lacan* (1986). MacCannell reads Lacan in the light of political theory – Rousseau, Kant, Hegel, Marx – in order to find a unifying factor in his otherwise 'anti-system' system, and identifies that unifying factor with what Lacan calls the 'forms of the social tie' (in Mitchell and Rose 1982: 152–3). In fact there seems to be some agreement between his commentators that for Lacan the symbolic order is a symbolic contract equivalent to the social contract.[5] Although such a position is not uncontroversial, I shall leave the arguments aside here, as I am primarily concerned to display the internal logic of Irigaray's texts, which assume, I think, an isomorphism between symbolic and social.

MacCannell converts the terminology of the social contract into Lacanian terms; the state of nature becomes the imaginary; civil society becomes the symbolic. Thus, she writes:

Hegel, like Rousseau before him, had shown how, with the power arrangement of the master and slave and their co-dependence, inter-human relationships move from the imaginary, the realm of prestige and the opinion of the other, into the symbolic; from the forms of 'love, contract, collaboration, passion and even the social contract . . .' to the forms of 'struggle and work' ([Lacan *Séminaire*] *I*, xviii: 248, 'L'Ordre symbolique'.) All that social life had possessed of an imaginary dimension (what Lacan calls the 'love-link') is converted into the symbolic of a law, a law imposed on the slave. (MacCannell 1986: 7)

In Lacan's version of the social contract, 'symbol means pact' (Lacan 1977: 61; 1966: 272). The symbolic is founded on a pact – a Word – or act of mutual recognition which defuses or sublimates the potentially murderous aggression of the imaginary or mirror stage.[6] David Macey in his recent book on Lacan comments that: 'Lacan's Word-as-pact can thus be translated into phenomenological terms as a discursive mode which permits recognition of the other and Being-with by re-enacting the establishment of a primordial pact' (Macey 1988: 148). Further, Lacan's account of this pact makes it clear that it is patriarchal: 'the symbolic order is, in its initial workings, androcentric. This is a fact' (Lacan 1978: 303).

MacCannell links Lacan's description of the entry into the symbolic order with political theory:

This mini-version of the founding of civil society as the founding of the form of individuation, with its dialectic of dependence on the presence of others whom one opposes to found one's own identity and of the simultaneous desire for independence from them [. . .] can also be read in Rousseau and Marx. (MacCannell 1986: 64)

Lacan's version of the Oedipus complex as the entry into language and into the symbolic order depends upon a sacrifice, and upon a metaphorical promise of future substitutive gratifications for the pleasures that have been renounced. But, MacCannell says:

the promise culture makes is never kept. The human forsakes the simple, combinatory (in structural terms, metonymic) mode, love *in* the familiar form, for the metaphorical promise of free and future combinations. But the promise is never kept. (p.69) [. . .] . . . the role that Oedipus enables us to play is not what it promised, that of our becoming members of a *community*, outside the family, in which we would be offered, in exchange for familial *eros*, the pleasure of being with others, 'combining with' them, according to the law. Culture promises such 'combinatories': 'love', 'procreation' . . . . Without these promises, would we devote our energies and defer our pleasures to 'civilisation'? (p.79)

From the point of view of political theory (Pateman), the social contract conceals the sexual contract, which is a contract between men giving them access to women. But Lacan adds a new twist to this story, by claiming that in fact there is no sexual relation and all that we have is a purely fraternal relation of hom(m)osexuality. From the point of view of Lacanian psychoanalysis, the Oedipus complex, seen as the 'form of the social tie', based upon common unhappiness, instinctual renunciation, and sacrifice, is fuelled by the *promise* of heterosexuality and access to women. But in fact, Lacan says, woman does not exist, and the promise is not kept.

We should now interpret 'woman does not exist' as: 'women are not parties to the social/symbolic contract'; in Irigarayan terms, they are outside the symbolic order, which they can enter only 'as men'; in Rousseauistic terms, they remain in the pre-contractual state of nature. (This is not the primordial state of nature, but that intermediate stage, prior to the social contract, in which the strong and powerful have taken advantage of the weak to foist upon them a contract which only empowers the powerful even more.)

In Lacan's version, the metonymic mode has to be sacrificed for the metaphorical substitution. So, taking the 'two lips' as a figure for metonymy, let us look in the next section at Irigaray's counter-version of the social/symbolic contract and the nature of the sacrifice.

Metaphor and metonymy: the symbolic division

First of all, here is Irigaray's alternative account of Rousseau's 'golden age', in which the metonymic mode replaces Rousseau's more patriarchal fiction:

> There was a time when mother and daughter were the figure of a natural and social model. This couple was the guardian of the fertility of nature in general and of the relations to the divine. At this time, food consisted of the fruits of the earth. The mother–daughter couple ensured the safeguard of human nourishment and the site of the oracular word. This couple protected the memory of the past: at that time the daughter respected her mother and her genealogy. It also concerned itself with the present: food was produced from the earth in calm and peace. Foresight for the future existed thanks to the relation of women to the divine, to the oracular word.
>
> Were men harmed by this organisation? No. In this respect for life, for love, for nature, neither of the two sexes was destroyed by the other. The two sexes loved each other, without needing the institution of marriage, without being required to have children – which has never suppressed reproduction – without taboos on sex or the body.
>
> This is probably what monotheistic religions narrate to us as the myth of earthly paradise. This myth corresponds to centuries of history known today as prehistory, primitive eras, etc. Those who lived in these so-called archaic times were perhaps more cultivated than we are. (SP: 206)

To understand this fiction, we need to look at the two terms *metaphor* and *metonymy*, to see what connotations and meanings they carry.

The meaning of metaphor and metonymy, two familiar figures of speech, has become vastly expanded and inflated in the wake of post-Saussurean linguistics and the theories indebted to the latter – Lévi-Strauss's anthropology, Lacan's work, and so on. In the 1950s Roman Jakobson appropriated them in a new way (see Jakobson 1962) in his essay on aphasia. He identified two types of aphasia. One type of aphasic patient suffered from deficiencies in the axis of substitution (that is, the ability to use meta-language, giving definitions, using words out of context and so on) while being able to string sentences together; the other type of aphasic suffered from deficiencies in the axis of combination, being unable to deal with syntax and sentence construction, but still deploying a range of words which could be substituted for each other (although sentences became monosyllabic or telegraphic). Jakobson mapped the axis of substitution/selection on to metaphor, and the axis of combination on to metonymy. He also pointed out (and this will become relevant later) that whereas the axis of substitution is dependent on the *code* (i.e. the complete linguistic system as a whole), and limited by certain constraints or rules governing the type of word which can be substituted, the axis of combination is related to *context*: although some constraints remain (word order, for example), it gives the possibility of limitless and open-ended combinations. The stock of words which can be selected from the code, although large, is finite; the stock of possible sentences is more or less infinite. Substitutions, then, are finite; they draw upon the available lexical stock; neologisms, for example, can only be introduced slowly. Combinations, on the other hand, are infinite.

Jakobson suggests that a link can be made between mechanisms of the unconscious, described by Freud, and the two linguistic axes of substitution and combination. Thus, relations of contiguity become a form of displacement (metonymy) or condensation (synecdoche), while relations of similarity become identification and symbol (Jakobson 1962: 878–9).

Following Jakobson, and conflating Freud, Saussure, and Jakobson, Lacan in turn appropriates the terms metaphor and metonymy, but redistributes the links that Jakobson had made, so that metonymy is now linked to displacement and the fetish, while metaphor is linked to condensation and the analytic symptom. However, Lacan's appropriations are notoriously idiosyncratic (see Macey 1988: 156 ff.; Ford 1985), and in a rather grandiose way, metaphor and metonymy come to characterize the human condition, and to bear the weight of a whole metaphysics of the subject.

There are in fact several associated pairs of concepts at work (see the top half of the chart on p.179). The most basic pair is probably the one defined by relations of similarity and contiguity. One can also distinguish condensation and displacement (i.e. a conceptual pair derived from psychoanalytic theory); metaphor and metonymy (deriving from rhetoric); and paradigm and syntagm (a conceptual pair from linguistic theory). A final pair is system and discourse. The paradigm, or the code, is equivalent to the system, i.e. the lexical stock from which one selects alternatives; the syntagm, the context, is the level of discourse and the creation of new sentences. But mapping these pairs on to each other is a conceptual leap; it is not something which goes without saying (Silverman 1983); the pairs are not precisely symmetrical. For example, in the case of displacement in the dream work, one can find instances of similarity as well as of contiguity. And condensation, although predominantly based on similarity, exploits contiguity as well (Silverman 1983, ch. 3).[7]

Irigaray's use of terms is no more rigorous than Lacan's. She uses them associatively rather than systematically – so that they bring with them a whole set of conceptual associations without being reducible to the the constraints of any of the conceptual systems from which they are borrowed. In addition, she complicates the picture, by adding a few more pairs of her own: male/female; sacrifice/fertility, substitution/contiguity, identification and genealogy.

similarity	contiguity
metaphor	metonymy
condensation	displacement
paradigm	syntagm
system	discourse
code	context
finite	infinite

Lacan	*Irigaray*
male	female
sacrifice	fertility
substitution	contiguity
↓	↓
identification	identification
paternal genealogy	maternal genealogy

Her use of these terms is quite coherent; she does not, for example switch sides. But it would be mistake to interpret any of them strictly in terms of the original conceptual frameworks (Freud, Jakobson, Lacan etc.) from which they are derived. (And, as already noted, Jakobson and Lacan, for example, do not agree on which side certain terms are to go.) She is staking out a symbolic territory on behalf of women.

Now Lacan, notoriously conservative, emphasizes the *code*, which is the domain of constraint: one is born into the symbolic order, one assumes it in order to become human, and Lacan seems to offer remarkably few possibilities for changing it in any way. Irigaray emphasizes the *context*, the possibility of limitless combination, a new syntax of culture which is creative and open-ended. Metaphor or predication fixes; the metonymic allows for process. (Here one can see an example of Irigaray's reclaiming of the symbolic and reconceptualization of the feminine, from its pre-Socratic version to its post-structuralist avatars. In the Pythagorean table of opposites mentioned in Chapter 3, the feminine was that which was limitless, without boundaries; in Derrida's *Spurs*, the feminine is contextualization carried to infinity and the open-endedness of all meaning. The limitless and the open-ended, seen in the light of the table of opposites shown on p.179, now take on the connotations of creative possibility, new social combinations, and social/symbolic change or innovation.)

In Lacan's economy, the founding sacrifice which underlies the social order is a relation of metaphor and substitution. It is the male position in the Oedipus complex, the instinctual renunciation made by the boy, and the identification with the father. What about the girl's relation to her mother? Irigaray is suggesting, on the maternal side, a different economy which would be metonymical, dependent on contiguity or association, in which fertility would take the place of sacrifice. The two lips, then, figure a different economy, in which the two (mother and daughter) are not *identified* in a movement of metaphoric substitution, but *contiguous*: they touch, or associate, or combine. Whereas the paternal genealogy is based on metaphoric identification, the maternal genealogy is, or could be, based on metonymic identification. What Irigaray is describing in the controversial descriptions in *This Sex* is the metonymic or contiguous, that which touches, associates, or combines. This is the context in which we need to understand expressions such as these:

> As for woman, she touches herself in and of herself without any need for mediation. . . . Woman 'touches herself' all the time, and moreover no one can forbid her to do so, for her genitals are formed of two lips in continuous contact [qui s'embrassent continûment]. (TS: 24; CS: 24)

> The *one* of form, of the individual, of the (male) sexual organ, of the proper name, of the proper meaning . . . supplants, while separating and dividing, that contact of *at least two* (lips) which keeps woman in touch with herself, but without any possibility of distinguishing what is touching from what is touched. (TS: 26; CS: 26)

> For if 'she' says something, it is not, it is already no longer, identical with what she means. What she says is never identical with anything, moreover; rather it is contiguous [contigu]. *It touches (upon)*. (TS: 29; CS: 28)

Contiguity, then, is a figure for the vertical and horizontal relationships between women, the maternal genealogy and the relation of sisterhood (since there are two pairs of two lips, of which one pair – the mouth – can be seen as horizontal, and the other pair – the labia – as vertical, each representing each other). It stands for women's sociality, love of self on the woman's side, the basis for a different form of social organization and a different economy.

Lacan links metonymy with *desire*, with the unconscious. Like the family in Rousseau's pastoral scene, the metonymic is incorporated as the basis for the contract between men. It is clear that Irigaray associates the domain of metaphor with the male economy and the paternal genealogy. The replacement of one metaphor with another is not what Irigaray has in mind; this is made quite clear in *This Sex*:

> But if [women's] aim were simply to reverse the order of things, even supposing this to be possible, history would repeat itself in the long run, would revert to sameness: to phallocratism. It would leave room neither for women's sexuality, nor for women's imaginary, nor for women's language to take (their) place. (TS: 33; CS: 32)[8]

What she is trying to conceptualize is the double syntax, the possibility of a relationship between *two* economies, of which one would be metaphorical (the paternal one) and one would be metonymical (the maternal one).

However, the term *contiguity* covers a broader area than the metonymic relations between women. When we look at how the term is used in *Speculum*, we see that contiguity is associated with the contiguity of parental intercourse. It is not only the metonymic relation of mother and daughter, but also the metonymic relation of mother and father. In *Speculum*, metaphor is what prevents contiguity, what cuts off/cuts out the maternal, leaving only one parental figure, the father, and only one genealogy, the paternal one. (This connection is obscured by the English translation which does not always translate contiguity literally.)

> But the genealogical conception [contiguïté généalogique] has been broken [tranchée]. The child ... will be cut off from any remaining empirical relation with the womb [le matriciel]. (SE: 293; SF: 365–6)

> Thus the orbit of the cave organized into cinematography everything that had been left outside its enclosure: the *hystera protera*. Other excess [outrance] to language. But these two 'terms' to the logic of discourse cannot/can no longer be related. A whole system of kinship – that is, in this case, of analogy – makes contact [contiguïté] between them impracticable. *The economy of metaphor that is in control keeps them apart* [écarte leur conjonction]. (SE: 346; SF: 434)[9]

By cutting off the maternal genealogy, metaphor also cuts off the possibility of the sexual relation. In this light we should interpret the statement: 'The division of labour prevents them from making love' (TS: 28; CS: 26), another reformulation of Lacan's dictum that the sexual relation does not exist. The Oedipal metaphor and organization of society cuts off so effectively the man from the woman/mother, that the two sexes do not meet or touch at all.

A further consequence for women is that women are forced by the patriarchal contract into becoming rivals. Girls learn to turn away from and even hate their mothers. As the woman is inserted into the male economy she, like men, learns to objectify her mother, take her mother as an object. As we saw in Chapter 2, this has consequences for women's identity. In so far as a woman identifies with her mother, she is forced to take herself as an object too: 'She cannot reduce her mother to an object without reducing herself to an object likewise because they are of the same sex' (SP: 210). By conceptualizing relations between women in terms of the two lips, Irigaray is proposing a metonymic, subject-to-subject relationship between women, based on contiguity or metonymic identification, but no longer outside discourse, outside the symbolic where Lacan places the metonymic. In this way, the two can be seen as together yet separate; both the girl and her mother can be separate beings, while remaining in relationship. The woman does not have to oust her mother in order to be. Hence Irigaray's stress on the word *with*:

> The mother agrees to be fertile *with her daughter*. (WSM: 9; SP: 93)

> These *like you, me too, I'm more (or less), like everybody else* do not have much relation to an ethic of love. They are the traces-symptoms of the *polemos* [struggle] between women. No *with you* [avec toi] in this economy. (E: 102)

> In sum, to free ourselves *with our mothers*. (CAC: 86; my emphasis)[10]

Under the regime of metaphor, there is the *place* of the mother, but so long as there is no maternal genealogy, and so long as the symbolic does not distinguish between mother and woman, it is a place which women have to fight over. Every woman then has to take the place of the mother in an aggressive rivalry that allows no possibility of the *with*. In this economy women are forced into substitution and hate for the mother (E: 100). Contiguity, on the other hand, allows for multiplicity, but on the woman's side. It is not that dissemination of the subject, or that sexual multiplicity which is a conceptualization from the male side, but a multiplicity which allows for subject-to-subject relations between women. So the 'two lips' or contiguity is the condition *both* of sexual difference (and thus of the sexual relation) *and* of a female homosexual economy. It stands for what is left outside the social contract, and the hidden unspoken underside of the contract between men.

Irigaray insists that patriarchy is built upon sacrifice, of which the primordial sacrifice is fertility. What has been sacrificed to the patriarchal economy is women's relationships with their mothers and daughters and with each other. Yet we cannot go back to the time of the myth, so the question which remains is that of creating or restoring a sociality based upon fertility rather than on sacrifice: 'How can we affirm together these elementary values, these natural fertilities, how can we celebrate them and turn them into currency while becoming or remaining women?' (WSM: 11; SP: 95).

This should not be misread as an injunction to go home and have children ('be fruitful and multiply'). As we saw in the Irigarayan myth (p.177), women should not be 'required to have children' (SP: 206). On the contrary it is a picture which allows women an identity *distinct* from motherhood. Here again the myth of Antigone is a resonant one; Antigone's story can be reinterpreted to stand for women's right to a distinct and separate *civil* identity (TD: 81–7). So *fertility* should be read, in terms of the table, as a counter-term to *sacrifice*, to indicate the possibility of a different mode of social organization in which women's difference is represented, symbolized, and codified.

This makes sense of all the things that Irigaray says about equality. If the social contract is based on a pact, in which fraternity is *constituted by* the exclusion of women from the fraternity, and access to women as objects of pleasure or exchange, then:

1. There is no place for women to be inserted into that contract, except as pseudo-men, so that demands for equality are profoundly misleading. What could equality mean?
2. Women need a sociality or solidarity of their own in order to resist that contract which works by separating women: 'all the norms of existing culture and society . . . rest . . . on the separation between women (E: 103).[11]
3. That solidarity cannot be based on anything *equivalent* to male fraternity, which would merely substitute one metaphorical order for another.
4. That solidarity or association has to be on a different basis: a metonymical form of association based on contiguity and the relation between women as subjects, that is, women who love themselves and each other.
5. This relationship *must* become a symbolic and cultural one. Metonymy must be brought into the sphere of discourse. 'Woman must be able to put herself into words, into images and symbols, within that inter-subjective relation with her mother, then with other women' (SP: 211). Simple contiguity is not sufficient. (This is a point which Irigaray would now emphasize strongly.) It must be translated into public and social forms.

A precipitate political involvement is always in danger of reproducing the same structure. Irigaray's feminism, then, is not primarily a political question of *emancipation* (which she sees as a question linked to the master–slave dialectic), but a question of symbolic change (though the two are not necessarily exclusive, since the first can be a precondition of the second, and vice versa). But the symbolic is put before the political in order to avoid a simple reproduction of the status quo. What typifies other independence movements is that they are all – potentially – in the same game (SP: 201), that of master and slave, i.e. in a reversible relationship in which each party can potentially become the other. What is different for Irigaray about the male–female relationship is that there is a sense in which it is *essentially* not reversible; one can never take the place of the other, either ethically or symbolically. In order to prevent sexual difference from being neutralized yet again, Irigaray argues that women-among-themselves should invent new forms of social organization which embody in a public form the metonymical subject-to-subject relations between women:

> . . . women merely 'equal' to men would be 'like them', therefore not women. Once more the difference between the sexes would be in that way cancelled out; ignored, papered over. So it is essential for women among themselves to invent new modes of organization, new forms of struggle, new challenges. The various liberation movements have already begun to do this, and a 'women's international' is beginning to take shape. But here too innovation is necessary: institutions, hierarchy, and authority, – that is, the existing forms of politics – are men's affairs. Not ours. (TS: 166; CS: 160) [12]

For this reason, Irigaray is more interested in right(s) (*droit*) than in power. And this is a concern which has been present from *Speculum* onwards. As I argued in Chapter 5, she does not regard philosophy in general (epistemology, metaphysics and so on) and right as dissociable. I suggested that in 'Plato's *Hystera*', Irigaray argues that the patriarchal family is written into Plato's metaphysics (SE: 301; SF: 375). Similarly in the section on Freud, she spells out the details of the sexual contract:

> The marriage contract will often have been *implicitly a work contract*, but one that is not ratified as such by law, thereby depriving woman of her right to perfectly legitimate social demands: salary, work hours, vacations etc. . . . . As well as being an undeclared work contract, the marriage contract will also have disguised *a purchase agreement for the body and sex of the wife*. (SE: 121; SF: 151)

So that equal rights may well be the first condition for the question of specific women's rights to be raised at all: 'Nonetheless, women have to advance to those same privileges (and to sameness perhaps) before any consideration can be given to the differences that they might give rise to' (SE: 119; SF: 149). But at the same time, she emphasizes: 'how can one participate in social exchange, when one has no available currency?' (SE: 119; SF: 149) (when one *is* the currency?). So it is necessary to distinguish between rights in the short term and rights in the long term.

The question she is now asking is: how to turn what she calls *fertility* into currency. There is no suggestion that women's sociality is a natural state. It needs to be mediated by the social/symbolic order, translated into rights and duties which are specific to women and concern their own bodies, and their children. Irigaray now thinks that the price paid for equal rights in an otherwise untransformed society can be too high, and is currently working with women in the Italian Communist Party to consider what kind of social order could encompass women's difference while admitting them to full participation as citizens.[13]

However, the point I want to make here is this. Myth or fiction is not simply, for Irigaray, a *reflection* of social organization, it also gives a shaping force to the conceptualization of rights and citizenship. The symbolic order is not a passive terrain on which different interest groups battle to make their mark. It is itself engaged in those battles. Plato's fiction is not just an expression of Ancient Greek class or sexual warfare; it actively contributes to women's exclusion from full citizenship. For Irigaray, it is a question of 'interpreting in a different way the impact of symbolic social labor in the analysis of relations of production' (TS: 191; CS: 185). I suggest, then, that it is in this light that we should read her fictions, whether the figure of the 'two lips' or the mini-utopias. What Irigaray is trying to offer or create is (a) images of the metonymic couple constituted by the mother and daughter, and (b) images of a creative parental couple. They are not literally social or political scenarios, but symbolic accounts, counter-myths to oppose the symbolic metaphors which relegate women to nature or to the unconscious and refuse to acknowledge the existence of, or the debt to, the maternal part of the couple. So in the final section I want to consider this point in relation to the figure of *exchange*. Although this is an apparently economic term, foregrounded by Irigaray rather than the more common emphasis on *production*, I shall suggest that it is also a figure for social/symbolic relationship in general.

Social/symbolic exchange

But what if these 'commodities' refused to go to 'market'? What if they maintained 'another' kind of commerce, among themselves?

Exchanges without identifiable terms, without accounts, without end. . . . Without additions and accumulations, one plus one, woman after woman. Without sequence or number. Without standard or yardstick [étalon]. *Red blood* [sang rouge] and *sham* [semblant] would no longer be differentiated by deceptive envelopes concerning their worth. Use and exchange would be indistinguishable. The greatest value would be at the same time the least kept in reserve. Nature's resources would be expended without depletion, exchanged without labour, freely given, exempt from masculine transactions: enjoyment without a fee, well-being without pain, pleasure without possession. As for all the strategies and savings, the appropriations tantamount to theft and rape, the laborious accumulation of capital, how ironic all that would be.

Utopia? Perhaps. Unless this mode of exchange has undermined commerce from the beginning. While *compulsory incest in the realm of pure semblance* [semblant] has prohibited a certain economy of abundance. (TS: 196–7; CS: 193 trans. adapted)[14]

It is a problem for Irigaray's readers how to deal with these utopian moments. The reading I am going to put forward suggests that one should see them in terms of the imaginary, rather than as literal accounts of a possible future, or engagement with current (economic or anthropological) theories of exchange. By this suggestion I do not mean to underestimate Irigaray's ability to contribute as a theorist, and I have been arguing throughout the book that she is intervening in philosophical debates in order to change the nature of philosophy itself. But one should also not forget her 'poetic' aspect, which she herself insists on, and to which I have arguably not given enough weight in this study. In *Le Corps-à-corps*, she writes:

> I think that one of the gestures that we have to make today, from the point of view of thought, is to refuse absolutely the opposition theory/fiction, refuse the opposition truth/art because it is a hierarchical opposition which is absolutely decisive for the establishment of metaphysics. (CAC: 45)

I showed that the 'two lips' related to the first utopia, that they could stand for mother and daughter. In the second utopia, just quoted, it is the two lips, 'continually interchanging' which underlie this vision of exchange. The exchanges 'without identifiable terms' correspond to the exchanges of the two lips: 'one can never determine of these two, which is one, which is the other' (WE: 65). They can stand for the interchange between lovers of the same sex, or of different sexes.

The 'other' kind of commerce raises the problem that a number of Irigaray's interviewers have asked her about: if there are *two* economies, how can there be exchange *between* them, as opposed to *within* them? *Exchange* should be understood in its most fundamental sense as the basis of sociality, at whatever level, economic, contractual, juridical, linguistic, interpersonal, moral, aesthetic and so on. One can exchange any kind of object, provided there is a *currency*, which may be money, but could also be language, goods or gifts, persons (slaves), animals, children, women. In its simplest structure, exchange requires, in addition to a currency, a yardstick or standard – the *étalon* which was discussed in Chapter 5 with reference to truth. Irigaray is making a very simple (but at the same time, in its implications, a very difficult) point: what if, she says, there were *more than one étalon*, or general equivalent, so that the two economies could not easily be translated into each other? Or what if there was a value (like the *sang rouge*) which was without price (AM: 96), or which could not be measured against an *étalon*: 'For her [woman], gold is not indispensable' (AM: 91). What if men and women were not commensurate? And what if our culture were to symbolize the 'double syntax' so that the logic of each was given full recognition? Then the 'same' could repossess its 'other', leaving the 'other woman' free to signify her own internal divisions, her own 'same' and her own 'other'. Irigaray seems to be arguing that not until this point is accepted and embodied will real exchange between men and women take place, or each be seen to have something the other admires and recognizes but does not possess. In this context, the figure of Antigone, again, represents the 'death' that ensues when only one law governs (E: 105–6).

As with the terms 'metaphor' and 'metonymy', I suggest that Irigaray is using *exchange* and related notions associatively, as well as with reference to the specific conceptual systems from which they are taken,[15] which tends to underline the fact that she sees certain presuppositions as embedded in western thought in general; the implicit juxtaposition of one conceptual system with another, brought about by the mobile signifier (for example exchange), is intended to shed light both on the imaginary of the system in its specificity, and also on what it shares with other systems which go to make up 'the symbolic order'. Like metaphor and metonymy, exchange belongs to a number of different conceptual systems, of which anthropology is perhaps the most obvious: the work of Marcel Mauss for example, whose highly influential 'Essay on the Gift' (1923–4) put forward the theory that exchange relations were a mode of social organization even when, or particularly when, there were no traders or currency properly speaking, exchanges taking the form of the gift; or the work of Lévi-Strauss, who put forward the view in *The Elementary Structures of Kinship* (1949), which Irigaray quotes in *This Sex* (TS: 170; CS: 167) that women are essential commodities in systems of exchange, exchangeable signs in kinship systems. Marx is also in the background, sometimes explicitly in *This Sex* and *Speculum*, but also wherever the terms *étalon* and gold are to be found (in *Amante marine* for example). A third conceptual system is Freud's 'anal economy', the series of symbolic equations (discussed in Chapter 3) between penis – faeces – baby – gift; the characteristic which each of these terms has in common is that they can be detached from the giver (or in the case of the penis, be imagined to be detachable) and thereby circulated from one person to another. Irigaray points out in *Parler n'est jamais neutre* how poorly this corresponds to women's bodies: it is much less easy to conceive of women's sexual organs as detachable 'parts' (PN: 270). In this context too, there is the Lacan connection, and the role of the phallus in linguistic exchange. Yet another conceptual system is that of philosophy, in which Irigaray discerns the desire for a standard of Truth against which everything else can be measured.

Thus, every time the terms of economy, currency, exchange, gold, standard, are used, they call up whole set of associations, those mentioned and probably others too, in an inextricable network in which language, patriarchal kinship systems, economic systems, and philosophical systems are all interwoven and interdependent: more or less the whole field of the symbolic is evoked each time. The epistemological demarcations between one field of enquiry and another are at times deliberately blurred, in an attempt to persuade the reader that among all these different fields there is a homogeneity constituted by the exclusion of woman/women except as object(s) of exchange. Irigaray's question is: what if women 'took part in elaborating and carrying out exchanges?' (TS: 191; CS: 185).

But her answer cannot be in the form of theory, since it is a question of beginning to imagine an entirely different social order. I see the myths or fictions of exchange as fictions of a different mode of social organization. These images of harmonious exchange, of absence of conflict or calculation, of free expenditure without hoarding or counting the cost, are not intended to be political programmes. They are putting into circulation an imaginary account of joyful intercourse between male and female partners, i.e. not a social organization itself, but its imaginary basis. When she says that truth is not women's affair, it is because she is addressing herself to the imaginary, or to the imagination. A 'clear univocal utterance' is 'trapped in the same regime' (SE: 143; SF: 178). Whereas philosophy in general, according to Michèle Le Doeuff (1980a), attempts to purify itself of images – in fact unsuccessfully – and yet remains secretly dependent on them in order to express what it is unable to say in other terms, Irigaray is using fictions *with intent*. The aim is to shift the position of the subject of enunciation through different kinds of writing: 'Two steps are important for the installation of new norms of life: the analysis of the formal structures of discourse and the creation of a new style' (SP: 191).

In her own writings, she says, she uses a double style: 'a style of amorous relations, and a style of thought, of exposition, of writing' (ibid.). She needs to produce writing that addresses, interpellates, seizes by the elbow, disturbs, and does not simply leave the subject secure in his positions. The difficulties of her writing are at least partly intentional:

> Make it impossible for a while to predict whence, whither, when how, why
> . . . something goes by or goes on: will come, will spread, will reverse,
> will cease moving. Not by means of a growing complexity of the same, of
> course, but by the irruption of other circuits, by the intervention at times
> of short circuits that will disperse, diffract, deflect endlessly, making energy
> explode sometimes, with no possibility of returning to one single origin.
> (SE: 142; SF: 177)

Although there may be some conflict between the desire to generate a new phantasy that her readers will share, and the desire to disturb the phantasmatic structures in which they presently live, the first is not possible without the second.

The problem with the creation of myths, however, is that it is an aleatory process. Who can tell in advance which reworking, which creation, is going to crystallize a potential shift in the collective vision and make a new configuration possible (or alternatively immobilize a tentative fluidity)? Again here, I think we need to return to the idea of the transferential reading, introduced in Chapter 1. Irigaray's writing has to work in good part by mobilizing a shared (though not necessarily static) phantasy between reader and writer, what Laura Mulvey calls a 'rêverie-generating image' (1989: 133–4). The problem is then what kind of rêverie is generated. To be politically effective, it must, as Mulvey suggests, appeal to a shared imaginary and symbolic structure, and in order to resonate widely, avoid idiolect. But at the same time, it must avoid a precipitate reconciliation which blunts the edge of the desire for change (Mulvey 1989: 134). As an example of rêverie-generating images, Mulvey cites from Buñuel's *Notes on the Making of 'Un Chien andalou'*. There is no 'correct' reading of this film; the images produce different responses in the viewer, according to the psychic resonances, which vary with individuals; at the same time it appeals to a psychic structure collectively shared because collectively structured. Here is the passage where Buñuel is describing how the images were generated. The images were taken from dream images:

> It should be noted that when an idea appeared the collaborators discarded it immediately if it was derived from a remembrance, or from their cultural pattern, or if, simply, it had a conscious association from an earlier idea. They accepted only those representations as valid which, although they moved them profoundly, had no possible explanation . . . NOTHING in the film SYMBOLISES ANYTHING. (Quoted in Mulvey 1989: 133)

The images either work or fail to work; they do not mean anything. Now I think it is clear that Irigaray is unlikely to want to trust to this process for producing images, which shows some of the difficulties with the appeal to the imaginary. The cultural reservoir of images, collectively structured by a patriarchal symbolic, is likely to be full of patriarchal symbols, while Irigaray needs to generate compelling images which crystallize or propel the desire for change. And there are a number of factors which complicate the process:

1. The generation of symbols is a collective process, which does not necessarily depend on the rational intellect; one can be moved by images that one does not understand (perhaps particularly by images that one does not understand). Irigaray is dependent on her readers for the dissemination of her vision. This is why Irigaray needs her readers; she is transmitting not only an idea but a phantasy. It is explicitly not a theory which the intellect might simply accept or reject, but an object of symbolic exchange which can be worked over like an image for a writer or artist. The phantasy is pliable; its force depends on a kind of collective reworking.
2. Since men and women are positioned differently in relation to the imaginary and symbolic order, it is possible that their collective or

individual responses to these images may be different. Irigaray is addressing two distinct audiences. And it may be that it is not possible to address both audiences simultaneously, through the same kinds of image. The reaction elicited may leave men and women out of phase with each other, since each sex has a different trajectory to make in the difficult journey towards exchange.

3. The timescale is unpredictable.
4. The response and interaction between different images and different visions is unpredictable. In culture, there are many different dialogues taking place.

Irigaray is difficult to assess because her persuasion does not lie in her arguments alone; it also lies in her appeal to the forces of change which the *logos* has attempted to exclude: to love, to the imagination which *desires*, to a possible female homosexual economy, to amorous exchange. Rhetorically, Irigaray is close to Rousseau in many ways. Rousseau's work displays an equally remarkable combination of rational and imaginary elements intertwined. It has been said that all of his work can be understood as the attempt to construct in imagination a society fit for him to live in, and in which he would be happy. Similarly, Irigaray could be said to be constructing in imagination a society that would be fit for women to live in. I said in Chapter 4 that one has to think the symbolic and the imaginary together. In Rousseau's case, he begins by appealing to an imaginary state of nature, as a yardstick to assess society. But he goes on in *The Social Contract* to conclude that the social (the law, the symbolic order) must act as a guarantee *against* nature. Formerly freedom, natural instinct is in the end slavery. Irigaray is also appealing in the first instance to 'nature' – to the possibility of a female imaginary. But in the same way, she also insists on bringing women out of 'nature' and into the symbolic order. It is contradictory perhaps, as Rousseau's account is contradictory. Rousseau writes that the state of nature probably never existed, but we have to posit its existence in order to understand society. 'Nature' in his work is both a primitive humanity that is simply 'buried' under layers of civilization and which might be found intact when the rubble is cleared away, and at the same time it is so distorted by society that it is like the statue in the desert whose original features have been lost for good, eroded by the elements. Similarly, for Irigaray women are not in a state of nature; they are not literally outside the social order, but one may have to posit the female imaginary, even though its nature and its existence are indeterminable. Rousseau put 'nature' into the future as well as in a primitive past; nature was something we also had to create. Similarly, Irigaray locates sexual difference in 'nature' but also puts it into the future, as a horizon of thought and action, as a transformation of the symbolic. Rousseau was thought eccentric for criticizing progress in the name of nature, though we might be more inclined today to be in sympathy with his critique of 'progress'.

Irigaray may be thought eccentric for insisting on difference (also partly in the name of nature) at a moment when it is being loudly and persuasively said that difference has been used to oppress women and not to liberate them, and that liberty lies in other directions – equality, or undecidability, or beyond sexual difference.

My reading of Irigaray leaves me with admiration for the complexity of her vision, but also with a series of questions to which the answers are completely open. Will her utopias in the twentieth century be as compelling as Rousseau's in the eighteenth? Is she sufficiently intuitive to catalyse changes in the symbolic? Will her address to the male subject of enunciation meet with any response?[16] Will the new vision of sexual difference be able to crystallize feminist political thought as Rousseau's egalitarian vision of the natural evidently focused revolutionary ideals in the eighteenth century? And most of all, but less ambitiously perhaps, will women collectively be able to find in her work some of the materials for the creation of their future?

Notes

Introductory remarks

1. Another Dutch publication, a collection of texts on epistemology edited by C. Schavemaker and H. Willemsen, *Over het weten van de mens [On Man's Knowing]*, Alphen aan den Rijn: Samson 1986, includes Irigaray in a panorama of philosophers as follows: Heraclitus, Plato, Aristotle, St Thomas Aquinas, Descartes, Hume, Kant, Marx, Nietzsche, Merleau-Ponty, Habermas, Levinas, Koningsveld, Popper, Irigaray, Ijsseling. (Source: *Bibliographie de la philosophie*, published by the Institut international de philosophie, Paris: Vrin.)
2. David Macey's translation of 'Misère de la psychanalyse' will appear in *The Irigaray Reader*, edited by Margaret Whitford (Oxford: Blackwell, forthcoming) under the title 'The poverty of psychoanalysis'.
3. For example, she appears in two collections of 'Exercices de la patience, Cahiers de Philosophie', published by Obsidiane, Paris: *Heidegger* (1962) (which included 'Le prix de la sérénité' – I have not seen this, but assume it is an earlier version of *L'Oubli de l'air*, Ch. 3), and *Le sujet exposé* (1983) (which included 'Fécondité de la caresse', later published in *Ethique de la différence sexuelle*). (Source: *Bibliographie de la philosophie*, published by the Institut international de philosophie, Paris: Vrin.)
4. See Le Doeuff (1980a) available in translation from the Athlone Press 1989), and the opening section of *L'Etude et le rouet* (1989) (currently being translated by Basil Blackwell).
5. Outstanding readings of Irigaray have been produced by Rosi Braidotti, Carolyn Burke, Diana Fuss, Jane Gallop, Elizabeth Grosz and Naomi Schor. Most of these are either hard to find, or only just published. I have been fortunate in being able to have access to unpublished work while writing this book.
6. See for example Bowlby (1983), Cameron (1985), Jones (1986), Le Doeuff (1989: 247 ff.) and Plaza (1978).
7. On the problems of stardom, and the question of women's differences (differences of *competence* and *talent* as well as those of race and class) see Cicioni (1989), which discusses the attempts of some Italian feminist groups to confront women's differences in an Irigarayan-influenced way through the practice of *affidamento*.
8. In Le Doeuff's book, this argument comes in the section on Simone de Beauvoir. An earlier version, in English, can be found in Le Doeuff (1980b: 278). (The reference to Irigaray is missing from the first, French, version – see Le Doeuff 1979.) Le Doeuff's position – from which the critique of Irigaray is made – can be found in *L'Imaginaire philosophique* (see note 4). Interestingly, Grosz (1989: 185) suggests that Le Doeuff may have been influenced by Irigaray's work.

Chapter 1 Feminism and utopia

1. But see Chalier's (1980) review of *Amante marine* which seems to me to understand it quite well.
2. '[T]he victim is supposed to have moral superiority or purity, because the exploitative terms in which her suppression is couched have been imposed on her by others' (Rosenthal 1973: 29).
3. This is made quite clear in *This Sex Which Is Not One* (TS: 166; CS: 160). See also 'Egales ou différentes?' (1988) which Irigaray wrote after the death of Simone de Beauvoir (trans. 'Equal or Different?' (1989)).
4. See Anne Phillips (1987). See also Maria Mies on equality:

   in a contradictory and exploitative relationship [i.e. capitalist patriarchy] the privileges of the exploiters can never become the privileges of all. If the wealth of the metropoles is based on the exploitation of colonies, then the colonies cannot achieve wealth unless they also have colonies. If the emancipation of men is based on the subordination of women, then women cannot achieve 'equal rights' with men, which would necessarily include the right to exploit others. (1986: 76)

   See also Scott (1988) for the argument that equality versus difference is a false polarity.
5. Haraway, in her exhilarating utopian article 'A Manifesto for Cyborgs' which argues against exclusionary politics, sees Irigaray as one of the storytellers whose work could inform late twentieth-century political imaginations (1985: 92).
6. 'Nonetheless, women have to advance to those same privileges (and to sameness, perhaps) before any consideration can be given to the differences that they might give rise to' (SE: 119; SF: 149).
7. See Fraser (1984) and Moi (1988) on the depoliticization involved in the attempt to avoid making choices, particularly with reference to Derridean deconstruction, and the avoidance of closure. Politics *is* closure, as Moi points out (1988: 18). I will develop this point in more detail in relation to Irigaray in Chapter 6.
8. See Shklar (1969).
9. In Jardine and Menke (forthcoming).
10. On taking essentialism seriously as a feminist strategy, see articles by Braidotti (1989), Fuss (1989) and Schor (1989). See also Fuss (1990). In an earlier article Schor remarks that:

    Denied sexual difference shades into sexual indifference and, following the same slippery path, into a paradoxical reinscription of the very differences the strategy was designed to denaturalize. [. . .] [W]hereas those who adopt the masculine position press for an end to sexual difference and only grudgingly acknowledge claims for feminine specificity, those who adopt the feminine position concede the strategic efficacy of undoing sexual oppositions and positionalities, all the while pursuing the construction of difference. The most active site of the feminine resistance to the discourse of indifference is a certain insistence on doubling, which may well be the feminine mode of subverting the unitary subject: mimeticism (Irigaray . . .)' (1987: 100, 110).

11. See for example Kuykendall (1984) or Ferguson (1989). See also Kuykendall (1988) where *Sexes et parentés* is reviewed together with Jeffner Allen's *Lesbian Philosophy: Explorations* (1986). Sayers (1986: 42–8) aligns her with Adrienne

Rich. Irigaray's appeal to the divinity of women, her emphasis on the mother, on blood and so on, have obvious resonances with radical feminist themes, and it may be because of the thematic similarities that she has been interpreted in terms of Rich or Daly, rather than in terms of the critique of essentialism which characterizes the philosophical tradition within which she is working.

12. Riley (1988) is particularly persuasive on the oscillations and ambiguities of post-Enlightenment feminism. Ramazanoglu (1989) gives a lucid account of the contradictions of 'second-wave' feminism. See also Harding (1986) and Gatens (forthcoming). Nicholson (ed.) *Feminism/Postmodernism* (1990) came out too late for me to discuss it here; however, discussion and critique of the Enlightenment inheritance is one of its central themes, and it is clearly going to be an important book. On Irigaray, see Johnson (1988), who points to the presence of contradiction in Irigaray's work between Enlightenment ideals and their deconstruction. It is a crucial issue, central to current feminist debates, and although I think that there is more to be said for Irigaray than Johnson suggests, none the less the contradiction is a real one.

13. For philosophical accounts of feminism and the inheritance of the Enlightenment, see the work of Grimshaw (1986, 1988), Hodge (1988, 1989) and Lovibond (1989).

14. See Taylor (1983).

15. Elaine Hoffman Baruch comments that 'a slight shift in perspective reveals that dystopia for men may be utopia for women and *vice versa*' (in Rohrlich and Baruch 1984: 204). See also the work of Kessler (1984), Albinski (1988), Rose (1988), and Bartkowski (1989).

16. Moi (1985: 121–3) discusses the view that the utopian project will always be marked by conflict and contradiction, but that this *justifies* it rather than discrediting it, since it arises out of the social contradictions of its time. See also the Hegelian position put forward by Rosenthal (1973).

17. See Silverman (1988, ch. 4) for a critical discussion of Kristeva's 'archaic mother'. Silverman also indicates the possible tensions between the need for phantasies and the problem of presenting women with strong images of themselves; she argues that the positive Oedipus complex, with its simultaneous devaluation of mother and (female) self, makes it difficult for women to recognize themselves in an idealizing 'mirror', and instead of inspiring them, can leave them anxious and brooding on their own insufficiences (1988: 175–6). She suggests in turn that feminism depends upon a maternal phantasy: 'I would even go so far as to argue that without activating the homosexual-maternal fantasmatic, feminism would be impossible – that it needs the libidinal resources of the negative Oedipus complex' (p.125).

18. See Weedon (1987) on points of convergence between socialist feminism and feminism influenced by contemporary French theory, for example Chapter 2 on the assumption that human nature is not essential but socially produced, and the necessity of creating the conditions for change and transformation; or pp.99 and 135 on their joint opposition to the fixation of meaning and therefore to the idea that masculinity and feminity are essentially 'given'. The phantasmatic element in the vision of the elimination of gender difference is sharply analysed by Elshtain (1987). Although aimed at a slightly different target, the article indicates clearly that the desire for the abolition of gender difference is not so much a *political* aim as a libidinal one.

19. See Cockburn (1988) for a socialist-feminist account sympathetic to the 'politics of difference', which argues (against Segal, for example) that a feminism of difference is not necessarily essentialist or idealist.

20.　On the materiality of the body in Irigaray's work, see Grosz (1986c, 1988a) and Schor (1989). On the materiality of language in Lacanian psychoanalytic theory, see Ragland-Sullivan (1989). It is interesting that when Moi puts forward the psychoanalytic dialogue as an epistemological model, she is able to refer to Freudianism as a 'materialism' (1989: 202). Yet as a 'materialist' feminist, influenced by the British Left tradition (Moi 1988: 3), she gives a materialist critique of Irigaray (Moi 1985) whose model is also psychoanalysis and the psychoanalytic dialogue. Admittedly, there is a difference of four years between Moi's two accounts. See Grosz (1989: 241–2) for a critique of Moi's account of Irigaray. Grosz argues that Moi's critique supposes (a) that discursive strategies are not material, and (b) that Irigaray is offering a *total* theory of women's oppression rather than a regional intervention at the level of the symbolic. Toril Moi has pointed out to me in correspondence that she and Grosz are working with quite different definitions of materialism. So the question of Irigaray and materialism still awaits a thorough elucidation, which will take into account the fact that 'materialism' is a political term, over which there is contest for rights and possession.

21.　One writer that Irigaray has drawn on here is Goux (1973). In Goux's interpretation of Marx, exchange is privileged over production, and social relations over relations between things. This allows him to address the symbolic function as a structuring mode, whatever the level of reality addressed, whether economic, political, juridical, moral, religious, philosophical, aesthetic, sexual, intersubjective, and so on. Any attempt to produce a materialist account of Irigaray should certainly look at her work in the light of Goux's arguments, particularly the idea that symbolic functions are mapped on to the bodies of men and women (the raw material).

22.　Irigaray makes it clear elsewhere that she does not regard the economic as irrelevant. See the following remarks from *Sexes et parentés*

> It appears to be impossible, at least in any profound and lasting way, to modify social relations, language, art in general, without modifying the economic system of exchange. They go hand in hand. Sometimes the one predominates, sometimes the other, but changes in both are indispensable for any social mutation. (WSM: 12; SP: 96)

See Benhabib and Cornell (1987) for the arguments that the categories of Marxist theory need to be replaced in their historical context and their gender subtext examined. Pollock's work in art history (1988) offers an example of the articulation of material and symbolic production. See Cocks (1989) for a recent attempt to theorize cultural transformation drawing on the work of Foucault, Gramsci, Edward Said, Stuart Hampshire, and Raymond Williams.

23.　The two main statements of the materialist critique of Irigaray can be found in Plaza (1978) and Moi (1985). Both these discussions, however, particularly Plaza's, were written at a time when available interpretations of Irigaray were still rather uncomprehending.

24.　She might here seem to have more in common with 'Rainbow Coalition' politics. See Haraway (1985) and Iris Marion Young in Benhabib and Cornell (1987). Although I have not discussed in this book the relation between Foucault and Irigaray, it is an area which would merit further exploration. The only work I have come across on Foucault and Irigaray is Braidotti (1986a). See also Collin (1984–5), which reviews together *Ethique de la différence sexuelle* and Foucault's *Histoire de la sexualité* vols. 2 and 3.

25.　This has led some people to see her as a cultural feminist, i.e. the proponent of a feminism which *replaces* political theory and struggle with the assertion of a female identity and culture which can potentially include all women whatever their politics (see Echols 1984a and 1984b for a more expanded definition of cultural feminism). For example Echols writes: 'Cultural feminist sexual politics really offers us nothing more than women's traditional sexual values disguised as radical feminist sexual values' (1984a: 64). This is rightly seen as a refusal to confront the real political and other differences *between* women. In so far as it is working with representations, it seems to some people to have become cut off from materialist politics. I hope that the interpretations of Irigaray that I am offering in this book will make the definition of 'cultural feminist' seem inappropriate and too limiting to describe Irigaray's project.

26. Gearhart (1985) offers an interpretation of Irigaray's counter-transference. See also Gallop (1982).

27. This remark comes from 'Misère de la psychanalyse' (see *Introductory Remarks*, note 2). This article was written in response to the death of a fellow analyst, a woman who had failed the 'passe', Lacan's 'rite de passage' qualifying analysts as theoreticians of his School (see Marini 1986: 138 ff. and Turkle 1979: 123 ff. for brief details of the 'passe').

28. See also Grosz (1986b: 74). Martindale (1987) also makes the link between Irigaray's polyvocality and the future world to be created: 'Irigaray seems to be speaking "as if". She writes in the optative mood, about a world that is not yet in existence' (1987: 18). Martindale usefully links the question of voice with that of ethics, the tensions between the need for a collective feminist 'we' and the feminist ethical imperative not to dominate the other (woman) by speaking for her or in her place.

Chapter 2 Subjectivity and language

1. It should also be pointed out that psychoanalytic culture in France is now very extensive. The first chapter of Marini's book on Lacan (1986) gives a survey of no less than *fifteen* different psychoanalytic societies or groups in France, in the Freudian tradition (not to mention the non-Freudian ones). Although Lacan's theory has obviously been highly influential, it is misleading to suppose that he is the only psychoanalyst that Irigaray has read or come into contact with. Monique Schneider (another analyst) comments: 'If one is a psychoanalyst, Lacan only occupies a part of the psychoanalytic field, but among those who are philosophers and interested in psychoanalysis, it is unthinkable not to be a Lacanian' (in Baruch and Serrano 1988: 168). I have not felt obliged to document the Lacanian origins of Irigaray's psychoanalytic concepts, and in fact in many cases I have found it more illuminating to use other psychoanalytic sources. In this respect, it is instructive to read the interviews in *Women Analyze Women* (Baruch and Serrano 1988). One can then see quite clearly that Irigaray is not an isolated figure, but is part of an analytic community with both shared and divergent preoccupations. She is normally seen in a limited number of contexts: against the background of Lacan (or sometimes Derrida); or as part of the triad Cixous–Irigaray–Kristeva. This collection of interviews frames her as a woman analyst in France, and allows one to glimpse a much denser array of intellectuals, analysts or other women (feminists and non-feminists) among whom she appears less startling and more connected to a wide range of her contemporaries than her writing itself (with its almost complete absence of references to specific contemporary texts or writers) admits.

2. See Turkle (1979) for an account of Irigaray's exclusion from Vincennes. Irigaray gives her own version, more succinctly, in *This Sex* (TS: 167; CS: 161)

and in 'Women's Exile' (WE: 71). Her rejected course proposal appears in *This Sex* (TS: 167–8; CS: 161–3). Irigaray describes what happened as being 'put into quarantine' by the psychoanalytic establishment (WWT: 224). For other accounts of the exclusion, see Nguyen (1975) and Deleuze and Lyotard (1975). See Favret-Saada (1977) and Baliteau (1975) for other critical accounts, by women psychoanalysts, of Lacan's procedures.

3.   On this point see for example Turkle (1979). For psychoanalytic accounts see Castoriadis (1978) and Roustang (1980).

4.   See *Introductory remarks*, note 2.

5.   Cf. *This Sex* (TS: 102–3; CS: 99), *Parler n'est jamais neutre*, (PN: 254), and 'Women's Exile' (WE 62–3). See *Speculum* (SE: 119–23; SF: 148–54) on the economic infrastructure underlying Freud's theories.

6.   See PN: 267 ff. See E: 120 or PN: 314 on the non-neutrality of psychoanalytic models.

7.   On the other hand, some critics find that she is *too* indebted to Lacan, e.g. Leland (1989):

> [The] defects in Irigaray's account of the alienation of women's desire illustrate two pitfalls associated with the appropriation of Lacanian psychoanalysis as a feminist theoretical tool. The first is the questionable empirical adequacy of Lacanian claims about universal structures of psychic life, particularly the Oedipus complex understood as the 'subjective' expression of exogamy. The second is the excessively abstract character of Lacan's account of these universals' (1989: 89).

See also Reineke: 'Much of my criticism is focused on a father of the new French feminism, Jacques Lacan, whose veiled presence in Irigaray's writing threatens to distort and to co-opt her aims' (1987: 67).

8.   She goes on to say that Freud began by listening to his women patients, his hysterics, but that once he had created his 'system', it prevented him from continuing to hear what women were saying.

9.   See 'Le Praticable de la scène' (PN: 239–52), 'La Limite du transfert' (PN: 293–305) and 'Le Geste en psychanalyse' (SP: 103–18). 'Le Geste en psychanalyse' appears in English in Brennan (1989: 127–38) under the title 'The gesture in psychoanalysis'. 'La Limite du transfert' will appear in *The Irigaray Reader* under the title 'The limits of the transference'.

10.   On the role of the poet, see particularly the final chapter of *L'Oubli de l'air*. (Other versions of this chapter can be found in *La Croyance même* (pp.68–77) and *Sexes et parentés* (SP: 61–5). An English version will appear in *The Irigaray Reader* under the title 'He risks who risks life itself'. On love, see particularly *Éthique de la différence sexuelle*.

11.   As she states herself explicitly in 'Egales ou différentes?' (see ch. 1 n. 3).

12.   But see Schor (1989) for the argument that the universe of science 'enjoys a strange privilege in Irigaray's conceptual universe'. This reading emphasizes Irigaray's *materialism* against her so-called *essentialism*.

13.   Gillian Rose (1984) points out that the idea of a Third Testament can be found in Deleuze, *Différence et répétition* (Paris: Presses Universitaires de France 1969). She writes: 'the idea of a "third" testament is taken from Joachim of Fiore, c. 1132–1202, who divided history into three periods: The Age of the Father (Old Testament), The Age of the Son (New Testament and 42 subsequent generations) and the Age of the Spirit, in which all humanity would be converted' (1984: 91, note 26). Irigaray adapts this scenario to include the woman too.

14.   On this point, Grosz comments:

Irigaray makes no suggestion of a causal connection between men's bodies and dominant representations, although it is not uncommon to see commentators assert that she directly links patriarchal domination to men's 'natures'. It is not the anatomy of the male body which seeks its own image in dominant discourses. Rather, the pre-existence of patriarchal social relations relies on the *production* of a specific form of male sexuality through internalisation of images, representations and signifying practices. In other words, men do not form discourses in their own image(s); rather, phallocentric discourses form male sexuality in their image(s). (1989: 112)

15. Ironically, given her project, she gives as the epigraph to 'Così fan Tutti' (TS: 85; CS: 86) Lacan's remark: 'Women don't know what they are saying.' Irigaray takes up this theme, but shows how it can be used with different effect.

16. In Benveniste's sense; see Benveniste (1966). She is pinning the division into two sexes on to Benveniste's division of language into two persons, the 'I' and the 'you'. Benveniste claims that only the 'I' and 'you' refer to persons; the third person is an absent person – it has a representational rather than an enunciatory or positional function (1971: 251–7).

17. This is made particularly clear in 'Communications linguistique et spéculaire: modèles génétiques et modèles pathologiques (PN: 15–34). On this point, see Macey (1988: 66), and Lecercle (1985: 55–62).

18. For a Lacanian critique of Irigaray's account of language, see Hamon who argues that *écriture féminine* (generically) is pre-Saussurean (1977: 47). See Silverman (1988: 144–5) for a similar critique.

19. Although I am in disagreement with Silverman's account of Irigaray, I find the rest of her book exceptionally interesting. I wonder if the problem with the Irigaray chapter is that it relies so heavily on Irigaray's early work, and so is unable to interpret Irigaray in the light shed by subsequent publications such as *Ethique de la différence sexuelle* or *Parler n'est jamais neutre*. Desire and subjectivity are obviously connected. But the conceptualization of subjectivity solely in terms of desire can lead to vision of a (male) sexual paradise where women still have no political, social, or cultural status. Malcolm Bowie indicates, in a splendid bravura flight of rhetoric, the limitations of desire as a would-be explanatory principle (1987: 2–5). See also Butler (1987) on the links between desire and subjectivity in the Hegelian and post-Hegelian subject.

20. See Hodge (1988).

21. This vision of exchange and blurring of subject boundaries can be found in *This Sex* (TS: 197; CS: 193) (a passage I discuss further in Chapter 8), and in 'Questions to Emmanuel Levinas' (also discussed in Chapters 7 and 8). It will be seen that my interpretation differs here from Nye's conclusion that:

Irigaray, . . . trapped in the metaphysics of Lacan's split self, cannot accept an interactional view of discourse. She sees feminist struggle as an internalized rebellion against the Law of the Father in one's own speech and thought. The goal of this struggle must be free expression of diffuse emotions and sensations, and a feminine speech that has affinities with the 'illogic' of hysterics and dreamers. . . . This is a language that women may '*parler-entre-elles*', but the revolutionary result is not the development of new forms of social life. It is a personal liberation that frees the subject from the symbolic Law of the Father. (Nye 1989b: 56–7)

22. See Freud, 'Beyond the Pleasure Principle', SE XVIII: 7–64, discussed by Irigaray in *La Croyance même* (reprinted in *Sexes et parentés*) and in 'Le Geste en psychanalyse' ('The Gesture in Psychoanalysis') (SP: 103–18).

23.   *Verbe* in French can mean 'verb'. It can also mean the word of God addressed
      to men, or God himself as the second person of the Trinity, as in the phrase:
      'the Word made flesh'. It can also mean language (*langue* or *langage*). The *Robert*
      dictionary gives this example from Victor Hugo: 'Car le mot c'est le Verbe, et le
      Verbe c'est Dieu' [For the word is the Word and the Word is God].
24.   The theorization of woman as predicate can also be found in the work of de
      Lauretis; see especially 1984, Ch. 5, and 1987, Ch. 2.
25.   Cf. an early reference to the conditions of women's access to subjectivity in *This
      Sex*, which appears to equate women's 'auto-affection' with their 'god':

      > That 'elsewhere' of feminine pleasure can be found only at the price of *crossing
      > back through the mirror that subtends all speculation.* . . . A playful crossing and
      > an unsettling one, which would allow woman to rediscover the place of her
      > 'self-affection'. Of her 'god', we might say. A god to which one can obviously
      > not have recourse – unless its *duality* is granted – without leading the feminine
      > right back into the phallocratic economy (TS: 77–8; CS: 75).

      This confirms my reading that 'auto-affection' should be taken as a *symbolic*
      process (or at least *requiring symbolization*) (see Chapter 4).
26.   See Burke (1987). See also Gallop's reading of Irigaray (Gallop 1982).
27.   In *Nietzsche aujourd'hui?* (1973: 299). One wonders what he *actually* said, since this
      is supposed to be a transcript. How did he put in the parenthesis?
28.   In Jardine and Menke (forthcoming).
29.   This idea of the optative mood, the 'as if', was first put forward by Burke (1981),
      about 'When our lips speak together'.

Chapter 3 Rationality and the imaginary

I should like to acknowledge my debt in this chapter to the work of Marion Milner.

1.   See Macey (1988), Ch. 6. Dews also comments on Lacan's social conservatism,
     e.g. 'Lacan does not believe . . . in the possibility of new forms of community'
     (1987: 238).
2.   '*Speculum* . . . begins to elaborate a phenomenological description by a woman:
     Luce Irigaray, whose name is on the book, of the auto-affection and auto-
     representation of her body.' Irigaray, in Jardine and Menke (forthcoming).
3.   See also: 'Originally I wanted to do a kind of tetralogy which would have tackled
     the problem of the four elements: water, air, fire, earth, applied to philosophers
     nearer our own time, and also to put into question the philosophical tradition,
     particularly from the point of view of the feminine' (CAC: 43). In the same
     interview (p.44) Irigaray adds that she was planning a book on Marx and fire,
     which has never appeared.
4.   Another woman philosopher whose work can be related to that of Bachelard
     is Le Doeuff (see Grosz, 1989: xviii–xix, for a brief definition of the difference
     between Lacan's imaginary and that of Le Doeuff). Interestingly, Le Doeuff
     partly assumes Bachelard's definition of the imaginary as thinking-in-images,
     and partly contests it; whereas Bachelard is concerned to purify scientific
     knowledge of all trace of the distorting imagination, Le Doeuff sees in the
     image, particularly in the philosophical text, the place where what has been
     excluded by the project of philosophy (which defines itself by exclusion, with
     reference to what it is not) returns to haunt the philosopher who refuses to
     acknowledge dependence on the image. (One can see why Grosz thinks that
     Le Doeuff might have been influenced by Irigaray.)
5.   See for example the discussion in the interview with Clément (1975) about the
     relation of her thought to Marxism.

6. The importance of morphology is discussed in Grosz (1989), pp.111, 113 ff.
7. It is interesting to compare her on this point with Kristeva. Although there are many points of convergence between them, partly because they both depend on the vocabulary and concepts of psychoanalysis, Kristeva appears to be politically rather pessimistic. See the critique of her in Moi (1985) and Leland (1989). See also Grosz (1989): 63 ff., 93 ff. for a discussion of Kristeva's rather equivocal stance vis-à-vis feminism.
8. Cf. Freud's account of hysterical symptoms, which do not correspond to neuro-physiological pathways but to symbolic or phantasmatic patterns: '*hysteria behaves as though anatomy did not exist or as though it had no knowledge of it*' (SE 1: 169). See Gallop's remarkable article (1983) on Irigaray's poetics of the body and the referential illusion.
9. '*The object of desire itself*, and for psychoanalysis, *would be the transformation of fluid to solid*? Which seals – this is well worth repeating – *the triumph of rationality*. Solid mechanics and rationality have maintained a relationship of very long standing, one against which fluids have never stopped arguing' (TS: 113; CS: 111). See also 'Le sujet de la science, est-il sexué?' (PN: 307–21) (translated under the title 'Is the subject of science sexed?', in *Cultural Critique* 1, Fall 1985 and in *Hypatia* 2, Fall 1987) and 'Ethique de la différence sexuelle' (E: 113–24), for an account of the 'maleness' of the human and physical sciences.
10. Hodge writes:

    As far as Irigaray is concerned, for women it makes no difference whether you talk about Freud or Lacan, Socrates or Plato; if you start in the twentieth century and tell history backwards, or start in the fifth century before the common era and talk about Socrates; it makes no difference if you talk about Freud and Socrates, and their emphasis on speech and talking, or if you write about Plato and Lacan and their written appropriations of the speech of psychoanalysis and of philosophical diagnosis. For Irigaray in *Speculum*, for women, there is no temporal direction, underpinned by a conception of progress, in which the project of modernity takes up the ideals of antiquity, and seeks to develop them, since those ideals are misogynist, and since the project of modernity has not been constructed to include women. History for women is a process from which women have been elided; it is not a process in which women, too, have been permitted to take up and develop the achievements of past generations. Thus with a gesture characteristic of philosophy, of radical feminism and of postmodernism . . . Irigaray denies the significance of temporal and historical difference. (1989: 109–10)

    One might relate this point to Irigaray's concern to install a maternal genealogy (see Section II, *passim*). In more general terms, I think Hodge is offering a Hegelian reading of Irigaray: if 'woman' is not internally self-contradictory (see Chapter 6), then woman's self-consciousness (or woman-as-subject) has no history.
11. In *Feminist Utopias* Bartkowski suggests that '[u]topian practice decenters questions of time and history, the angle of long-standing criticism from the Left' (1989: 12). A study of the question of time in Irigaray's work (historical, linear time, women's time etc.) has not, as far as I know, been undertaken, but would clearly shed light on a lot of issues.
12. There has been considerable debate about the concept of patriarchy since Kate Millett relaunched it in 1969 in *Sexual Politics* as an explanatory concept. Coward (1983), providing a conceptual history of the term, looks at some of its limitations and suggests that it should be treated with caution. Others, particularly Marxist feminists, find it has ahistorical, universalizing, biologically deterministic

implications which make it unsuited to feminist use. A brief account of
the debates can be found in Ramazanoglu (1989). Ramazanoglu points out
however that: 'It was the crude universality of the radical feminist conception of
patriarchy which forced marxist feminists to rethink their marxism' (1989: 38). I
tend towards the side of those who would retain it (see e.g. Mies, 1986, for whom
it is a 'struggle concept' or Walby, 1986, 1990, who gives a useful account of its
trajectory in Marxist feminist thinking and makes a persuasive case for putting
it to use.) Since concepts have a history they can bring with them unacceptable
implications; this is the danger of which Coward and others warn. But they can
also be redefined and put to work analytically in different ways. I think this is
what Irigaray has done with the imaginary – she has turned it into a 'struggle
concept'. It is only to be expected that the sources of the concept make it a
double-edged weapon, with risks to the user. I wonder if the male imaginary
does not replace the concept of patriarchy in certain of its functions (particularly
since, as I will show later, it has come to have social and not merely individual
application). In particular what it would do is to suggest a different alternative.
The alternative to *patriarchy* might present itself as matriarchy (which is how
feminism is often interpreted, in terms of a simple desire for reversal of power,
an interpretation Irigaray is anxious to steer clear of). The alternative to the *male
imaginary* is conceptualized as a sexual partner, in an amorous relationship. This
presents a completely different picture which does, however, leave unexplained
the dimension of power and force (as Irigaray's critics have pointed out).

13. When I first wrote on Irigaray in 1986, I noted the connection between the
     imaginary and the elements, but at that time was unable to take it further. In
     the mean time, I have been able to benefit from work by Burke (1987) and Grosz
     (1986c, 1989), and this section is indebted to their insights.

14. Grosz (1989) discusses together Irigaray's work on the divine, on the cosmic, on
     space and time, on the elements, and on Greek mythology. I think she is right
     to treat these aspects all together, under the heading of Irigaray's attempts to
     create alterity. Since the discussion in the present book has been organized along
     different lines, I have allocated these issues to different chapters, but this does not
     imply that I disagree with the links that Grosz makes.

15. See Rose (1986: 166–97); Benvenuto and Kennedy (1986: Ch. 2). See also Dews
     (1987: 55–60) on the differences between Freud's theory of the Ego and Lacan's.
     He argues that Freud's concept of the Ego is at variance with Lacan's principally
     in that Lacan's account is of an alienating Ego. For Irigaray, the alienation is
     primarily for the woman; she does not seem to see the imaginary per se as
     inherently alienating, perhaps because she is engaged in the process of *unbinding*
     the rigid masculine Ego and (re)binding the fragmentary feminine. Laplanche
     (1989) is helpful on this:

     day-to-day psychoanalytic experience reveals that [psychic conflict] is a
     conflict between binding and unbinding processes. This does not mean that
     we have to promote binding, or that we have to conclude that binding always
     works to the advantage of biological life or even psychical life; extreme binding
     means extreme immobilization. In that sense, Lacan's denunciations of the ego
     as an agency of fascination and immobilization, outrageous though they may
     be, are still valid. The psyche will certainly die if it disintegrates or comes under
     the sway of the death drive, but it can also die if it becomes too rigidly synthetic.
     The ego too can be a source of death. (1989: 148)

     These comments also help us to understand the tension between the global
     and the specific in Irigaray's analysis (see Chapter 1). On the death drive,
     see Chapters 4 to 7.

16. For a moving and almost entirely non-technical account of the operations of unconscious phantasy and their possible effects on the personality and activities of adult life, see Milner (1969).

17. Lacan's 'imaginary' is, of course, a much more far-reaching notion than this remark indicates. It should be pointed out that, as various commentators have indicated, Lacan's terms and concepts are not completely stable (Bowie 1987: 105; Benvenuto and Kennedy 1986: 102; Macey 1988: 201); they are mutually self-defining and their implications alter in different contexts,

18. This point was first noted by Gallop (1982: 68–9).

19. My translation. Castoriadis gives as examples of social imaginary significations: religious belief; reification (in slavery or under capitalism); the modern bureaucratic universe and its pseudo-rationality. To call institutions like slavery or capitalism 'imaginary' might give the misleading impression that they are 'all in the mind'. Castoriadis stresses that 'the social imaginary, as we understand it, is more real than the "real"' (p.197). The problem is rather that 'society lives its relation with institutions in the form of the imaginary; . . . it does not recognise the institutional imaginary as its own product' (p.184).

20. I say 'relatively subordinate', because I think it is in fact essential to the understanding of *Speculum*. But the *term* is not used a lot, and the dimension of the imaginary has often passed unnoticed in accounts of Irigaray.

21. Compare this with Lacan's statement that: 'Strictly speaking . . . there can be no symbolisation of the female sex [sexe] . . . the female sex [sexe] has the character of an absence, a void or a hole' (Lacan 1981: 198–9). (*Sexe* in French usually refers to the sexual organs; it is unusual for it to signify what English usually means by sex, although Foucault sometimes seems to be using it in that way, and it can refer to women: the 'fair sex'.) But whereas Lacan appears to leave the issue at that, implying that nothing can be done about it, Irigaray is attempting to *shift* the structure of the imaginary.

22. Cf. Brown and Adams 1979: 37:

    In any case, the attempt to find an existent state of nature cannot, in principle, succeed. This is not a problem of the limitations of our existing knowledge (the possibility of an as-yet undiscovered people living in a purely natural state). The reason why it cannot succeed is . . . that the term 'nature' is in the end defined only by reference to the social, as that which is the non-social.

23. See Castoriadis (1975) pp.372 ff. for a discussion of the essential heterogeneity of the unconscious on the one hand, and the logic of identity on the other.

24. Castoriadis defines the magma as follows:

    A magma is that from which one can extract (or in which one can construct) an indefinite number of ensemblist organisations, but which can never be reconstituted (ideally) by an ensemblist composition (finite or infinite) of these organisations. . . . We assert that everything that can be effectively given – representations, nature, signification – exists in the mode of a *magma*; that the social-historical institutions of the world, things, and individuals, insofar as it is the institution of the *Legein* and the *Teukhein*, is always also the institution of identitary logic and thus the imposition of an ensemblist organisation on a first stratum of givenness which lends itself interminably to this operation. But also, that it is never and can never be *only* that – that it is also always and necessarily the institution of a magma of imaginary social significations. And finally, that the relation between the *Legein* and the *Teukhein* and the magma of imaginary social significations is not thinkable within the identitary-ensemblist frame of reference – no more than are the relations between the *Legein* and representation, *Legein* and nature, or between representation and signification, representation and world, or 'consciousness' and 'unconscious'. (Castoriadis 1975: 461–3, trans. in Howard 1977: 297) Howard provides a useful introduction to Castoriadis's ideas.

25.   See Mitchell and Rose (1982). See Hamon (1977) and Mitchell and Rose (1982) for a Lacanian critique of Irigaray. Cf. also Bannet (1989). Bannet, while finding Lacan himself limited in this respect, thinks that he has a creative effect on his readers: 'Lacan's emphasis on the dominance of the symbolic order and on the inevitability of repetition preclude him from really understanding creativity' (1989: 40). However, 'Lacan's work and Lacan's impact on the often innovative work of others demonstrates that it is still possible for subjects to transform what they have received. . . . This contradiction in Lacan has been no less fruitful than anything else in his system' (p.48). The oscillation between the positive and negative approaches to Lacan's work is nicely illustrated by MacCannell, who begins by thinking that 'Lacan's discovery of the phallogocentric roots of our subjectivity . . . has the effect of perpetuating it, and not . . . of overthrowing it to renew it in a more perfect condition' (1982: 49), but then later changes her mind and thinks that a lot of his critics have been unfair to Lacan: 'The tendency . . . of his readers has been to over-identify Lacan's analysis of the culture of the signifier with Lacan, with his own stance *on* that culture' (1986: 19). She accuses herself of the same mistake (ibid.: 15–16, notes 2 and 4).

26.   Macey also makes a diagnosis of Lacan's imaginary; he suggests (1988: 201, 206) that Lacan is a fetishist.

27.   Silverman (1988: Ch. 1) provides a clear and helpful discussion of the meaning of the term 'symbolic castration' and its relation to the claim that 'there is no pre-discursive reality' (see especially pp.7–8). Subjectivity in language is *constituted by* the loss of the object:

When we say that language takes the place of the real, we mean that it takes the place of the real for the subject – that the child identifies with a signifier through which it is inserted into a closed field of signification. Within that field of signification, all elements – including the first-person pronoun which seems transparently to designate the subject – are defined exclusively through the play of codified differences. Not one of these elements is capable of reaching beyond itself to reestablish contact with the real. The door thus closes as finally upon the subject's being as upon the object. Lacan conveys the extremity of the opposition between language and the phenomenal realm when he describes it as a choice between meaning and life. (p.8).

This process has come to be referred to as symbolic castration.

28.   For two conceptualizations which indicate that the rigidity of Oedipal formulations might be giving way slightly, see Silverman (1988) and Adams (1989). Silverman suggests the possible symbolic adequacy of the negative Oedipus complex (1988: 136). What she means by this is that the Oedipal *mother* could occupy the third symbolic term which breaks up the imaginary dyad of mother and daughter; it is not necessary for the father to intervene. This would enable the activation of the negative Oedipus complex (the girl's love for the parent of the same sex), identification with the parent of the same sex, and at the same time open up the distance necessary to desire. Adams theorizes lesbian sadomasochism as a practice which has detached itself from the phallic referent and organizes sexuality outside the phallic field, thereby divorcing sexuality from gender.

29.   This is Irigaray's interpretation of Lacan's view that there is no relation between the sexes since 'woman does not exist' (see Mitchell and Rose 1982: 137–71). Irigaray's discussion is in 'Così fan Tutti' in *This Sex*.

30. The traps of the symbolism that one inherits are usefully discussed in Lloyd
     (1984: Ch. 7). See also Gatens (forthcoming).
31. Stanton (1986), though indicating, correctly I think, the echoes of Rimbaud
     in Irigaray and other women writers, does not problematize Irigaray's use of
     metaphor: 'the three exponents of difference, who are the subject of this study
     [Cixous, Irigaray, and Kristeva], have privileged metaphor, the trope upheld
     from classical to modernist times as the optimal tool for transporting meaning
     beyond the known' (1986: 157–8). Fuss (1989) recognizes the problem, though
     she concludes that:

> One wonders to what extent it is truly possible to think of the 'two lips' as
> something other than a metaphor. I would argue that, despite Irigaray's
> protestations to the contrary, the figure of the 'two lips' never stops functioning
> metaphorically. . . . But, what is important about Irigaray's conception of
> this particular figure is that the 'two lips' operate as a metaphor for
> *metonymy*; through this collapse of boundaries, Irigaray gestures towards
> the deconstruction of the classic metaphor/metonymy binarism. In fact, her
> work persistently attempts to effect a historical displacement of metaphor's
> dominance over metonymy. (1989: 72)

This seems to me an astute and perceptive comment. For further discussion of
     metaphor, metonymy, and the 'two lips', see Chapter 8, p.177ff.
32. Schor (1989) indicates that Irigaray distinguishes in *This Sex* between two
     different kinds of mimesis (TS: 131; CS: 129–30) and relates this to (1) the
     old mimesis (parrotting), and (2) a second level, in which parrotting becomes
     parody, a masquerade. Schor then suggests that one can also see a third level
     (3) mimesis, signifying difference as possibility. I would relate (1) to the 'other
     of the same', and (3) to the 'other of the other', discussed further in Section II;
     (2) and (3) would then correspond to the two moments of Irigaray's work, the
     strategic and the utopian.
33. In the technical language of Freud's metapsychology, this point is expressed as
     follows:

> the conscious presentation comprises the presentation of the thing plus the
> presentation of the word belonging to it, while the unconscious presentation
> is the presentation of the thing alone. The system *Ucs.* contains the thing-
> cathexes of the objects, the first and true object-cathexis; the system *Pcs.* comes
> about by this thing-presentation being hypercathected through being linked
> with the word-presentations corresponding to it. It is these hypercathexes,
> we may suppose, that bring about a higher psychical organisation and make
> it possible for the primary process to be succeeded by the secondary process
> which is dominant in the *Pcs.* . . . . A presentation which is not put into words,
> or a psychical act which is not hypercathected, remains thereafter in the *Ucs.*
> in a state of repression. (SE XIV: 200–1)

Chapter 4 Maternal genealogy and the symbolic

1. For a clear theoretical account of the difference, see Laplanche (1989: 54 ff.).
2. According to Derrida, *déréliction* is sometimes used in French to translate
    Heidegger's *Geworfenheit* (1986a: 427). Irigaray also defines it as the original
    state of loss and separation constituted by being born (E: 122–3), losing
    one's original home. But her main point is that the symbolic provides
    alternative homes for men, while women lack an adequate symbolization to
    house them.

3. Recent accounts from a variety of psychoanalytic and therapeutic perspectives (feminist and otherwise) stress women's difficulty in effecting separation. See for example Eichenbaum and Orbach (1982), Ernst and Maguire (1987), Kristeva (1987), Herman (1989). But the fact that they agree on the *symptom* should not lead one into concluding without further investigation that there is any similarity between Irigaray and these other accounts in their theoretical presuppositions.
4. A recent work by Olivier (1980) reaches much the same conclusion. Although Olivier has clearly been inspired by Irigaray, she discusses the wider society only in so far as it helps or hinders the possibility of shared parenting.
5. Cf. Heidegger's well-known statement that (poetic) language is the 'house of being'. One might see *L'Oubli de l'air* as an expanded version of the implications of this statement for women. See Chapter 7, p.156 ff.
6. There have been some serious misformulations of Irigaray's position here, perhaps arising from a non-structural interpretation of the pre-Oedipal which is equated with the imaginary. Look for example at the following statements by Kuykendall:

    > we can see that an ethic which Irigaray can develop from her perception of women as experiencing ourselves as paralyzed, unable to act, must begin by healing what she believes is a life-destroying breach between mother and daughter. . . . The ethical imperative that Irigaray would draw . . . is to cease to pursue the psychic separation between mother and daughter required by patriarchy. . . . Suppose, then, that we consider the possibility of a matriarchal ethic to replace that patriarchal imperative to separate mother from daughter. (1984: 267)

    These statements are correct, provided that one does not equate the 'patriarchal imperative to separate' with the psychic separation essential for separate identity; what Irigaray regards as life-destroying is the *failure to separate* and the consequent lack of distinction between the identity of the mother and that of the daughter. But in that case, how is one to interpret Kuykendall's statements that: 'Recent feminist arguments emphasize recognition rather than equality as a mark of mutuality, and some, like Luce Irigaray's, verge on a conception of mutuality as identity, as in the identity of mother with daughter' (1984: 264–5); or: 'But it is not clear, either, what more general interpretation can be offered to support a psychological interpretation of that relationship [between women] as conducive of fusion, rather than separation, with the ensuing mutuality and empowerment' (p.269) which, by taking fusion to be empowerment, simply claims the opposite of what Irigaray is actually writing? Such imprecision in terminology can only perpetuate misreading. But in more general terms, it is difficult, I think, for the Anglo-American reader familiar with feminist psychoanalytic theory through the work of Chodorow and object-relations theory, to understand what is different in Irigaray's theory unless considerably more theoretical context is supplied. (See Jardine 1985 on the problems of reading French theory out of context.)

    Again, Suleiman may not be wrong to write that:

    > 'When Our Lips Speak Together' is a text that celebrates love between women. What is most specific about such a love? . . . . In the perfect reciprocity of this relation, there is no place for an economy of exchange, or of opposition between contraries. The lovers are neither two nor one, neither different nor the same, but un-different (in-différentes). (1986: 13)

But without further explanation it is difficult for the reader to know exactly what is being celebrated; Suleiman's description could just as easily be read as an account of what for Irigaray is the symptom.

One final example from Doane:

> The image of the woman 'wrapped' in contiguity, deprived of the phallus as signifer of desire, has been taken up by French theorists such as Irigaray, Cixous, Montrelay, and Kofman in a sometimes hyperbolic celebration of the only picture of feminine 'subjectivity' available from psychoanalysis. These theorists activate the tropes of proximity, overpresence or excessive closeness to the body, and contiguity in the construction of a kind of 'ghetto politics' which maintains and applauds women's exclusion from language and the symbolic order. (1987: 12)

The *one* thing Irigaray is *not* celebrating is women's exclusion from language and the symbolic order: such an exclusion constitutes their dereliction.

7. There appears to be a growing consensus that this move is characteristic of postmodernism. See for example Battersby (1989), Hodge (1989), Morris (1988), Lovibond (1989).

8. Despite the differences between them, I think this is the position that unites Irigaray critics as diverse as Jacqueline Rose, Ellie-Ragland-Sullivan, Marie-Christine Hamon and Kaja Silverman.

9. For a brief account, see the item 'Foreclosure' in Laplanche and Pontalis (1967). I have found Green's 'The borderline concept' (1986: 60–83) helpful as a non-Lacanian discussion of the different mechanisms which might be involved. In particular, Green distinguishes between repression and splitting, and between splitting in psychosis and splitting in borderline disorders. However one conceptualizes the process of non-symbolization which Irigaray discusses in *Speculum* (and to which I refer in the present section), it is clear that it is not repression; as Irigaray points out: 'can one speak at this stage of repression when the processes that make it possible have not yet come into being?' (SE: 84; SF: 101). Some more radical inaccessibility of representation is at work here. It is important to note that Irigaray locates it primarily not in the psyche of the individual woman but in the symbolic order itself. It is the female imaginary which is psychotic – in bits and pieces – rather than individual women. This makes it difficult for individuals to find an identity *as women*, i.e. as a different sex (see Chapter 6).

10. Brennan (1988) points out that if the lack of a penis meant the complete inability to effect symbolic castration, then all women would be psychotic, which is obviously not the case. See also her discussion of the 'Lacanian muddle':

> 'the idea that the phallus is represented by the penis implies, according to some thoroughly criticised Lacanian accounts, that men are more capable of differentiating themselves. For those same Lacanians, this explains the empirically greater incidence of psychoses among women; women are more likely to be undifferentiated, goes this reasoning, thus psychotic. Hence a paradox. The patriarchal symbolic is a condition of sanity for both sexes, women excepted' (1989: 5).

11. This is the reading given by Montefiore (1987).

12. Brennan (1990), 'An impasse in psychoanalysis and feminism' in Sneja Gunew (ed.), *Feminist Knowledge: Critique and Construct*.

13. This issue is discussed in Gallop (1982: ch. 1); Rose (1986: 49–81); Brennan (1990).

14. See Brennan (1990).

15.   Laplanche and Pontalis give a useful summary (1967: 371–8) (in English under
the heading 'Death instincts'). See also Hinshelwood (1989) on its avatars
in Kleinian theory (under the headings of 'Superego' and 'Death Instinct').
Irigaray's Freudian sources are: 'Instincts and their vicissitudes' (SE XIV),
'Beyond the pleasure principle' (SE XVIII) and 'The economic problem of
masochism' (SE XIX).

16.   If I am right in thinking that Irigaray's politics is to a considerable extent
psychoanalytically derived, then Borch-Jacobsen's (1989) discussion of Freudian politics would be relevant here. According to Borch-Jacobsen, there is
a complicity in Freud between subject-form and political form, so that what
threatens the subject also threatens the political. The unity of the social body
and the unity of the subject cannot be dissociated. The Oedipus complex is in
fact a political myth – a myth with a political function, while the subject is 'born'
in myth, fantasy, and art. Viewed from this perspective, Irigaray's work could
readily be perceived as a simultaneous threat to the male subject and to the
social order (an interpretation one sometimes comes across). As I read her, she
is *deeply* concerned with the question of social order, and with binding rather than
dissolving. Borch-Jacobsen's interpretation of Freud supports my hypothesis
to the extent that I see the economy of the subject and the organization of the social
world as inextricably linked in Irigaray's thought.

Chapter 5 The same, the semblance, and the other

1.   I use this term as a sort of catachresis (without a literal referent) since whatever
it is that women have been excluded from obviously varies a lot.

2.   I am not sure what sort of causality, if any, is being posited here. Sometimes in
interviews, Irigaray makes it sound as though the symbolic had primacy. But
in her more cautious moments she merely claims that the symbolic goes hand
in hand with other determinants. I suggest two possible directions for further
exploration here. (1) See 'Dialectique et histoire' in Goux (1973) for a discussion
of causality which could shed some light on the kind of conception Irigaray might
be working with, since Goux, like Irigaray, is specifically addressing the symbolic
function, but within a more traditionally materialist framework than Irigaray.
(2) See Copjec, who links the notion of cause with that of the death drive: 'Cause
is a concept that must be forged anew if we are to build some understanding of
the relation between the social order and psychical existence' (1989: 244). Since
the death drive seems to me to be central for Irigaray, this is a direction which
should clearly be investigated further.

3.   Sexual difference is not an opposition or a contradiction, and in this
respect Irigaray does not accept Hegel's opposition mediate/immediate. See
'L'Universel comme médiation' in *Sexes et parentés*.

4.   See Judovitz (1988) for a remarkable discussion of the links in Descartes between
truth, representation, subjectivity, and the scopic economy. Her argument is
that:

> Although Descartes uses representation in its ordinary sense to designate
> any image or presentation, corresponding to our current use of the
> term in literary criticism and art history, he contends that the only
> valid philosophical representation is one based on the criterion of
> certitude. In this study, representation will be in question as the
> concept that governs axiomatically the conditions of possibility of all
> the representations as objects. As a schema, representation defines how
> the subject comes to know the world, by describing it according to its

norms. The truth of representation will be shown to emerge as a result of adequation, not between ideas and the world, but rather, between ideas and the conventions that define the validity of those ideas.... The efforts to go beyond these terms [subjectivity and representation], as postmodernity has tried to do, imply more often than not the preservation of their metaphysical underpinnings. Although postmodernism is posited as the overcoming of subjectivity and representation, upon closer scrutiny it becomes clear that its critiques do nothing more than reinforce the contradictions of their original articulation. (1988: x–xi)

5. The Form or Idea in Plato is not consistently defined. See for example Murdoch (1972: 25–31).

6. Irigaray, in her interpretation of Plato, appears to follow the line that Greek thinkers around the time of Plato had become preoccupied with measurement as an exact science. As Nussbaum explains:

> Evidently, then, a science of deliberative measurement would be an enormous advantage in human social life. And this is an idea for which the tradition of Greek reflection about *techne* and human understanding has by Plato's time prepared the way. The connection between numbering and knowing, the ability to count or measure and the ability to grasp, comprehend or control, runs very deep in Greek thought about human cognition. Already in Homer, the poet associates knowing with the ability to enumerate: the Muses give him their knowledge of the warring armies by imparting a catalogue of their numbers and divisions. To answer a 'how many?' question is to demonstrate a praiseworthy grasp of that to which one's attention is directed. We find in Homer contrasts between the *andrōn arithmos*, the denumerable army of heroes whose story can therefore be told, and the *dēmos apeirōn*, the mass of the undemarcated, whose lives will never be grasped and set down in a definite way. The denumerable is the definite, the graspable, therefore also the potentially tellable, controllable; what cannot be numbered remains vague and unbounded, evading human grasp. (1986: 107)

One of the central concerns that emerged out of this preoccupation, Nussbaum continues, was the necessity for a single measure or standard against which everything could be measured; a single standard would enable even apparently disparate things to be measured against each other as having *more* or *less* of whatever the standard was. This measure is preferably quantitative, therefore, allowing precise and accurate judgements to be made. And one can see Plato's ethical thought in this way; if agreement could be reached on the nature of the Good, and if it could be shown that certain activities essentially had more of, or were closer to, the Good, then there could be no real disagreement about what to do. According to Nussbaum, this picture replaces the more complex one, enacted by Greek tragedies, where the necessity of choosing between two actions, each equally demanded and yet incompatible, was the source of tragic conflict. In Plato's version, the conflict would be solved by agreement on a single standard so that the two actions could be shown to approach, to a greater or lesser extent, to the idea of the Good. It would then make sense to choose the action which had *more* rather than *less* of the Good:

> We readily grasp the relevance of measurement to the removal of serious value conflict. For instead of choosing, under circumstantial pressure, to neglect a different value with its own separate claim, one will merely be giving up a smaller amount of the same thing. (1986: 109)

Nussbaum does point out in a footnote that not everyone agrees with her interpretation of Greek thought (p.449, note 44), but it is an interpretation which illuminates clearly the issues with which Irigaray is concerned, particularly the question of the *single standard* (the One, the Same) and the claims of the different value. For Irigaray, women and men are ontologically *incommensurable*; they cannot, except by reduction of one sex to the other, be measured as greater or lesser approximations of the One.

7. On this point see Judovitz (1988: ch. 2). For other feminist accounts of the relation between phallocentrism and oculocentrism, see for example Keller and Grontkowski (1983) in philosophy, and the work of feminist film theorists, e.g. Kaplan (1984), Kuhn (1982, 1985), Doane (1987), de Lauretis (1984, 1987), Mulvey (1989), Silverman (1988). See also Kappeler (1986).

8. For another feminist account of the incorporation of the maternal function in Plato, and in the beginnings of modern science, see Keller, (1985). See also Benjamin (1980), Hartsock (1983: ch. 11), and O'Brien (1981).

9. See Lovibond (1989) on Nietzsche, feminism, castration, and truth. Also helpful are Speidel's notes to her translation of 'Veiled lips' (1983) from *Amante marine*.

10. Perhaps following Freud's hypothesis that one always finds in analysis: 'the invariable presence of the castration complex' (SE X: 8 note 2).

11. And also to Derrida's *Spurs* (1978, trans. 1978). Speidel (see note 9) suggests that in Irigaray's text: 'In a sense . . . Derrida seems to become 'woman' in *Veiled Lips* – his expression veiled, silenced and effaced, mediating between Irigaray and Nietzsche' (p.123, note 8).

12. Speidel helpfully provides the following gloss:

> Pallas Athene was born without her mother, emerging fully-grown from the head of Zeus. . . . According to Hesiod, Athena was the child of Zeus and Metis (Wisdom, Cunning) but her birth presupposed the disappearance of her mother. . . . [T]he father-gods who preceded Zeus – Ouranos and Kronos – both fell victim to sons who acted as embodiments of their mothers, of the mother's power to outwit and replace the father. Fearful of the children that Gaia, the Earth, would bear him, Ouranos, the Sky, tried to force her offspring back into her womb, but Gaia tricked him. To her son Kronos she gave a sickle, and when Ouranos entered her, Kronos – hiding in the earth – castrated his father. Kronos, in turn, fearful of his children, ate each at birth, but Rheia, their mother – in league with Gaia – deceived him, feeding him a stone instead of Zeus. Zeus survived to overthrow Kronos. Faced with the cunning of Metis, Zeus evaded the destiny of his father and grandfather by devouring – not the children – but the mother herself. He ate Metis and, having made her his cunning, produced from his own head a child, Athena, the transformation of the mother's guile into an instrument of the father's policy and will' (Speidel, op.cit.: 119–20, note 1)

In the text, Irigaray is referring to Aeschylus, *The Oresteia*, from which the quotations are taken. On Irigaray's use of the myth of Athena, see also Grosz (1989: 163 ff).

13. On the relation between death and castration in Freud, see particularly SE XIX: 57–9 and SE XX: 128–30 ('The Ego and the Id' and 'Inhibitions, Symptoms and Anxiety'). Klein revises Freud's view that the fear of death and the fear of castration are analogous, and states even more strongly that 'the fear of death enters into and reinforces castration fear' (Klein 1988: 30).

14. To give a concrete example, which Irigaray uses in 'Misère de la psychanalyse': in psychoanalysis, analysts analyse women's phantasies and fears of being raped. It is easier to address rape in terms of women's phantasies than it is to address

the relation between *men's* rape phantasies and social reality, between men's aggressive desires and the social and symbolic distribution of sadism and masochism. It is easier to put the social reality down to 'nature'.

15. And *not*, as the English translation gives it, 'a dream that is *also* truth'.

16. For the principal discussions of Antigone in Irigaray's work, see *Speculum* (SE: 214–26, 117–18; SF: 266–81; 146–7), *Ethique de la différence sexuelle* (E: 105–6, 113 ff.), *Sexes et parentés* (SP: 13 ff., 124 ff.) and *Le Temps de la différence* (TD: 81 ff.).

17. *Sang* is also a semi-homophone of *sens* (sense – as in the five senses – or meaning), and this pun is also used by Irigaray.

18. When Simone de Beauvoir identified woman as the Other, she was, in Irigarayan terms, pointing to their status as 'other of the same'. The only alternative she could see was to argue for Sameness: women should accede to the world of men. Thus she accepts a basically Hegelian view of transcendence, which does not challenge the dominance of the transcendence/immanence split. Irigaray's difference from Simone de Beauvoir can be clearly seen here, in that Irigaray is staking on the possibility of an 'other of the other' which would recast the Hegelian problematic altogether. See Schor (1989).

Chapter 6 Identity and violence

1. This dilemma is formulated in Moi (1985, 1988), de Lauretis (1987) and Braidotti (1989).

2. The phrase is used by de Lauretis (1984: 7) and Grosz (1986a: 134).

3. See especially 'Le V(i)ol de la Lettre' [The rape/plunder of the letter] in *Parler n'est jamais neutre* (a response to Derrida's *Of Grammatology, Writing and Difference*, 'Différance' in *Margins of Philosophy* and 'The double session' in *Dissemination*; the title echoes 'The violence of the letter' in Derrida's *Of Grammatology*) and *La Croyance même* (a response to Derrida's *The Post Card* and first given as a paper at a conference on Derrida's work called 'The Ends of Man'). See also *Amante marine* (where Derrida's *Spurs* is part of the intertext), *Ethique de la différence sexuelle* (where traces of Derrida can also be found). This is not an exhaustive list. Derrida is clearly an intertextual figure in *Speculum*, and no doubt in other places too, such as *L'Oubli de l'air*.

4. I have in mind Spivak (1983, 1989). In 1983, Spivak indicates (firstly and secondly) what the strengths are seen to be and (thirdly) what the limitations are:

> My attitude towards deconstruction can now be summarised: first, deconstruction is illuminating as a critique of phallocentrism; second, it is convincing as an argument against the founding of a hysterocentric to counter a phallocentric discourse; third, as a 'feminist' practice itself, it is caught on the other side of sexual difference. At whatever remove of 'différance' (difference/deferment from/of any decidable statement of the concept of an identity or difference) *sexual difference is thought*, sexual *differential* between 'man' and 'woman' remains irreducible. (1983: 184)

In 1989 she explains that women need not abandon deconstruction, but that the name 'woman' is not one that they can use as a deconstructive device:

> I explain in the essay why feminism should keep to the critical ways of deconstruction but give up its attachment to that specific name for the problem/solution of founded programmes . . ., also named 'writing' [p.206]. The claim to deconstructive feminism (and deconstructive anti-sexism – the political claim of deconstructive feminists) cannot be sustained in

the name of 'woman'. Like class consciousness, which justifies its own
production so that classes can be destroyed, 'woman' as the name
of writing must be erased in so far as it is a necessarily historical
catachresis. . . . It should be a lesson to us that *if* we do not watch out
for the historical determinations for the name of woman as catachresis in
deconstruction, and merely seek to delegitimize the name of man, we legitimize
what is diagnosed by Nietzsche and acted out by Foucault. (1989: 218)

5.   I am indebted in this section to the work of other scholars who have written
on Derrida and feminism, in particular the work of Rosi Braidotti, Elizabeth
Grosz, Alice Jardine, and Gayatri Chakravorty Spivak. See also Allen (1989),
Bartkowski (1980), de Lauretis (1987), Doane (1989), Findlay (1989), Fraser
(1984), Kintz (1989), McGraw (1984), Ragland-Sullivan (1989), Rose (1989)
and *Feminist Studies* (1988).
     Elizabeth Grosz has pointed out to me in correspondence that I have been
rather unfair to Derrida in this section. She comments:

> Whilst I think you do raise some serious reservations about and valid feminist
> criticisms of Derridean deconstruction, I also think that you have not accorded
> his position the generosity you show to others, particularly to Irigaray's own
> work. Many of your claims and criticisms regarding Derrida's position seem
> rather too close to the objections raised by other feminists against Irigaray's
> position.

I think this is probably true, and no doubt some reader of this book will want
to show in detail the extent of my unfairness. What I have tried to do is to focus
on Derrida's explicit position vis-à-vis feminism (thus in a Derridean-influenced
way, choosing the *marginal* remarks, the interviews, the off-the-cuff or at least less
reflective comments, as a lever), to highlight the erasure of women in favour of
woman. However, I readily accept that the value of Derrida's work for feminism
lies in what feminists – of which Irigaray is a foremost example – can make of
it.

6.   On this point, Bannet (1989: 202 ff.) is helpful.
7.   Derrida's 'third woman' in *Spurs*. It would be instructive to compare Derrida's
formulations here with Irigaray's conceptualization of woman as the 'other of
the other'.
8.   Fuss (1990) argues for Derrida's implication in essentialism.
9.   See for example Barbara Christian in Kauffman (1989). This diagnosis of
'narcissism' from a Black feminist critic states fairly clearly the kind of position
that Irigaray is taking up:

> These writers did announce their dissatisfaction with some of the cornerstone
> ideas of their own tradition . . . But in their attempt to change the orientation
> of Western scholarship, they, as usual, concentrated on themselves and were
> not in the slightest interested in the worlds they had ignored or controlled.
> Again I was supposed to know *them*, while they were not at all interested in
> knowing *me*. Instead they sought to 'deconstruct' the tradition to which they
> belonged even as they used the same forms, style, language of that tradition,
> forms that necessarily embody its values. . . . [T]hey always harkened back
> to the masterpieces of the past, again reifying the very texts they said they
> were deconstructing. Increasingly, . . . *their* way, *their* terms, *their* approaches
> remained central' (p.230)

10. On feminism, Derrida, and the death drive, see Jacqueline Rose's brilliant
(1989) article: 'Where does the misery come from? Psychoanalysis, feminism
and the "event"', and Ragland-Sullivan (1989).

11.   See Rey Chow in Weed (1989):

> one is tempted to see a kind of uncanny repetition of the treatment of the 'other' that was in Hegel – a treatment that privileges the eventfulness, the motility, and thus the 'self-consciousness' of the 'universal subject' to the detriment of the represented or colonized object, who, by implication, has not even begun to be contradictory.... And yet ... critics often elaborate on domination-as-structure in such a way as to repeat precisely this asymmetry. (p.160)

Her point is about the (necessary) limitations of the anti-imperialist discourse of the First World critic of imperialism, but the point seems to me to apply equally to the male deconstructor of phallogocentrism. Irigaray expresses a similar point in *Speculum* as follows:

> But perhaps beyond this specular surface which sustains discourse is found not the void of nothingness but the dazzle of a multifaceted speleology. A scintillating and incandescent concavity.... We need only press on a little further into the depths, into that so-called dark cave which serves as hidden foundation to their speculations. For there where we expect to find the opaque and silent matrix of a logos immutable in the certainty of its own light, fires and mirrors are beginning to radiate. (SE: 143–4; SF: 178–9)

12.   Spivak (1983, 1984) explains clearly the family relationships here.
13.   See also: 'we do need to ask ourselves how to give an identity to scientific, religious and political discourses, and to situate ourselves in these discourses as subjects in our own right.' Irigaray in Jardine and Menke (forthcoming).
14.   There is an interesting disagreement between two of Irigaray's most acute and sympathetic interpreters, Rosi Braidotti and Elizabeth Grosz. Grosz takes Irigaray to be operating entirely within the field of the discursive; everything she writes is a discursive strategy. Braidotti takes Irigaray to be positing sexual difference as an ontological category – like mortality, always already there – and to be founding her strategies on a politics of essentialism. I would be inclined here to go for the logic of the both/and. Why assume that she is doing *either* one *or* the other? Particularly as *both* see her as employing *strategies*, – so that positing ontological difference might itself be a mimetic or discursive tactic.
15.   The recent collection edited by Linda J. Nicholson, *Feminism/Postmodernism* (1990), provides a brilliant collection of current debates in the States around the question of the politics of identity. Many of the contributors – but by no means all – conclude that the presuppositions of the notion of identity make it politically and theoretically dubious.
16.   See Copjec (1989) for a non-Derridean view of identity which sees its internal scission as *constitutive* of identity rather than undermining it:

> When psychoanalysis speaks of the hysteric's failure of identity, it accounts for this failure ... by means of the materiality of language, which always cuts the subject off from a complete identity. Yet the necessary failure of social discourses in their representations of the subject is not taken by psychoanalysis – as it is by Derrida and Weber – as the subversion of the subject's identity. Rather this failure, the very *impossibility* of representing the subject to the subject, is conceived as that which *founds* the subject's identity. *The failure of representation produces rather than disrupts identity*. That missing part which representation, in failing to inscribe, cuts off is the absence around which the subject weaves its fantasies, its self-image, not in imitation of any ideal vision, but in response to the very impossibility of ever making visible this missing part. We are constructed, then, not in conformity to

social laws, but in response to our inability to conform to or see ourselves
as defined by social limits. Though we are defined and limited *historically*, the
absence of the real, which founds these limits, is not *historicizable*. It is only
this distinction which informs the Lacanian definition of cause that allows
us to think the construction of the subject without thereby being obliged to
reduce her *to* the images social discourses construct *of* her. (1989: 241–2)

As I shall argue later, Irigaray sees *male* identity (which Derrida deconstructs)
as founded on a non-acknowledgement of its own scission; the reorganization
of the death drive would involve recasting the problematic of identity, so that
the Same reincorporated its own Other, thus splitting the unicity [= 'unicité']
of Sameness internally, and allowing the possibility of woman as both Same
and Other for-herself.

17.   The problematics of identity, becoming, and the death drives has obvious
Hegelian and post-Hegelian overtones (see Butler 1987; see pp.14–15 on the
question of the desire for identity as a kind of philosophical death wish). I have
not considered here the question of Irigaray's Hegelianism. But provisionally,
my argument would be that Irigaray reformulates the problem of identity and
the death drive in terms of the split subject and of gender, and that in so doing
she opens up the Hegelian perspective while still remaining to a certain extent
within its problematic. The question to ask of Irigaray's work, then, would be
whether and to what extent she has succeeded in reformulating the question of
generic identity without falling back into the stasis of the metaphysical economy
of the death drive. She is certainly aware of this as an issue.

18.   I therefore disagree with Frances Bartkowski's (1986) assessment of Irigaray's
ethics. Bartkowski quotes Kristeva to the effect that the 'habitual and in-
creasingly explicit attempt to fabricate a scapegoat victim as foundress of
a society or a counter-society' should be replaced by the 'analysis of the
potentialities of *victim/executioner* which characterize each identity, each subject,
each sex' (quoted p.28). Bartkowski continues:

How are we to take comfort and find challenge in contemporary writings like
Irigaray's that seem so thoroughly disconnected from the lives of real human
beings – female and male? What of those women who may still be 'more
cruel than their masters', as Beauvoir did not fail to see? . . . What Irigaray
seems neither to acknowledge nor to represent is the return of the hierarchical
struggle among those who have not yet had their full say (pp.28–9).

On the contrary, it seems to me, Irigaray is confronting precisely that problem.
Only by *symbolizing* their own negativity – whether one calls it death drive,
sadomasochism, cruelty, exclusion or hierarchical struggle – can women
collectively find ways to address it.

19.   On the *retouche*, see Chapter 7 and the beginning of Chapter 8.

20.   Another direction to explore, which I have not discussed here, is her use of the
work of Eliade on the sacred. See also Irigaray's discussion of a book by the
feminist theologian Elisabeth Schüssler Fiorenza, *In Memory of Her* (New York:
Crossroad Publishing Co. 1983) in 'Equal to Whom?' (1989).

21.   See the interview with Irigaray in *Hecate* (1983).

22.   If she is, as I hypothesize, also using the work of Goux, this reading is
supported by Goux's attempt to read Marxism and psychoanalysis as
structurally homologous. According to Goux, God is like gold, or the
phallus, a 'general equivalent'. The question of God is thus framed in
terms both of the imaginary and symbolic order, and of the economic order.
Quoting Descartes, he concludes that 'the *ego* [moi] and *the idea of God* are

the two sides of the same reality of the soul' (1973: 65), reading Descartes here in terms of the specular relationships of the mirror stage, with God as a sort of divine mirror.

23.   Self-love = *amour de soi*. This term has a history. Against the pessimism of La Rochefoucauld (1613–80), for whom there was no altruism, only a ravening self-interest, Rousseau defined two meanings of self-love, *amour de soi* and *amour propre*. The first was positive, to do with self-esteem, self-preservation and self-respect. The second was negative, to do with unhealthy dependence on the opinion of others, leading to vanity, seeing oneself as the centre of the world.

24.   Interestingly, we sometimes find the phrase *advenir-femme* (the advent of woman) rather than *devenir-femme* (becoming-woman) which is associated with Derrida or Deleuze for example. Thus *Ethique* (E: 124) uses *advenir* for the coming-to-be of the sensible transcendental. See also *This Sex* (TS: 141; CS: 139) where *advenir* is translated into English as 'coming-to-be-woman'.

25.   See Borch-Jacobsen (1989) for a sophisticated discussion of the relation between the 'same' and conflict which draws on both Freud and Girard, (but not Irigaray for some reason).

26.   The ending of Zoë Fairbairns's *Benefits* (1979) allows us to raise in imagination the question of what might happen and what women might do if the supply of mothers, for whatever reason, did dry up, and if women were no longer mothers.

27.   This point has been taken up by some Italian feminist groups, using Irigaray's work – see the discussion of *affidamento* in Cicioni (1989) – as an attempt to give public form to a particular kind of relationship between women which would recognize the *differences* between women and mediate them symbolically. As Cicioni explains, *affidamento* has been both practically and theoretically controversial, however.

28.   For a longer and excellent discussion of Irigaray on religion, see Grosz (1986c, 1989).

Chapter 7 Ethics, sexuality, and embodiment

1.   In their introduction to *Desire: The Politics of Sexuality*, the editors write

> Foucault gives a subtle rendering of the general argument that sex and capitalism have gone hand-in-hand for too long for sex to be interpreted at face value as a radical force. Foucault suggests that the public discussion of sex constitutes a chief way in which modern social institutions manipulate the consciousness and intimate experience of great masses of people . . . To advance the cause of sexual freedom, then, may paradoxically tighten the grip of the system. But while Foucault raises important questions against which to test the current talk about sex, his analysis rests, as it must, on the obsessive male sexual discourse that runs through the centuries from St Augustine to Philip Roth. Women's relationship to the sexual – like that of people of color and sexual minorities – has been very different. It has been tacit. To close a discussion that began for some only very recently is to leave those speakers once again beyond consideration . . . It is too soon, then, for silence. (Snitow et al. 1984, pp.1–2).

2.   See for example *Parler n'est jamais neutre* (PN: 268–9); the first interview in *Les Femmes, la pornographie et l'érotisme* (e.g. pp.44, 48–9); *This Sex* (TS: 23–3; CS: 23–32); 'Questions to Emmanuel Levinas' (first question).

3.   See for example Butler (1989a).

4.   On Heidegger: 'As long as Heidegger does not leave the "earth", he does not leave metaphysics' (OA: 10);

Where he exists, she is no longer. . . . The ek-stase is the exit-entry outside of her. But at the same time, outside of him. Is it thus that his being, as sexed being, destines itself? Throwing-projecting him always there? At a distance? In the distancing? . . . He forgets that there are in the there two different ek-stases. That the there of the destiny of his being is not the there of her subsistence. He folds them back into the same, in the eternal return to the same. (OA: 62)

On Merleau-Ponty: see *Ethique* (E: 143–71, especially 148, 162 and 167–8. Cf.: 'The whole analysis of Merleau-Ponty is marked by this . . . solipsism. Without the other and above all the other of sexual difference, it is impossible to get out of this description of the visible, doubled with [redoublée de] that of the tactile of the touching hands?' (E: 148). 'So I might say that Merleau-Ponty's seer remains in a prenatal incestuous situation with the whole. This mode of existence or of being is probably that of all men, at least in the West' (E: 162). 'For a sublimation of the flesh, what is lacking is a passage through silence and solitude which leads to the existence, the emergence of a *parole* of a person who is born in a space still to be defined by him, to be marked by him, in order that, speaking (of) himself, he might also be able to speak himself to the other and hear him' (E: 167). 'If reversibility is not interrupted, the sublimation of the flesh cannot be accomplished' (E: 168). On Levinas: see E: 173–99 (translated as 'The fecundity of the caress' in Cohen (ed.), *Face-to-Face with Levinas* (1985): 231–56) and 'Questions to Emmanuel Levinas'. Cf.:

> To caress, for Levinas, consists, therefore, not in approaching the other in its most vital dimension: the touch, but in the reduction of that vital dimension of the other's body to the elaboration of a future for himself. To caress could thus constitute the hidden intention of philosophical temporality. . . . This description of the caress . . . is a good example of the way in which the temporality of the male subject, of Emmanuel Levinas at any rate, makes use of the support of the feminine in the intentionality of pleasure for its own becoming. In this transformation of the flesh of the other into his own temporality, it is clear that the masculine subject loses the feminine as other (QEL: 112).

Irigaray does not discuss Simone de Beauvoir (except briefly in the interview 'Egales ou différentes?') though I suspect that a comparison would reveal more debt than she acknowledges. She does not discuss Sartre either, as far as I know, although she must be aware of his version of the imaginary. But his philosophy of ek-stasis, with the for-itself fleeing from an engulfing and more or less explicitly feminine in-itself, clearly fits her analysis of the male imaginary.

I am not acquainted with the full range of feminist work on phenomenology. However, the following might be of interest: On Sartre: Collins and Pierce (1976); on Merleau-Ponty: Butler (1989b); McMillan (1987); Reineke (1987). On Levinas: articles by Alison Ainley, Tina Chanter and Noreen Connor in Bernasconi and Wood (1989); Chalier (1982).

5.   For Kant, the transcendental is the conditions of possibility of experience (and therefore, by definition, not experience itself). For Husserl, the transcendental is reached through the bracketing of the empirical and the contingent, in the gesture of the *epoche* in order to reach the structure of the constituting ego which for Husserl constitutes itself *in and through* the constitution of its objects. What is left, after the bracketing has been performed, is the pure structure of the subject in universal form. With Sartre, the transcendental ego is empty of content; the empirical ego is its object. In each case, there is a rigorous split or exclusion of the sensible, of experience, of the empirical or psychological.

6. One might also see here a response to Levinas in part. If Levinas uses the language of the 'feminine' to support his temporality, perhaps Irigaray is using the language of the masculine, at times, to support *her* becoming. And how to refer to the masculine, the transcendentally neutral, *except* in sexual terms? Chalier (1982) gives a number of examples of Levinas's deployment of the 'feminine' in his ethical account.

7. Glossed by Krell in his editorial remarks on Heidegger's 'Building Dwelling Thinking' (1978: 321).

8. 'Comment et où habiter?' in *Cahiers du Grif* 26 (March 1983).

9. See Grosz's brilliant article on 'Desire, the body and recent French feminisms' (1988a) and her discussion of alternative modes of spatialization and temporality. Some of the same ideas can also be found in her article 'Notes towards a corporeal feminism' (1987) which develops a conception of the social/political body which avoids mind/body dualism and could usefully be compared with Irigaray's conception of the sensible transcendental.

10. There is possibly an oblique reference to Derrida here, since for Derrida, *différance* or espacement (which is neither space nor time – see Derrida, 1972: 59) is the condition of Kant's *a priori*, not the maternal-feminine.

11. See *L'Oubli de l'air*, where Irigaray suggests that the structure of Heidegger's *Sorge* (= *souci* or care) exemplifies this.

Chapter 8 Women and/in the social contract

1. Cf. MacCannell:

   Well before Freud, Rousseau saw that cultural man has the capacity to generate a norm out of the most norm-free of situations and to serve, in the name of maintaining itself, the 'death instinct'. In short, 'culture' seems always to tend to become 'nature', i.e. an *ordered* set of principled, fixed behaviour and structures. It can only 'progress', then, if resubjected to the radical reflection on 'natural' cultural arrangements by which semiosis originates (1982: 31).

   MacCannell may not agree, but I certainly think that this is what Irigaray is doing: her work is a 'radical reflection on "natural" cultural arrangements'.

2. See for example her 'Mythes religieux et civils' in *Rinascita* 18 April 1987, forthcoming in *Je-Tu-Nous*.

3. Saussure thought that language use was a 'sort of contract' (quoted in Rose 1984: 115). This may well be where Lacan derived the idea of 'the word' as 'the pact that transforms [subjects] and establishes them as human communicating subjects' (Lacan 1975a: 126). Gillian Rose also points out that writing is Derrida's name for the social contract (1984: 143). For Derrida, she says, 'the "subject" is identical with the "social" or "moral"' (ibid.) though she argues that his reading of Rousseau is to some extent a *mis*reading. Kristeva takes a similar line on the social contract: 'the symbolic contract which *is* the social contract' (1986: 196).

4. The social contract was criticized by Hegel on a number of grounds (see Pateman 1988: 173 ff. for a discussion), but primarily because it reduces the person to a single dimension, that of the ability to make and enter contracts. Pateman points out that despite Hegel's objection to the social contract, he paradoxically and at the same time accepts a form of marriage contract which excludes women from political life and relegates them to the private sphere of the family, so that although he appears to be opposed to social contract theory, he retains its hidden underside: the sexual contract which keeps women out of public

life. Irigaray makes much the same objection, though on different theoretical grounds.

5.   See Dews (1987), Macey (1988).

6.   Macey shows how much this reading is indebted to Kojève's account of Hegel. In this version of the social contract, the imaginary seems to correspond not to Rousseau's primordial state of nature, in which humans, although isolated from each other, are naturally compassionate, but rather to the 'pastoral stage' where aggression first makes its appearance, or to the 'second state of nature' (despotism) which makes the need for the new contract obvious.

7.   I leave out here the complications of metaphor and the contract in Hegel and Derrida, but on this, see the discussion in Rose (1984: ch. 8).

8.   Cf. also: 'It clearly cannot be a matter of substituting feminine power for masculine power. Because this reversal would still be caught up in the economy of the same, in the same economy – in which, of course, what I am trying to designate as "feminine" would not emerge' (TS: 129–30; CS: 128).

9.   See also *Speculum* (SE: 351, 348), where 'contact' translates 'contiguïté' (SF: 439–440 and 437), and *Speculum* (SE: 352) where 'being close to' translates 'contiguïté à' (SF: 442). See also *Amante marine* (AM: 104).

10.   Among numerous other examples, see the title of *Le Corps-à-corps avec la mère* [*Body-to-body with the mother*], or the '*have a fling with the philosophers*' (TS: 150; CS: 147), or *Amante marine* passim, e.g. 'to reflect you with her in the river which together you would make flow' (AM: 39) or '[Persephone] does not "want" herself except with the other' (AM: 123).

11.   And cf. in a recent book: 'Education, the social world of men-amongst-themselves, patriarchal culture function for little girls like Hades for Kore-Persephone' (TD: 122) – a stark modern rereading of this myth.

12.   I am not quite sure what she means here by 'institutions' (in French in the singular – *institution*) since the principal definition of this word is: social forms or structures established by law or custom, especially those in the domain of public law/right (*droit public*). It's much more likely to mean *the* institution, e.g. Parliament, and to be referring to questions like the number of women MPs within the existing structure. Perhaps it is worth reiterating that Irigaray is not opposed to tactical struggles, but does see them as long-term aims.

13.   This work can be found in *Le Temps de la différence*.

14.   The exchange without *étalon* is one of her most persistent images. Cf. the following passage from 'When our lips speak together':

> Exchange? Everything is exchanged, yet there are no transactions. Between us, there are no proprietors, no determinable objects, no prices. Our bodies are nourished by our mutual pleasure. Our abundance is inexhaustible: it knows neither want nor plenty . . . our exchanges are without terms, without end. (TS: 213–14; CS: 213)

15.   See Chapter 2, point 6 pp. 36–7. Owens (1987: 224) criticizes Irigaray for her imprecise understanding of Lévi-Strauss. Leland argues that Irigaray's appropriation of 'empirically suspect Lévi-Straussian and Lacanian claims' is 'uncritical', and that her 'account of psychological oppression lacks cultural and historical specificity' (1989: 83); Moi (1985: 141) finds her use of Marx disappointing. As in Chapter 1, I would argue that one cannot address Irigaray's critiques without *first* taking into account her interrogation of the presuppositions underlying each system and its conceptualization. It is not

enough simply to reiterate in one's objections the categories which Irigaray is putting into question.

16.   I had already completed the present book when I read Gemma Corradi Fiumara's remarkable *The Other Side of Language: A Philosophy of Listening* (London: Routledge 1990) which seems to me to put forward, in a much more fully elaborated form, many of the ideas I was trying to work out in relation to Irigaray: in particular ideas about the psychoanalytic session as a philosophical model; knowledge and reason as ideally 'connubial' rather than 'predatory' or 'grasping'; the possibility of bringing to birth the as yet unspoken, unexpressed, and even unthought.

Bibliography

1. Luce Irigaray

French

1965   J. Dubois, L. Irigaray, and P. Marcie, 'Transformation négative et organisation des classes lexicales', *Cahiers de Lexicologie* 7: 1–32.
        J. Dubois, P. Marcie, L. Irigaray, H. Hécaen, and R. Angelergues, 'Analyse distributionnelle en neurolinguistique: le comportement verbal des aphasiques et des déments dans les épreuves de langage répété', *Langage et comportement* 1: 111–34.

1966   J. Dubois and L. Irigaray, 'Approche expérimentale de la constitution de la phrase minimale en français', *Langages* 3: 90–125.
        L. Irigaray and J. Dubois, 'Les Structures linguistiques de la parenté et leurs perturbations dans les cas de démence et de schizophrénie', *Cahiers de Lexicologie* 8: 47–69.

1967   'Approche psycholinguistique du langage des déments,' *Neuropsychologia* 5: 25–52.
        'La Production de phrases chez les déments', *Langages* 5: 49–66.

1973   *Le Langage des déments*, Collection 'Approaches to Semiotics', The Hague: Mouton.

1974   *Speculum. De l'autre femme*, Paris: Minuit.

1975   'La Femme, son sexe et le langage' [interview with Catherine Clément], *La Nouvelle Critique* 82 (March): 36–9.

1977   '"Ce Sexe qui n'en est pas un": Les Femmes entre deux mondes' [interview with Martine Storti], *Histoires d'elles* 0 (March): 21.
        Ce Sexe qui n'en est pas un, Paris: Minuit.

1978   Interview (1) and Interview (2) in Marie-Françoise Hans and Gilles Lapouge (eds) *Les Femmes, la pornographie et l'érotisme*, Paris: Seuil, pp.43–58 and 302–4.

1979   'Elle appelle toujours la nuit', *Sorcières* 18: 26–7 [on Marguerite Duras's film *Navire Night*].
        'Etablir une généalogie de femmes', *Maintenant* 12 (28 May).
        'Mères et filles vues par Luce Irigaray', *Libération* (21 May).
        Et l'une ne bouge pas sans l'autre, Paris: Minuit.

1980   'L'Autre de la nature', entretien entre Luce Irigaray, Xavière Gauthier, Anne-Marie de la Vilaine, and Françoise Clédat, *Sorcières* 20: 14–25.

'La Femme n'est rien et c'est là sa puissance', *Histoires d'elles* 21 (March): 3 [review of Baudrillard's *De la séduction*].
'Grève de la parano', *Histoires d'elles* 22 (April): 3. [Reprinted in *Paris-Féministe* 24 (1–15 April 1986): 13–15, under the title 'Les grêveuses'.]
Amante marine. De Friedrich Nietzsche, Paris: Minuit.

1981   *Le Corps-à-corps avec la mère*, Montreal: Editions de la pleine lune.
1982   *Passions élémentaires*, Paris: Minuit.
1983   'Où et comment habiter?,' *Cahiers du Grif* 26 (March): 139–43.
L'Oubli de l'air chez Martin Heidegger, Paris: Minuit.
La Croyance même, Paris: Galilée. [Reprinted in *Sexes et parentés*.]
1984   *Ethique de la différence sexuelle*, Paris: Minuit.
1985   'Sur l'éthique de la différence sexuelle', *Cahiers du Grif* 32 (Winter): 115–19.
Parler n'est jamais neutre, Paris: Minuit.
1986   'Créer un Entre-Femmes', *Paris-Féministe* 31–2 (September): 37–41 [first published in *Rinascita* 28 September 1985].
'Le Religieux comme droit féminin', followed by 'Le Christianisme, religion de l'incarnation?' [open Letter to the Pope on the occasion of his visit to France], *Paris-Féministe* 34 (1–15 November): 15–16.
1987   'Egales à qui?' *Critique* 480 (May): 420–37 [review of Elisabeth Schüssler Fiorenza's book *In Memory of Her*].
Special issue of *Langages*, 'Le Sexe Linguistique', ed. Luce Irigaray, no. 85.
'Présentation', *Langages* 85: 5–8.
'L'Ordre sexuel du discours', *Langages* 85: 81–123.
'C'est quoi ou qui, ta santé?', *Paris-Féministe* 41 (1–15 March): 13–15.
'Mythes religieux et civils', *Rinascita* 18 April.
Sexes et parentés, Paris: Minuit.
1988   'Egales ou différentes?', *Paris-Féministe* 61 (1–15 April): 14–16 [first published in *Tageszeitung*, Berlin, 19 April 1986].
'"Le Sida ne passera pas par moi"', *Paris-Féministe* 74 (December): 24–7.
'Sujet de la science, sujet sexué?', *Sens et place des connaissances dans la société*, éditions du CNRS.
1989   'A Quand notre devenir femmes?', *Paris-Féministe* 77 (1–15 February): 25–7 [first published in *Fluttuaria*, Milan, November 1987].
Le Temps de la différence: pour une révolution pacifique, Paris: Librairie générale française (livre de poche).
Forthcoming 'Questions à Emmanuel Levinas' in *Critique*.
Je, tu, nous: pour une culture sexuée [provisional title], Paris: Grasset 1990.
Sexes et genres à travers les langues, Paris: Grasset [collective work on sex in language: English, French and Italian, edited by Irigaray].
Dieu Qui? Dieu Quoi? Le Divin conçu par nous, Paris: Grasset [collective work on the divine, edited by Irigaray, which appeared in Italian under the title *Il Divino Concepito da Noi* in *Inchiesta* 85/86 (July–December 1989)].

(Collected articles, and works published in languages other than English and French, have not been listed separately.)

English

1977   'Women's exile' (trans. Couze Venn), interview in *Ideology and Consciousness* 1: 62–76. [Reprinted in Deborah Cameron (ed.) *The Feminist Critique of Language: A Reader*, London: Routledge 1990, pp. 80–96.]

1978   'That sex which is not one', trans. Randall Albury and Paul Foss, in P. Foss and M. Morris (eds) *Language, Sexuality and Subversion*, Sydney: Feral Publications, pp.161–71.

1980   'When our lips speak together', trans. Carolyn Burke, *Signs* 6(1): 69–79.

1981   'This sex which is not one', trans. Claudia Reeder, in Elaine Marks and Isabelle de Courtivron (eds) *New French Feminisms*, Brighton: Harvester, pp. 99–106.
    'When the Goods get together,' trans. Claudia Reeder, in Elaine Marks and Isabelle de Courtivron (eds) *New French Feminisms*, Brighton: Harvester, pp.107–10.
    'And the one doesn't stir without the other', trans. Hélène Vivienne Wenzel, *Signs* 7 (1): 60–7.

1982   'One does not move without the other', trans. Rosi Braidotti and Mia Campioni, *Refractory Girl* 23: 12–14.

1983   'Luce Irigaray', interview with Lucienne Serrano and Elaine Hoffman Baruch, in Janet Todd (ed.) *Women Writers Talking*, New York and London: Holmes and Meier, pp.230–45. [Reprinted in Elaine Hoffman Baruch and Lucienne Serrano, (eds) *Women Analyze Women*, London: Harvester Wheatsheaf 1988, pp.147–64.]
    'An interview with Luce Irigaray', interview with Kiki Amsberg and Aafke Steenhuis, trans. Robert van Krieken, in *Hecate* 9 (1–2): 192–202. [This interview is usually referred to under the title 'For centuries we've been living in the mother–son relation'.]
    'Veiled lips', trans. Sara Speidel, in *Mississippi Review* 11 (3): 98–119 [extracts from the 'Lèvres voilées' section of *Amante marine*].

1985   'Is the subject of science sexed?', trans. Edith Oberle, *Cultural Critique* 1.
    'Any theory of the "subject" has always been appropriated by the "masculine"', *Trivia* (Winter).
    'The fecundity of the caress', trans. Carolyn Burke, in Richard A. Cohen (ed.) *Face to Face with Levinas*, Albany: SUNY Press, pp.231–56.
    Speculum of the Other Woman, trans. Gillian C. Gill, Ithaca: Cornell University Press.
    This Sex Which Is Not One, trans. Catherine Porter with Carolyn Burke, Ithaca: Cornell University Press.

1985–6   'Language, Persephone and sacrifice', interview with Luce Irigaray, conducted and trans. Heather Jon Maroney, *Borderlines* 4 (Winter): 30–2.

1986   'Women, the sacred and money', trans. Diana Knight and Margaret Whitford, *Paragraph* 8 (October): 6–18.
    Divine Women, trans. Stephen Muecke, Sydney: Local Consumption Occasional Papers, no. 8.

1987   'Sexual difference', trans. Seán Hand, in Toril Moi (ed.) *French Feminist Thought*, Oxford: Blackwell, pp.118–30.
    'Is the subject of science sexed?', trans. Carol Mastrangelo Bové, *Hypatia* 2 (Fall): 65–87.

1988   Extracts from interview with Alice Jardine and Anne Menke in 'Exploding the issue: "French" "women" "writers" and "the canon"', *Yale French Studies* 75: 229–58 [complete interview in Alice Jardine and Anne Menke (eds) *Shifting Scenes: Interviews on Women, Writing and Politics in Post '68 France*, New York: Columbia University Press, forthcoming, 1991].

1989   'Is the subject of science sexed?', trans. Carol Mastrangelo Bové, in Nancy Tuana (ed.) *Feminism and Science*, Bloomington: Indiana University Press, pp.58–68.

'Sorcerer love: A reading of Plato's *Symposium*, Diotima's speech', trans. Eléanor Kuykendall, *Hypatia* 3 (3) (Winter): 32–44.
'The Gesture in Psychoanalysis', trans. Elizabeth Guild, in Teresa Brennan (ed.) *Between Feminism and Psychoanalysis*, London: Routledge, pp.127–38.
'Equal to whom?' in *differences* vol.1 (2): 59–76.

1990   Interview in *French Philosophers in Conversation: Derrida, Irigaray, Levinas, Le Doeuff, Schneider, Serres*, interviews with Raoul Mortley, London: Routledge.
'The Culture of Difference', trans. Alison Martin, in *Pli* 3(1) (formerly *Warwick Journal of Philosophy*) Spring issue, pp.44–52.

Forthcoming 'Questions to Emmanuel Levinas', trans. Margaret Whitford, in Robert Bernasconi and Simon Critchley (eds) *Rereading Levinas*, Bloomington: Indiana University Press, 1991, and in *The Irigaray Reader* (see next item).
The Irigaray Reader, ed. Margaret Whitford, Oxford: Blackwell.
The Ethics of Sexual Difference, trans. Carolyn Burke, Ithaca: Cornell University Press.

2. Secondary texts and other works consulted

Articles wholly or partly about Irigaray, and books containing one or more chapters on Irigaray, have been marked with an asterisk. I would be grateful if readers would draw my attention to substantial discussions of Irigaray's work that I may have missed.

Adams, Parveen (1978) 'Representation and sexuality', *m/f* 1: 65–82.
Adams, Parveen (1986) 'Versions of the body', *m/f* 11–12: 27–34.
Adams, Parveen (1989) 'Of female bondage', in Brennan (ed.) pp. 247–65.
*Adlam, Diana and Venn, Couze (1977) 'Introduction to Irigaray', *Ideology and Consciousness* 1:57–61.
Albinski, Nan Bowman (1988) *Women's Utopias in British and American Fiction*, London and New York: Routledge.
Allen, Jeffner (1989) 'Women who beget women must thwart major sophisms', in Garry and Pearsall (eds), pp.37–46.
Allen, Jeffner and Young, Iris Marion (1989) *The Thinking Muse: Feminism and Modern French Philosophy*, Bloomington: Indiana University Press.
Allen, Judith and Grosz, Elizabeth (eds) (1987) 'Feminism and the body', *Australian Feminist Studies* 5.
Bachelard, Gaston (1943) *L'Air et les songes*, Paris: José Corti.
Baliteau, Catherine (1975) 'La Fin d'une parade misogyne: La psychanalyse lacanienne', *Les Temps modernes* 30 (348) (July): 1933–53.
Bannet, Eve Tavor (1989) *Structuralism and the Logic of Dissent: Barthes, Derrida, Foucault, Lacan*, London: Macmillan.
Barrett, Michèle (1987) 'The Concept of difference', *Feminist Review* 26 (Summer): 29–41.
Bartkowski, Frances (1980) 'Deconstruction: a union forever deferred', *enclitic* 4 (2): 70–7.
*Bartkowski, Frances (1986), 'The question of ethics in French feminism', *Berkshire Review* 21: 22–9.
Bartkowski, Frances (1989) *Feminist Utopias*, Lincoln and London: University of Nebraska Press.
*Baruch, Elaine Hoffman and Serrano, Lucienne (1988) *Women Analyze Women: in France, England and the United States*, New York and London: Harvester Wheatsheaf.
Battersby, Christine (1989) *Gender and Genius: Towards a Feminist Aesthetics*, London: The Women's Press.

Baudrillard, Jean (1981) *De la séduction*, Paris: Denöel Gonthier.
Benhabib, Seyla and Cornell, Drucilla (eds) (1987) *Feminism as Critique: Essays on the Politics of Gender in Late-Capitalist Societies*, Cambridge: Polity Press.
Benjamin, Jessica (1980) 'The bonds of love: rational violence and erotic domination', in Hester Eisenstein and Alice Jardine (eds) *The Future of Difference*, Boston, Mass.: G.K. Hall, pp.41–70.
Benveniste, Emile (1966) *Problèmes de linguistique générale 1*, Paris: Gallimard. [English trans. *Problems in General Linguistics*, trans. Mary Elizabeth Meek, Coral Gables, Fla.: University of Miami Press, 1971.]
Benvenuto Bice and Kennedy, Roger (1986) *The Works of Jacques Lacan: An Introduction*, London: Free Association Books.
*Berg, Elizabeth L. (1982) 'The third woman', *Diacritics* 12 (2): 11–20. [Review of *Speculum* and *Amante marine*.]
*Berg, Maggie (1988) 'Escaping the cave: Irigaray and her feminist critics', in Gary Wihl and David Williams (eds) *Literature and Ethics*, Toronto: University of Toronto Press.
*Berg, Temma F. (1989) 'Suppressing the language of (wo)man: the dream of a common language', in Temma F. Berg, A.S. Elfenbein, J. Larsen and E.K. Sparks (eds) *Engendering the Word: Feminist Essays in Psychosexual Politics*, Chicago: University of Illinois Press.
Bernasconi, Robert and Wood, David (eds) (1989) *The Provocation of Levinas: Rethinking the Other*, London: Routledge.
Bernheimer, Charles and Kahane, Claire (1985) *In Dora's Case: Freud – Hysteria – Feminism*, London: Virago.
Borch-Jacobsen, Mikkel (1989) *The Freudian Subject*, trans. Catherine Porter, London: Macmillan.
Bowie, Malcolm (1987) *Freud, Proust and Lacan: Theory as Fiction*, Cambridge: Cambridge University Press.
*Bowlby, Rachel (1983) 'The feminine female', *Social Text* 7: 54–68.
*Braidotti, Rosi (1981) 'Féminisme et philosophie: La philosophie contemporaine comme critique du pouvoir par rapport à la pensée féministe' [dissertation], Université de Paris – 1.
Braidotti, Rosi (1982), 'Femmes et philosophie, questions à suivre', *La Revue d'en face* 13: 23–33.
*Braidotti, Rosi (1986a) 'The ethics of sexual difference: the case of Foucault and Irigaray', *Australian Feminist Studies* 3: 1–13.
Braidotti, Rosi (1986b) 'Ethics revisited: women and/in philosophy', in Pateman and Gross (eds), pp.44–60.
Braidotti, Rosi (1987) 'Envy: or with your brains and my looks', in Jardine and Smith (eds), pp.233–41, 283–4.
*Braidotti, Rosi (1989) 'The politics of ontological difference', in Brennan (ed.), pp.89–105.
*Braidotti, Rosi (forthcoming) *Patterns of Dissonance*, Cambridge: Polity Press.
Brennan, Teresa (1988) 'Controversial discussions and feminist debate', in Edward Timms and Naomi Segal (eds) *Freud in Exile: Psychoanalysis and Its Vicissitudes*, New Haven and London: Yale University Press, pp.254–74.
*Brennan, Teresa (ed.) (1989) *Between Feminism and Psychoanalysis*, London: Routledge.
Brennan, Teresa (1990) 'An impasse in psychoanalysis and feminism', in Sneja Gunew (ed.) *Feminist Knowledge: Critique and Construct*, London: Routledge.
*Brown, Beverley and Adams, Parveen (1979) 'The feminine body and feminist politics', *m/f* 3: 33–50.

*Brun, Odette (1987) 'Sexes et parentés' (review), *Paris-Féministe* 49 (September): 22–25.

*Burchill, Louise (1984) 'Either/or: peripeteia of an alternative in Jean Baudrillard's *De la séduction*', in André Frankovits (ed.) *Seduced and Abandoned: The Baudrillard Scene*, Glebe NSW: Stonemoss Services.

*Burke, Carolyn (1980) 'Introduction to Luce Irigaray's "When Our Lips Speak Together"', *Signs* 6 (1): 66–8.

*Burke, Carolyn (1981) 'Irigaray through the looking glass', *Feminist Studies* 7 (2): 288–306.

*Burke, Carolyn (1987) 'Romancing the philosophers: Luce Irigaray', *The Minnesota Review* 29. [Reprinted in Dianne Hunter (ed.) *Seduction and Theory: Feminist Readings on Representation and Rhetoric*, Chicago: University of Illinois Press.]

Butler, Judith P. (1987) *Subjects of Desire: Hegelian Reflections in Twentieth-Century France*, New York: Columbia University Press.

Butler, Judith (1989a) 'Gendering the body: Beauvoir's philosophical contribution', in Garry and Pearsall (eds), pp.253–62.

Butler, Judith (1989b) 'Sexual ideology and phenomenological description: a feminist critique of Merleau-Ponty's *Phenomenology of Perception*', in Allen and Young (eds), pp.85–100.

*Cameron, Deborah (1985) *Feminism and Linguistic Theory*, London: Macmillan.

*Campioni, Mia and Braidotti, Rosi (1982) 'Mothers/Daughters/Feminists: the darkest continent', *Refractory Girl* 23: 9–12.

Castoriadis, Cornelius (1975) *L'Institution imaginaire de la société*, Paris; Seuil. [English trans. *The Imaginary Institution of Society*, trans. Kathleen McLaughlin, Cambridge: Polity Press 1987.]

Castoriadis, Cornelius (1978) *Les Carrefours du labyrinthe*, 2nd edn, Paris: Seuil. [English trans. *Crossroads in the Labyrinth*, Brighton: Harvester 1984.]

*Chalier, Catherine (1980) 'Amante marine' (review), *Sorcières* 20: 26–30.

Chalier, Catherine (1982) *Figures du féminin: Lecture d'Emmanuel Levinas*, Paris: La Nuit surveillée.

Chapman, Rowena and Rutherford, Jonathan (1988) *Male Order: Unwrapping Masculinity*, London: Lawrence & Wishart.

Chodorow, Nancy (1978) *The Reproduction of Mothering: Psychoanalysis and the Sociology of Gender*, Berkeley: University of California Press.

Chow, Rey (1989) '"It's you and not me": domination and "othering" in theorizing the Third World' in Weed (ed.), pp.152–61, 277–8.

Christian, Barbara (1989) 'The race for theory' in Kauffman (ed.), pp.225–37.

*Cicioni, Mirna (1989) '"Love and respect, together": the theory and practice of *affidamento* in Italian feminism', *Australian Feminist Studies* 10: 71–83.

Cixous, Hélène (1981) 'Castration or decapitation' (trans. Annette Kuhn), *Signs* 7 (1): 41–55.

Cockburn, Cynthia (1988) 'Masculinity, the left and feminism' in Chapman and Rutherford (eds), pp.303–29.

Cocks, Joan (1989) *The Oppositional Imagination: Feminism, Critique and Political Theory*, London & New York: Routledge.

*Collin, Françoise (1984–5) 'Repenser l'éthique', *Cahiers du Grif* 29 (Winter): 97–9.

Collins, Margery and Pierce, Christine (1976) 'Holes and slime: sexism in Sartre's psychoanalysis' in Carol C. Gould and Marx W. Wartofsky (eds) *Woman and Philosophy: Toward a Theory of Liberation*, New York: Putnam's Sons, pp.112–28.

Copjec, Joan (1989), 'Cutting Up' in Brennan (ed.), pp.227–46.

Cornell, Drucilla and Thurschwell, Adam (1987) 'Feminism, negativity, Intersubjectivity' in Benhabib and Cornell (eds), pp.143–62, 185–9.

Coward, Rosalind (1983), *Patriarchal Precedents: Sexuality and Social Relations*, London: Routledge & Kegan Paul.

*Dallery, Arleen B. (1985) 'Sexual embodiment: Beauvoir and French feminism (*écriture féminine*)', in *Women's Studies International Forum* 8 (3): 197–202.

*Dallery, Arleen B. (1989), 'The politics of writing (the) body: *écriture féminine*', in Alison M. Jaggar and Susan R. Bordo (eds) *Gender/Body/Knowledge: Feminist Reconstructions of Being and Knowing*, New Brunswick and London: Rutgers University Press, pp.52–67.

Daly, Mary (1984), *Pure Lust: Elemental Feminist Philosophy*, London: The Women's Press.

De Lauretis, Teresa (1984) *Alice Doesn't: Feminism, Semiotics, Cinema*, London: Macmillan.

De Lauretis, Teresa (ed.) (1986) *Feminist Studies/Critical Studies*, Bloomington: Indiana University Press.

De Lauretis (1987) *Technologies of Gender*, Bloomington: Indiana University Press.

Deleuze, Gilles and Lyotard, Jean-François (1975) 'A Propos de département de psychanalyse à Vincennes', *Les Temps modernes* 30 (342) (January): 862–3.

Derrida, Jacques (1967) *De la grammatologie*, Paris: Minuit.

Derrida, Jacques (1972) *Positions*, Paris: Minuit. [English trans. *Positions*, trans. Alan Bass, London: Athlone Press 1981.]

Derrida, Jacques (1974) *Of Grammatology*, trans. Gayatri Chakravorty Spivak, Baltimore and London: Johns Hopkins University Press.

Derrida, Jacques (1978) *Eperons: Les styles de Nietzsche*, Paris: Flammarion. [English trans. *Spurs: Nietzsche's Styles*, trans. Barbara Harlow, Chicago: University of Chicago Press 1978.]

Derrida, Jacques (1985) 'Deconstruction in America: an interview with Jacques Derrida', James Creech, Peggy Kamuf and Jane Todd, *Critical Exchange* 17 (Winter): 1–33.

Derrida, Jacques (1986a) 'Geschlecht: différence sexuelle, différence ontologique', *Cahiers de l'Herne* 45: 419–30. [Reprinted in Derrida, *Psyché: inventions de l'autre*, Paris: Galilée 1987, pp.393–414.]

Derrida, Jacques (1986b) 'On colleges and philosophy', *Postmodernism*, ICA Documents 4 and 5: 66–71.

Derrida, Jacques (1987) 'Women in the beehive: a seminar with Jacques Derrida', in Jardine and Smith (eds) pp.189–203.

Derrida, Jacques and Conley, Verena Andermatt (1984) 'voice ii', *Boundary 2*, 12(2): 68–93.

Derrida, Jacques and McDonald, Christie V. (1982) 'Choreographies' *Diacritics* 12 (Summer): 66–76.

Dews, Peter (1987) *Logics of Disintegration: Post-structuralist Thought and the Claims of Critical Theory*, London: Verso.

Doane, Mary Ann (1987) *The Desire to Desire: The Woman's Film of the 1940s*, Bloomington: Indiana University Press.

Doane, Mary Ann (1989) 'Veiling our desire: close-ups of the woman', in Feldstein and Roof (eds) pp.105–41.

*Duchen, Claire (1986) *Feminism in France from May '68 to Mitterrand*, London: Routledge & Kegan Paul.

Duchen, Claire (ed.) (1987) *French Connections: Voices from the Women's Movement in France*, London: Hutchinson.

Echols, Alice (1984a) 'The taming of the id: feminist sexual politics 1968–83', in Carole S. Vance (ed.) *Pleasure and Danger: Exploring Female Sexuality*, London: Routledge & Kegan Paul, pp.50–72.

Echols, Alice (1984b) 'The new feminism of yin and yang', in Snitow et al. (eds) pp.62–81.

Edelman, Lee (1989) 'At risk in the sublime: the politics of gender and theory', in Kauffman (ed.) pp.213–24.

Eichenbaum, Luise and Orbach, Susie (1982) *Outside In, . . . Inside Out . . . Women's Psychology: A Feminist Psychoanalytic Approach*, Harmondsworth: Penguin.

Elshtain, Jean Bethke (1987) 'Against androgyny', in Phillips (ed.) pp.139–59. [First published in *Telos* 47 (1981): 5–21.]

Ernst, Sheila and Maguire, Marie (1987) *Living With the Sphinx: Papers from the Women's Therapy Centre*, London: The Women's Press.

Fairbairns, Zoë (1979) *Benefits*, London: Virago.

*Fauré, Christine (1981) 'The twilight of the goddesses, or the intellectual crisis of French feminism', trans. Lilian Robinson, *Signs* 7 (1) (Autumn): 81–6.

Favret-Saada, Jeanne (1977) 'Excusez-moi, je ne faisais que passer', *Les Temps modernes* 371 (June): 2089–103.

Feldstein, Richard and Roof, Judith (eds) (1989) *Feminism and Psychoanalysis*, Ithaca and London: Cornell University Press.

*Felman, Shoshana (1975), 'Women and madness: the critical phallacy', *Diacritics* (Winter): 2–10 [includes review of *Speculum*].

Felman, Shoshana (1977) 'To open the question', *Yale French Studies* 55–6 pp.5–10.

Feminist Studies (1988) 14 (1): special issue on feminism and postmodernism.

*Féral, Josette (1978) 'Antigone or the irony of the tribe', *Diacritics* (Fall): 2–14 [review of *Speculum* and *This Sex Which Is Not One*].

*Féral, Josette (1981) 'Towards a theory of displacement', *Sub-Stance* 32: 52–64.

Ferguson, Ann (1989) *Blood at the Root: Motherhood, Sexuality and Male Dominance*, London: Pandora.

Feuerbach, Ludwig (1893) *The Essence of Christianity*, trans. Marian Evans from the 2nd German edn, London: Kegan Paul, Trench, Trübner.

Findlay, Heather (1989) 'Is there a lesbian in this text? Derrida, Wittig and the politics of the three women', in Weed (ed.) pp.59–69.

Ford, Katherine Jane (1985) 'Lacan's debt to Saussure', PhD dissertation, Queen Mary College, London University [forthcoming from Harvester Wheatsheaf].

*Foss, Paul (1978) 'On the value of that text which is not one', in P. Foss and M. Morris (eds) *Language, Sexuality and Subversion*, Sydney: Feral Publications, pp.173–91.

*Franklin, Sarah (1985) *Luce Irigaray and the Feminist Critique of Language*, Women's Studies Occasional Papers no. 6, Canterbury: University of Kent.

Fraser, Nancy (1984) 'The French Derrideans: politicizing deconstruction or deconstructing politics', *New German Critique* 33: 127–54.

*Fraser, Nancy (1989) 'Introduction' [editorial], *Hypatia* 3 (3): 1–10.

*Freeman, Barbara (1986) 'Irigaray at *The Symposium*: speaking otherwise', *Oxford Literary Review* 8 (1–2): 170–7.

Freud, Sigmund (1951–73) *Standard Edition of the Complete Psychological Works of Sigmund Freud*, trans. and ed. James Strachey, London: The Hogarth Press.

*Fuss, Diana J. (1989) '"Essentially speaking": Luce Irigaray's language of essence', *Hypatia* 3 (3) (Winter): 62–80.

*Fuss, Diana J. (1990) *Essentially Speaking*, London: Routledge.

*Gallop, Jane (1982) *Feminism and Psychoanalysis: The Daughter's Seduction*, London: Macmillan.

*Gallop, Jane (1983) '*Quand nos lèvres s'écrivent*: Irigaray's body politic', *Romanic Review* 74: 77–83. [Reprinted in Jane Gallop (1988) *Thinking Through the Body*, New York: Columbia University Press, pp.92–100, 117–18.]

Gallop, Jane (1985) *Reading Lacan*, Ithaca and London: Cornell University Press.

Gardiner, Judith Kegan (1985) 'Mind mother: psychoanalysis and feminism', in Gayle Green and Coppélia Kahn (eds) *Making a Difference: Feminist Literary Criticism*, London and New York: Methuen, pp.113–45.

Garry, Ann and Pearsall, Marilyn (eds) (1989) *Women, Knowledge and Reality: Explorations in Feminist Philosophy*, Boston and London: Unwin Hyman.

Gasché, Rodolphe (1986) *The Tain of the Mirror: Derrida and the Philosophy of Reflection*, Cambridge, Mass. and London: Harvard University Press.

Gatens, Moira (1986) 'Feminism, philosophy and riddles without answers', in Pateman and Gross (eds) pp.13–29.

*Gatens, Moira (forthcoming) *Feminism and Philosophy*, Cambridge: Polity Press.

*Gearhart, Suzanne (1985) 'The scene of psychoanalysis: the unanswered questions of Dora', in Bernheimer and Kahane (eds) pp.105–27.

*Gelfand, Elissa D. and Hules, Virginia Thorndike (1985) *French Feminist Criticism: Women, Language and Literature. An Annotated Bibliography*, New York and London: Garland Publishing.

Girard, René (1972) *La Violence et le sacré*, Paris: Grasset. [English trans. *Violence and the Sacred*, trans. Patrick Gregory, Baltimore: John Hopkins University Press 1977.]

*Godard, Linda (1985) 'Pour une nouvelle lecture de la question de la "Femme": essai à partir de la pensée de Jacques Derrida', *Philosophiques* 12 (1) (Spring): 147–64.

Goux, Jean-Joseph (1973) *Economie et symbolique: Freud, Marx*, Paris: Seuil.

Green, André (1986) *On Private Madness*, London: The Hogarth Press.

*Griffiths, Morwenna and Whitford, Margaret (eds) (1988) *Feminist Perspectives in Philosophy*, London: Macmillan.

Grimshaw, Jean (1986) *Feminist Philosophers: Women's Perspectives on Philosophical Traditions*, Brighton: Wheatsheaf.

Grimshaw, Jean (1988) 'Autonomy and identity in feminist thinking', in Griffiths and Whitford (eds) pp.90–108.

*Gross, Elizabeth (1986a) 'Philosophy, subjectivity and the body: Kristeva and Irigaray', in Pateman and Grosz (eds) pp.125–43

*Gross, Elizabeth (1986b) 'Irigaray and sexual difference', *Australian Feminist Studies* 2 (Autumn):63–77 [review of *Speculum* and *This Sex Which Is Not One*].

*Gross, Elizabeth (1986c) *Irigaray and the Divine*, Local Consumption Occasional Paper no. 9, Sydney.

*Gross, Elizabeth (1986d) 'Derrida, Irigaray and deconstruction', in 'Leftwright', *Intervention* 20: 70–81.

Grosz, Elizabeth (1987) 'Notes towards a corporeal feminism', *Australian Feminist Studies* 5 (Summer): 1–16.

*Grosz, Elizabeth (1988a) 'Desire, the body and recent French feminisms', *Intervention* 21–2: 28–33.

*Grosz, E. A. (1988b) 'The hetero and the homo: the sexual ethics of Luce Irigaray', *Gay Information* 17–18 (March): 37–44.

*Grosz, Elizabeth (1989) *Sexual Subversions: Three French Feminists*, Sydney: Allen & Unwin.

*Hamon, Marie-Christine (1977) 'Le langage-femme, existe-t-il?', *Ornicar?* 11: 37–50.

Haraway, Donna (1985) 'A manifesto for cyborgs: science, technology and socialist feminism in the 1980s', *Socialist Review* 80: 65–107. [Reprinted in Weed (ed.) (1989) pp.173–204, 279–88 and in Nicholson (ed.) (1990) pp.190–233.]

Harding, Sandra (1986) *The Science Question in Feminism*, Milton Keynes: Open University Press.

Harding, Sandra and Hintikka, Merrill B. (eds) (1983) *Discovering Reality: Feminist Perspectives on Epistemology, Metaphysics, Methodology and Philosophy of Science*, Dordrecht: Reidel.

Hartsock, Nancy (1983) *Money, Sex and Power*, New York and London: Longman.
Harvey Irene E. (1986) *Derrida and the Economy of Différance*, Bloomington: Indiana University Press.
Haug, Frigga et al. (1987) *Female Sexualization: A Collective Work of Memory*, trans. Erica Carter, London: Verso.
Heath, Stephen (1978) 'Difference', *Screen* 19 (3): 51–112.
Heaton, John (1989) 'The other and psychotherapy', in Bernasconi and Wood (eds) pp.5–14.
Herman, Nini (1989) *Too Long a Child: The Mother–Daughter Dyad*, London: Free Association Books.
Hinshelwood, R. D. (1989) *A Dictionary of Kleinian Thought*, London: Free Association Books.
Hodge, Joanna (1988) 'Subject, body and the exclusion of women from philosophy', in Griffiths and Whitford (eds) pp.152–68.
*Hodge, Joanna (1989) 'Feminism and post-modernism: misleading divisions imposed by the opposition between modernism and post-modernism', in Andrew Benjamin (ed.) *The Problems of Modernity: Adorno and Benjamin*, London: Routledge, pp.86–111.
*Holmlund, Christine (1989) 'I love Luce: the lesbian, mimesis and masquerade in Irigaray, Freud and mainstream film', *New Formations* 9 (Winter): 105–23.
*Homans, Margaret (1986) 'Reconstructing the feminine', *The Woman's Review of Books* (6 March): 12–13 [review of *Speculum* and *This Sex Which Is Not One*].
Howard, Dick (1977) 'Ontology and the political project: Cornelius Castoriadis', in Dick Howard, *The Marxian Legacy*, New York: Urizen, pp.262–301, 328–33.
*Jacobus, Mary (1986) *Reading Woman: Essays in Feminist Criticism*, London: Methuen.
Jaggar, Alison (1983) *Feminist Politics and Human Nature*, Brighton: Harvester.
Jakobson, Roman (1962) 'Deux aspects du langage et deux types d'aphasie', *Les Temps modernes* 17 (188): 853–80. [English trans. in Roman Jakobson and Halle Morris, *Fundamentals of Language*, The Hague: Mouton 1956.]
Jardine, Alice A. (1985) *Gynesis: Configurations of Woman and Modernity*, Ithaca and London: Cornell University Press.
Jardine, Alice and Menke, Anne (eds) (forthcoming, 1991) *Shifting Scenes: Interviews on Women, Writing and Politics in Post '68 France*, New York: Columbia University Press.
Jardine, Alice and Smith, Paul (eds) (1987) *Men in Feminism*, New York and London: Methuen.
*Johnson, Pauline (1988), 'The Dilemmas of Luce Irigaray' in *Australian Feminist Studies* no. 6 (Autumn), pp.87–96.
*Jones, Ann Rosalind (1985), 'Inscribing Femininity: French Theories of the Feminine' in *Making a Difference: Feminist Literary Criticism*, ed. Gayle Greene and Coppélia Kahn, London and New York: Methuen, pp.80–112.
*Jones, Ann Rosalind (1986), 'Writing the Body: Towards an Understanding of *l'Ecriture féminine*' in *The New Feminist Criticism: Essays on Women, Literature and Theory*, ed. Elaine Showalter, London: Virago, pp.361–377.
Judovitz, Dalia (1988), *Subjectivity and Representation in Descartes: The Origins of Modernity*, Cambridge: Cambridge University Press.
Kant, Immanuel. See Norman Kemp Smith.
Kaplan, E. Ann (1984) 'Is the gaze male?', in Snitow et al. (eds) pp.321–38.
Kappeler, Susanne (1986) *The Pornography of Representation*, Cambridge: Polity Press.
Kauffman, Linda (ed.) (1989) *Gender and Theory: Dialogues on Feminist Criticism*, Oxford: Blackwell.
Keller, Evelyn Fox (1985) *Reflections on Gender and Science*, New Haven and London: Yale University Press.

Keller, Evelyn Fox and Grontkowski Christine R. (1983) 'The mind's eye', in Harding and Hintikka (eds) pp.207–24.

Kessler, Carol Farley (ed.) (1984) *Daring to Dream: Utopian Stories by United States Women: 1836–1919*, London: Pandora.

Khanna, Lee Cullen (1984) 'Change and art in women's worlds: Doris Lessing's *Canopus in Argos: Archives*', in Rohrlich and Baruch (eds) pp.269–79.

Kintz, Linda (1989) 'In-different criticism: the deconstructive "parole"', in Allen and Young (eds) pp.113–35.

Klein, Melanie (1988) *Envy and Gratitude and Other Works 1946–1963*, London: Virago.

Kofman, Sarah (1980) *L'Enigme de la femme: La Femme dans les textes de Freud*, Paris: Galilée. [English trans. *The Enigma of Woman: Woman in Freud's Writings*, trans. Catherine Porter, Ithaca: Cornell University Press 1985.]

Krell, David Farrell (ed.) (1978) *Martin Heidegger: Basic Writings*, London: Routledge & Kegan Paul.

Kristeva, Julia (1986) 'Women's time', in Toril Moi (ed.) *The Kristeva Reader*, Oxford: Blackwell, pp.187–213.

Kristeva, Julia (1987) *Soleil noir: Dépression et mélancolie*, Paris: Gallimard.

Kuhn, Annette (1982) *Women's Pictures: Feminism and Cinema*, London: Routledge & Kegan Paul.

Kuhn, Annette (1985) *The Power of the Image: Essays on Representation and Sexuality* London: Routledge & Kegan Paul.

*Kuykendall, Eléanor (1984) 'Toward an ethic of nurturance: Luce Irigaray on mothering and power', in Joyce Trebilcot (ed.) *Mothering, Essays in Feminist Theory*, Totowa, NJ: Rowman & Allanheld.

*Kuykendall, Eléanor (1989) '*Sexes et parentés*, by Luce Irigaray' [review], *Hypatia* 3 (2) (Summer): 172–4.

*Kuykendall, Eléanor H. (1989) 'Introduction to "Sorcerer Love" by Luce Irigaray', *Hypatia* 3 (3) (Winter): 28–31.

Lacan, Jacques (1966) *Ecrits*, Paris: Seuil.

Lacan, Jacques (1975a) *Le Séminaire, livre I: Les Ecrits techniques de Freud*, Paris: Seuil.

Lacan, Jacques (1975b) *Le Séminaire, livre XX: Encore*, Paris: Seuil.

Lacan, Jacques (1977) *Ecrits: A Selection*, trans. Alan Sheridan, London: Tavistock.

Lacan, Jacques (1978) *Le Séminaire, livre II: Le moi dans la théorie de Freud et dans la technique de la psychanalyse*, Paris: Seuil.

Lacan, Jacques (1981) *Le Séminaire, livre III: Les psychoses*, Paris: Seuil.

Laplanche, Jean (1970) *Vie et mort en psychanalyse*, Paris: Flammarion, collection Champs. [English trans. *Life and Death in Psychoanalysis*, London and Baltimore, Johns Hopkins University Press 1976.]

Laplanche, Jean (1989) *New Foundations for Psychoanalysis*, trans. David Macey, Oxford: Blackwell.

Laplanche, Jean and Pontalis, J.-B. (1964) 'Fantasme originaire, fantasmes des origines, origine du fantasme', *Les Temps modernes* 215 (April): 1833–68.

Laplanche, Jean and Pontalis, J.-B (1967) *Vocabulaire de la psychanalyse*, Paris: Presses universitaires de France. [English trans. *The Language of Psychoanalysis*, trans. David Nicholson-Smith, London: The Hogarth Press 1973.]

*Lasvergnas, Isabelle (1986) 'La Trace du féminin dans la pensée: quelques échos des débats contemporains sur l'altérité', *Bulletin d'Information des Etudes féminines* 18 (June): 85–113.

Lecercle, Jean-Jacques (1985) *Philosophy Through the Looking Glass: Language, Nonsense, Desire*, London: Hutchinson.

Le Doeuff, Michèle (1979) 'De l'existentialisme au deuxième sexe', *Magazine littéraire* 145 (February):18–21.

Le Doeuff, Michèle (1980a) *Recherches sur l'imaginaire philosophique*, Paris: Payot. [English trans. *The Philosophical Imaginary*, London: Athlone Press, 1989.]

Le Doeuff, Michèle (1980b) 'Simone de Beauvoir and existentialism', *Feminist Studies* 6 (2) (Summer): 277–89.

Le Doeuff, Michèle (1987) 'Women and philosophy', trans. Debbie Pope, in Toril Moi (ed.) *French Feminist Thought: A Reader*, Oxford: Blackwell pp.181–209.

Le Doeuff, Michèle (1989) *L'Etude et le rouet*, Paris: Seuil.

*Leland, Dorothy (1989) 'Lacanian psychoanalysis and French feminism: toward an adequate political psychology', *Hypatia* 3 (3) (Winter): 81–103.

Lemaire, Anika (1977) *Jacques Lacan*, trans. David Macey, London: Routledge & Kegan Paul.

Levi-Strauss, Claude (1949) *Les Structures élémentaires de la parenté*, Paris: Presses universitaires de France.

Lloyd, Genevieve (1984) *The Man of Reason: 'Male' and 'Female' in Western Philosophy*, London: Methuen.

Lorenz, Maria (1953) 'Language as expressive behaviour', *Archives of Neurology and Psychiatry* 70 (3): 277–85.

Lorenz, Maria and Cobb, Stanley (1953) 'Language behaviour in psychoneurotic patients', *Archives of Neurology and Psychiatry* 69: 684–94.

Lovibond, Sabina (1989) 'Feminism and postmodernism', *New Left Review* 178 (November–December): 5–28.

Lovibond, Sabina (forthcoming) 'An ancient theory of gender: Plato and the Pythagorean table', in Léonie Archer, Susan Fischler, and Maria Wyke (eds) *An Illusion of the Night: Women in Ancient Societies*, London: Macmillan.

*Lyon, Elisabeth (1979) 'Discourse and difference', *Camera obscura* 3–4: 14–20.

MacCannell, Juliet Flower (1982) 'Phallacious theories of the subject', in Dean MacCannell and Juliet Flower MacCannell (eds) *The Time of the Sign: A Semiotic Interpretation of Modern Culture*, Bloomington: Indiana University Press, pp.36–52.

MacCannell, Juliet Flower (1986) *Figuring Lacan: Criticism and the Cultural Unconscious*, London and Sydney: Croom Helm.

MacCormack, Carol and Strathern, Marilyn (eds) (1980) *Nature, Culture and Gender*, Cambridge: Cambridge University Press.

McGraw, Betty R. (1984) 'Splitting subjects/splitting seduction', *Boundary 2* 12 (2): 143–52.

*McLuskie, Kate (1983) 'Women's language and literature: a problem in women's studies', *Feminist Review* 14 (Summer): 51–61.

McMillan, Elizabeth (1987) 'Female difference in the texts of Merleau-Ponty', *Philosophy Today* 31: 359–66.

Macey, David (1988) *Lacan in Contexts*, London: Verso.

*Marini, Marcelle (1978) 'Scandaleusement autre', *Critique* 373–4 (June–July): 603–21 [review of *This Sex Which Is Not One*].

Marini, Marcelle (1986) *Lacan*, Paris: Belfond.

Marks, Elaine and De Courtivron, Isabelle (eds) (1981) *New French Feminisms*, Brighton: Harvester.

Martindale, Kathleen (1987) 'On the ethics of "voice" in feminist literary criticism', *Resources for Feminist Research/Documentation sur la recherche féministe*, special issue on Women and Philosophy/Femmes et philosophie, 16 (3): 16–19.

Mauss, Marcel (1923–4) 'Essai sur le don: Forme et raison de l'échange dans les sociétés archaïques', reprinted in *Sociologie et anthropologie*, Paris: Presses universitaires de France 1950, pp.143–279.

Merleau-Ponty, Maurice (1964) *Le Visible et l'invisible*, Paris: Gallimard.

Mies, Maria (1986) *Patriarchy and Accumulation on a World Scale: Women in the International*

Division of Labour, London: Zed Books.

Millett, Kate (1971) *Sexual Politics*, London: Rupert Hart-Davis [first published 1969].

Mills, Patricia Jagentowicz (1987) *Woman, Nature and Psyche*, New Haven and London: Yale University Press.

Milner, Marion (1969) *The Hands of the Living God: An Account of a Psycho-analytic Treatment*, London: The Hogarth Press.

Mitchell, Juliet (1975) *Psychoanalysis and Feminism*, Harmondsworth: Penguin.

Mitchell, Juliet and Rose, Jacqueline (eds) (1982) *Feminine Sexuality: Jacques Lacan and the Ecole Freudienne*, London: Macmillan.

*Moi, Toril (1985) *Sexual/Textual Politics: Feminist Literary Theory*, London: Methuen.

Moi, Toril (ed.) (1987) *French Feminist Thought*, Oxford: Blackwell.

Moi, Toril (1988) 'Feminism, postmodernism and style: recent feminist criticism in the United States', *Cultural Critique* 9 (Spring): 3–22.

Moi, Toril (1989) 'Patriarchal thought and the drive for knowledge', in Brennan (ed.) pp.189–205.

*Montefiore, Jan (1987) *Feminism and Poetry: Language, Experience, Identity in Women's Writing*, London: Pandora.

Moore, Suzanne (1988) 'Getting a bit of the other – the pimps of postmodernism', in Chapman and Rutherford (eds), pp.165–92.

Morris, Meaghan (1988) *The Pirate's Fiancée: Feminism, Reading, Postmodernism*, London: Verso.

Mulvey, Laura (1989) *Visual and Other Pleasures*, London: Macmillan.

*Munster, Anna (1986) 'Playing with a different sex: between the covers of Irigaray and Gallop', in E.A. Grosz et al. (eds) *Futur*Fall: Excursions into Post-Modernity*, University of Sydney: Power Institute of Fine Arts, pp.118–27.

Murdoch, Iris (1977) *The Fire and the Sun: Why Plato Banished the Artists*, Oxford: Oxford University Press.

Nguyen, M. (1975) 'Les Exclues du département de psychanalyse de Vincennes', *Les Temps modernes* 30 (342) (January): 858–61.

Nicholson, Linda J. (ed.) (1990) *Feminism/Postmodernism*, New York and London: Routledge.

Nietzsche, Friedrich (1966) *Beyond Good and Evil: Prelude to a Philosophy of the Future*, trans. Walter Kaufmann, New York: Vintage Books [first published 1886].

Nietzsche, Friedrich (1974) *The Gay Science*, trans. Walter Kaufmann, New York: Vintage Books [first published 1882].

Nietzsche Aujourd'hui? (1973) Paris: Union générale des éditions, 10/18.

Norris, Christopher (1982) *Deconstruction: Theory and Practice*, London: Methuen.

Norris, Christopher (1987) *Derrida*, London: Fontana.

Nussbaum, Martha (1986) *The Fragility of Goodness: Luck and Ethics in Greek Tragedy and Philosophy*, Cambridge: Cambridge University Press.

*Nye, Andrea (1988) *Feminist Theory and the Philosophies of Man*, London: Croom Helm.

*Nye, Andrea (1989a) 'The hidden host: Irigaray and Diotima at Plato's *Symposium*', *Hypatia* 3 (3) (Winter): 45–61.

*Nye, Andrea (1989b) 'The voice of the serpent: French feminism and philosophy of language', in Garry and Pearsall (eds) pp.233–49.

O'Brien, Mary (1981) *The Politics of Reproduction*, London: Routledge & Kegan Paul.

Olivier, Christiane (1980) *Les Enfants de Jocaste: L'Empreinte de la mère*, Paris: Denoël/Gonthier. [English trans. *Jocasta's Children: The Imprint of the Mother*, trans. George Craig, London: Routledge 1989.]

Owens, Craig (1987) 'Outlaws: gay men in feminism', in Jardine and Smith (eds) pp.219–32, 279–83.

Pateman, Carole (1988) *The Sexual Contract*, Cambridge: Polity Press.

Pateman, Carole and Gross, Elizabeth (eds) (1986) *Feminist Challenges: Social and Political Theory*, Sydney and London: Allen & Unwin.

Phillips, Anne (ed.) (1987) *Feminism and Equality*, Oxford: Blackwell.

Plato *see* Paul Shorey.

*Plaza, Monique (1978) "'Phallomorphic power" and the psychology of "woman"' trans. Miriam David and Jill Hodges, *Ideology and Consciousness* 4 (Autumn):4–36.

Plumwood, Val (1986) 'Ecofeminism: an overview and discussion of positions and arguments', *Australasian Journal of Philosophy*, 64, suppl. (June): 120–38.

Pli (formerly *Warwick Journal of Philosophy*) (1990) 3(1) (Spring). Special issue on feminist philosophy.

Plumwood, Val (1988) 'Women, humanity and nature', *Radical Philosophy* 48 (Spring): 16–24.

Pollock, Griselda (1988) *Vision and Difference: Femininity, Feminism and the Histories of Art*, London: Routledge.

Poovey, Mary (1988) 'Feminism and deconstruction', *Feminist Studies* 14 (1) (Spring): 51–65.

Ragland-Sullivan, Ellie (1986) *Jacques Lacan and the Philosophy of Psychoanalysis*, Urbana and Chicago: University of Illinois Press.

Ragland-Sullivan, Ellie (1989) 'Seeking the third term: desire, the phallus and the materiality of language', in Feldstein and Roof (eds) pp.40–64.

Ramazanoglu, Caroline (1989) *Feminism and the Contradictions of Oppression*, London: Routledge.

*Reineke, Martha J. (1987) 'Lacan, Merleau-Ponty and Irigaray: reflections on a specular drama', *Auslegung: A Journal of Philosophy* 14 (Winter): 67–85.

Riley, Denise (1988) *'Am I that Name?': Feminism and the Category of 'Women' in History*, London: Macmillan.

Rohrlich, Ruby and Barauch, Elaine Hoffman (eds) (1984) *Women in Search of Utopia: Mavericks and Mythmakers*, New York: Schocken Books.

Rose, Gillian (1984) *Dialectic of Nihilism: Post-Structuralism and Law*, Oxford: Blackwell.

Rose, Hilary (1988) 'Dreaming the future', *Hypatia* 3 (1) (Spring): 119–37.

Rose, Jacqueline (1986) *Sexuality in the Field of Vision*, London: Verso.

Rose, Jacqueline (1989) 'Where does the misery come from? Psychoanalysis, feminism and the "event"', in Feldstein and Roof (eds) pp.25–39.

Rosenthal, Abigail (1973) 'Feminism without contradictions', *The Monist* 57 (1): 28–42.

Rousseau Jean-Jacques (1755) *Discours de l'origine de l'inégalité*. [English trans. *Discourse on the Origin of Inequality*, trans. Maurice Cranston, Harmondsworth, Penguin 1984.]

Rousseau, Jean-Jacques (1762) *Du Contrat social*. [English trans. *The Social Contract*, trans. Maurice Cranston, Harmondsworth: Penguin 1968.]

Roustang, François (1980) . . . . *Elle ne le lâche plus*, Paris: Minuit. [English trans. *Psychoanalysis Never Lets Go*, Baltimore: Johns Hopkins University Press 1983.]

Rowbotham, Sheila, Segal, Lynne, and Wainwright, Hilary (1979) *Beyond the Fragments: Feminism and the Making of Socialism*, London: Merlin Press.

*Rowe, John Carlos (1985–6) "'To live outside the law you must be honest": the authority of the margin in contemporary theory', *Cultural Critique* 2: 35–70.

Rycroft, Charles (1986) 'An enquiry into the function of words in the psycho-analytic situation', in Gregorio Kohon (ed.) *The British School of Psychoanalysis*, London: Free Association Books, pp.237–52.

Sartre, Jean-Paul (1940) *L'Imaginaire*, Paris: Gallimard. [English trans. *The Psychology of the Imagination*, trans. Bernard Frechtman, London: Rider 1949.]

Sayers, Janet (1982) *Biological Politics: Feminist and Anti-feminist Perspectives*, London: Tavistock.

Sayers, Janet (1986) *Sexual Contradictions: Psychology, Psychoanalysis and Feminism*, London: Tavistock.

Schor, Naomi (1987) 'Dreaming dissymetry: Barthes, Foucault and sexual difference', in Jardine and Smith (eds) pp.98–110.

*Schor, Naomi (1989) 'This essentialism which is not one: coming to grips with Irigaray', *differences* 1 (2): 38–58.

Scott, Joan W. (1988) 'Deconstructing equality-versus-difference: or, the uses of poststructuralist theory for feminism', *Feminist Studies* 14 (1) (Spring): 33–50.

*Segal, Lynne (1987) *Is The Future Female? Troubled Thoughts on Contemporary Feminism*, London: Virago.

Sharpe, Ella (1940) 'Psycho-physical problems revealed in language: an examination of metaphor', reprinted in Ella Sharpe, *Collected Papers on Psychoanalysis*, London: The Hogarth Press, 1950, pp.155–69.

Shklar, Judith (1969) *Men and Citizens: A Study of Rousseau's Social Theory*, Cambridge: Cambridge University Press.

Shorey, Paul (ed.) (1980) *Plato: the Republic*, 2 vols, Loeb edn, London: Heinemann.

Silverman, Kaja (1983) *The Subject of Semiotics*, New York and Oxford: Oxford University Press.

*Silverman, Kaja (1988) *The Acoustic Mirror: The Female Voice in Psychoanalysis and Cinema*, Bloomington: Indiana University Press.

Smith, Norman Kemp (trans.) (1933) *Immanuel Kant's Critique of Pure Reason*, London: Macmillan.

Smith, Paul (1988) *Discerning the Subject*, Minneapolis: University of Minnesota Press.

Snitow, Ann, Stansell, Christine, and Thompson, Sharon (1984) *Desire: The Politics of Sexuality*, London: Virago.

Spivak, Gayatri Chakravorty (1974) 'Translator's Preface', in Derrida (1974) pp.ix–lxxxvii.

Spivak, Gayatri Chakravorty (1983) 'Displacement and the discourse of woman', in Mark Krupnick (ed.) *Displacement: Derrida and After*, Bloomington: Indiana University Press.

Spivak, Gayatri Chakravorty (1984) 'Love me, love my ombre, elle', *Diacritics* (Winter): 19–36.

Spivak, Gayatri Chakravorty (1987) *In Other Worlds: Essays in Cultural Politics*, New York and London: Methuen.

Spivak, Gayatri Chakravorty (1989) 'Feminism and deconstruction, again: negotiating with unacknowledged masculinism', in Brennan (ed.) pp.206–23.

*Stanton, Domna C. (1986) 'Difference on trial: a critique of the maternal metaphor in Cixous, Irigaray and Kristeva', in Nancy K. Miller (ed.) *The Poetics of Gender*, New York: Columbia University Press, pp.157–82. [Reprinted in Allen and Young, 1989, pp.156–79.]

*Stenstad, Gail (1989) 'Anarchic thinking: breaking the hold of monotheistic ideology on feminist philosophy', in Garry and Pearsall (eds) pp.331–9.

*Suleiman, Susan Rubin (1986) '(Re)Writing the body: the politics and poetics of female eroticism', in Susan Rubin Suleiman (ed.) *The Female Body in Western Culture: Contemporary Perspectives*, Cambridge: Harvard University Press, pp.7–29.

Taylor, Barbara (1983) *Eve and the New Jerusalem: Socialism and Feminism in the Nineteenth Century*, London: Virago.

*Threadgold, Terry (1988) 'Language and gender', *Australian Feminist Studies* 6 (Autumn): 41–70.

*Tibbett, Frederick (1988) 'Irigaray and the languages of Wittgenstein', *Critical Matrix*,

Princeton Working Papers in Women's Studies 4 (Fall/Winter): 83–110.

Turkle, Sherry (1979) *Psychoanalytic Politics: Jacques Lacan and Freud's French Revolution*, London: Burnett Books.

Walby, Sylvia (1986) *Patriarchy at Work*, Cambridge: Polity Press.

Walby, Sylvia (1990) *Theorizing Patriarchy*, Oxford: Blackwell.

Weed, Elizabeth (ed.) (1989) *Coming to Terms: Feminism, Theory, Politics*, New York and London: Routledge.

Weedon, Chris (1987) *Feminist Practice and Poststructuralist Theory*, Oxford: Blackwell.

*Wenzel, Hélène Vivienne (1981) 'Introduction to Luce Irigaray's *And the One Doesn't Stir Without the Other*', *Signs* 7 (1) (Autumn): 56–9.

*Whitford, Margaret (1986) 'Speaking as a woman: Luce Irigaray and the female imaginery', *Radical Philosophy* 43, pp.3–8.

Wollheim, Richard (1973) *Freud*, London: Fontana.

Wood, D. C. (1979) 'An introduction to Derrida', *Radical Philosophy* 21: 18–28.

Wood, David (1985) 'Difference and the problem of strategy', in David Wood and Robert Bernasconi (eds) *Derrida and Differance*, University of Warwick: Parousia Press, pp.93–106.

*Yaeger, Patricia (1989) 'Toward a female sublime', in Kauffman (ed.) pp.191–212.

Index